Sense & Nonsense in Australian History

Published by **Black Inc. Agenda**
Series Editor: Robert Manne

Other books in the Black Inc. Agenda series:

Whitewash: On Keith Windschuttle's Fabrication of Aboriginal History ed. Robert Manne

The Howard Years ed. Robert Manne

Axis of Deceit Andrew Wilkie

Following Them Home: The Fate of the Returned Asylum Seekers David Corlett

Civil Passions: Selected Writings Martin Krygier

Do Not Disturb: Is the Media Failing Australia? ed. Robert Manne

SENSE & NONSENSE in AUSTRALIAN HISTORY

John HIRST

Black Inc.
Agenda

Published by Black Inc. Agenda,
an imprint of Schwartz Publishing Pty Ltd
Level 5, 289 Flinders Lane
Melbourne Victoria 3000 Australia
email: enquiries@blackincbooks.com
http://www.blackincbooks.com

Book design: Thomas Deverall
Typeset by J&M Typesetting Pty Ltd
Index by Michael Ramsden

The cover features a detail of *The Crow Trap* by Russell Drysdale (1941).
© Estate of Russell Drysdale

Printed in Australia by McPherson's Printing Group

Contents

Preface

For over twenty years I have been quarrelling in print with the standard left-liberal view of Australian history. I have also been puzzling over how best to write the history of societies that were colonies. The history of the mother country cannot be left behind; it remains the context in which colonial society forms and lives.

When Robert Manne invited me to assemble my essays for publication, I was pleased to find that they deal with important themes throughout our history since 1788, from convict society to the republic. Taken together they provide the interpretative framework for an alternative history of Australia – which frees me from the obligation of writing it.

The essays appear here without footnotes. Readers who want to check the evidence should go to the original versions, whose locations are given in an appendix. The essay 'How Sorry Can We Be?' appears here for the first time. In this case I have given more indication in the text of the works on which I am drawing.

I thank Robert Manne, the editor of Black Inc.'s Agenda series, for the invitation to produce this book and for his launching of me as historian-cum-controversialist when he was editor of *Quadrant*. At La Trobe University I have enjoyed great support from many colleagues and have been instructed and stimulated at the seminar on the Sociology of Culture founded by Claudio Veliz and in my time run by John Carroll. At Black Inc. I have been fortunate again to work with Chris Feik who is a sensitive and supportive editor.

John Hirst

Introduction: *Changing My Mind*

Historians write from the evidence, but also from their understanding of how the world works and how they would like it to work. A historian who thinks large impersonal forces have shaped our destiny will write a different history from one who thinks that great leaders have turned the tide – or made a tide. A socialist will not write approvingly of the rise of modern capitalist society. A free marketeer will be hard put to treat socialists sympathetically.

The great majority of the historians of Australia over the last forty or fifty years have been left-leaning, progressive people. I was taught Australian history by them and their books. I was brought up on Russel Ward *The Australian Legend* (1958) and Robin Gollan *Radical and Working Class Politics* (1960); my first teacher at the University of Adelaide in the early 1960s was Ian Turner. These three, as it happens, were more than left-leaning: they had all been members of the Communist Party. They were all properly trained academic historians and none was a crude propagandist. They wrote under tighter control of their discipline than the next generation of radicals. I still value and draw on their books. But their sympathies were plain.

My sense of how the world works and my political allegiance were at first those of my teachers. They are now different. With this change, my history-writing has changed. I am not sure how these two changes relate to each other. I wonder if my study of history has changed my views or whether my views changed and then my history-writing.

*

By the time I acquired my BA I believed that the Labor Party was the only party decent people could support. Labor promised a new, just social order; Liberals were the tools of big business, selfish and stupid.

I proceeded immediately to study for a PhD. The topic I chose for my thesis required me to study the South Australian history of both the Labor and Liberal parties. They both had their origins in Adelaide; the Labor Party in the trade unions and the Liberals among the city's businessmen and large property holders. If either group was to be a governing party, it had to gain support in the country. It took them some time to realise that country people were not automatically going to support a city organisation and its program.

The Labor Party had to drop its plan to tax all land, big farms and small, and it had to give country branches a real say at conferences. With these concessions made, it did win office in its own right for the first time in 1910. But the hard men in the trade unions were disgusted at the moderation of the Labor government. They turned on the Labor politicians, one of whose offences was to have made these concessions to the country. During World War I the hard men expelled the leading Labor politicians (for supporting conscription) and they reduced country branches to a nullity at Labor conferences. In future delegates had as many votes as the number of members they represented. A trade union delegate might have 10,000 votes and a country branch delegate ten.

As I followed this struggle, I found my sympathies were very much with parliamentarians. I was a Labor supporter (I was never a party member) but I was perfectly happy for parliamentarians to accept the restraints that winning government required.

The Liberal Party in South Australia took final shape in 1910, the year Labor first ruled. Most of its money came from big business and large landholders, but they had no influence over the choice of candidates. In the countryside, which was the Liberals' stronghold, party members insisted on selecting their own candidates without interference from head office. The farmers who wanted more land for themselves and their sons had also insisted that the party program include the compulsory purchase by the government of large pastoral estates and their subdivision into farms. It was to resist just such a measure that the big businessmen and landowners had first formed a political organisation. Now they were bankrolling a party that supported it! They were not happy.

*

The discipline of studying the evidence had led me to put aside the view that Liberals were just the voice of big business. But I was unusual among Australian historians in spending time on the Liberal Party. When they write political history, they generally study causes with which they sympathise. Some years ago an American colleague of mine expressed his amazement at this narrowness: 'There are shelves of books in the library on the Labor Party, even a small shelf on Communists and the Communist Party, but you are lucky to find two or three volumes on the Liberal Party – but haven't they governed the country for most of its history?' The imbalance is not quite as bad as this. Part of the difference arises because Liberals themselves are not as interested in their history and write fewer memoirs and reminiscences. But I think academic historians can be criticised for their lack of interest in the Liberals or for simply adopting the Labor view of them. You might think that left-leaning historians would study them if only to understand the enemy. Fortunately we now have two very revealing books on the Liberals written by left-leaning Judith Brett: *Robert Menzies' Forgotten People* and *The Australian Liberals and the Moral Middle Class*.

So why was I more ready to spend time on the Liberals? Was it just that I was writing a general history and I needed to look at them as well as Labor? Or was it that my mother was a Liberal voter and did not appear to be the willing tool of big business? She voted Labor for the first time in 1966 (against the landslide for Harold Holt) because she did not want my younger brother to be conscripted for Vietnam. She was not a passionate or a vocal Liberal; she did not take much interest in politics. She was calm and non-judgmental; very unwilling to see wickedness. This is a useful trait for a historian who first of all has to understand.

If I was now less prejudiced about the Liberal Party, my political sympathies still lay with Labor and they strengthened when Gough Whitlam became leader. I was as elated by his 1972 victory and as angry at his 1975 dismissal as any party member.

My bedrock assumptions about the world changed while I was writing my book on convict society in New South Wales. It was published in 1983 when I was forty years old. I began my researches with the usual assumption that convict society was cruel and degraded with masters being corrupted by the power they held over the convicts. The question I posed for myself was how had this brutalised society been transformed into a free, democratic society. My conclusion was that I had asked the wrong question. This was not a brutalised society; it was much more a normal British colony which had convicts as part of its labour force and which had always preserved crucial legal rights and economic opportunities for convicts and ex-convicts. I was one of what is now called 'the normalising school' on convict society.

At the centre of the book were musings on the nature of power. As my ideas formed, I found I was contesting the liberal view that power corrupts and that if subordinates complain or rebel it is because they have been badly treated. I began the section in the book on masters and servants by questioning how much power the masters of convict servants had. They had the power to get their convicts flogged, but they got poorer service than the masters back in England with servants who were kept in line by the threat of being sacked without a reference. Even under threat of flogging, convict servants were inclined to be stroppy, to get drunk or run away. A minority were absolutely incorrigible. I explored the idea that some masters were driven to cruelty not by lust for power but through the frustrations of getting work out of convicts, of not having enough power. Cruelty was a standing temptation for those who began by thinking that gentle treatment would bring good service. The commonly accepted formula for success with convicts was a combination of kindness and firmness (that could include flogging). This was the practice of those known – by convicts and others – as 'good masters', an old notion of power being exercised justly that survived even in the convict colony.

I was more open to think in new ways about convict society because I had read the recent books on slavery in the United States which described a complex relationship between masters and slaves. In law slaves might be property to be bought and sold but slaves were not things, for things do not answer back, go slow or run away. I had also learnt the paradox that when you 'own' your labour force you are more responsible for its welfare than when you hire free workers for wages. More important, I think, was the fact that I was now a 'master' myself – of a very rebellious teenager. I was of course a decent and understanding parent but that did not lessen the ferociousness of the rebellion. I was under siege myself as I watched masters trying to control convicts. My fellow-spirit in convict Sydney was the very decent Christian master George Allen. He was reluctant to send his servants to court for punishment, but when John Crawley ignored his orders on the pretence that he was deaf, he felt he had no option. On the day Crawley returned after receiving twenty-five lashes, Allen noted in his diary: 'It is very strange that when Men are well treated they will not behave themselves.'

My family, without having read my convict book, but having some sense of its argument, mocked me for claiming that flogging did not hurt. Some of my colleagues made the same criticism in a different way. But in fact I pointed out that flogging did injure some convicts so badly that they were admitted to hospital. It was not true, as is sometimes alleged, that flogging was used as a punishment because it did not take the convict away from his work. What I did not do in my book was to denounce flogging and be constantly outraged by it. By our standards it is an outrage, but I have this historian's quirk of knowing that the people who flogged criminals would think our practice of locking criminals up in all male institutions for thirty years or more cruel and unnatural. So I hesitate to condemn the past, but I recognise that I run the danger of not seeing horror when it is truly there.

*

The writing of my convict book set my mind in a new direction. Like a good historian I can offer the evidence for this in the notable sayings I have recorded in a little notebook I always have with me:

History shows there is no such thing as absolute power. —F. Eggleston, *State Socialism in Victoria*, p. 315

Mild, just, but exact in discipline; he was father to his people who were attached to him from affection and obedient from confidence.

—Tribute to James Cook on contemporary monument, copy in Maritime Museum Greenwich

Surely of all the 'rights of man', this right of the ignorant man to be guided by the wiser, to be gently or forcibly held in the true course by him is the indisputablest. —Thomas Carlyle, *Chartism*, chapter 6

Thomas Carlyle, the historian-philosopher of the nineteenth century, became my favourite guide. He lived through the industrial revolution and hated its tendency to reduce all human relations to a cash nexus. But he did not believe that the liberal and democratic programs of his day would meet humankind's deepest needs. I was myself living in a new age of revolution, the libertarianism of the 1970s and after. I could not believe its promise that the loosening of social ties and the questioning of all authority would produce a better world. It was on this issue that I parted company with left-leaning, progressive people. I was, and am still, a supporter of the old left causes of a fairer distribution of wealth and opportunity.

I do not have the temperament of the liberationist. When authority is attacked my instinct is to come to its defence. I am very sympathetic to the problems of governing. I think our society has become too suspicious of authority and forgetful that we have cultural restraints on power that have produced and may still produce good leaders, bosses and teachers. The modern formula for governing is to be open and accountable and to consult widely and be inclusive. But the pleasures of sitting in committees can be exaggerated. In a committee we are instantly aware that some people are more fluent, forthright and determined than others; that we are not equals. With a good boss we are all equals in that he or she is equally concerned for us and will judge us equitably. That is a very satisfying environment in which to work.

I was not favouring a more authoritarian government for the state. There we need the checks and balances. The danger, as I saw it, was that democratic principles and rights were being applied to all subordinate institutions, which rendered them less able to do their job. A school that has so little control over its pupils that it has to call the police is a failed institution.

From Carlyle, who was much influenced by German idealist philosophy, I received the encouragement to think differently about human motivation and the course of history. Here are some extracts from my notebook:

It is a calumny on men to say that they are roused to heroic action by ease, hope of pleasure, recompense – sugar plums of any kind, in this world or the next. In the meanest mortal there lies something nobler. The poor swearing soldier, hired to be shot, has his 'honour of the soldier', different from drill regulations and the shilling a day. It is not to taste sweet things, but to do noble and true things, and vindicate himself under God's heaven as a god-made Man that the poorest son of Adam dimly longs … Difficulty, abnegation, martyrdom, death are the *allurements* that act on the heart of man. —Carlyle, *On Heroes and Hero-Worship*, Lecture 2

It is not what a man outwardly has or wants that constitutes the happiness or misery of him … The real smart is the soul's pain and stigma, the hurt inflicted in the moral self. —Carlyle, *Chartism*, chapter 5

From my teachers in Australian history I learned a sort of debased Marxism which looked to economic interests to explain events. This was somewhat offset by the lectures Professor Hugh Stretton gave on European history. I was probably not well attuned to his message. I do remember gaining a sense that the world was more open than is sometimes portrayed and that men with fresh ideas can be influential. In an aside he declared that the trouble with the Labor Party was that it had stopped thinking, which was no doubt true of the Labor Party circa 1963, pre Whitlam. We students were in the dark about Stretton. He had written nothing, though he was rumoured to be working on a magnum opus of whose subject there were conflicting reports. It was only later that all became clear when I read *The Political Sciences* and *Ideas for Australian Cities*.

The Australian historians had done a regular job on the history of the making of the Australian Commonwealth. I can remember at university reading on the economic interests that underlay the federation movement.

Many times thereafter I had to read that federation was a business deal with very little idealism about it. It gave me great satisfaction for the celebration of the hundredth anniversary in 2001 to write a book that inverted this claim, and put the ideal before the material.

My book began with the idealists, the people who worked for federation who called it, publicly and privately, a noble, holy or sacred cause. That was the first sign that the old interpretation had missed the animating spirit of the movement. My job then was to explain why the making of a nation could be viewed this way. I hope I was not too starry eyed about these people. They had an interest in the creating of a nation, not an economic interest but a status interest, the quintessential selfish interest, what Carlyle called the moral self. They wanted to avoid the stigma of being thought second-rate. While the colonies were separate those who lived in them were known as colonists, a second-class people. If the colonies combined, the colonists would become citizens of a nation and share the standing of other nations round the globe.

Businessmen wanted the colonies to combine. My knock-down case against their influence on federation was that they wanted a customs union, not a federation. A customs union would yield immediate economic benefits: this was the practical proposal. Federation would deliver a customs union but since it involved the setting up of a whole new system of government it would be immensely difficult and would take too long. Until the very last, businessmen opposed moves to federation.

Over many years the businessmen advanced plans for a customs union, but they always failed because of the different economic interests and policies of the different colonies. It was the 'impractical' men, the politicians, the patriots and the poets, who created the union, which then delivered a customs union.

I called my book *The Sentimental Nation*. I think of it as a tribute to Carlyle. It has of course to pass the test of the discipline: has the evidence been produced to support this interpretation? But the making of an interpretation of this sort is also evidence of what has happened to my mind and self since I left my first teachers.

2004

WHAT SORT OF HISTORY?

Australia's Absurd History

Multiculturalism, with contradiction at its heart, has a great capacity for the absurd. Its exponents are now developing an absurdist history of Australia. This is how it runs: Once upon a time there was a small, inward looking, intolerant, racist Anglo-Celtic nation. It began to take migrants from Europe and then Asia. The migration program was an outstanding success. The nation turned into a diverse, open, tolerant society. The new migrants created the tolerance.

Where is the absurdity in this? That a nation which hated 'wogs' invited hundreds of thousands of Italians and Greeks to come to its shores? No, nations, like individuals, may under urgent necessity do what is distasteful to them. The rationale for the migration policy was to boost Australia's population and economy as a defence against a renewed threat from the north. Better the dark-skinned Greek than the Japanese. No, the absurdity lies in the claim that the migrants created the tolerance. The more benighted and bigoted we make the Australian people of the 1940s, the less likely it is that the migration program would have had a successful outcome. If the Anglo-Celts were so bad – and in the current demonology there is no-one worse than an Anglo-Celt circa 1940 – why did they not savagely oppress and permanently marginalise the incoming strangers, a process all too common and very easy to accomplish?

But if the strangers are numerous and carry with them a very different value system, could they then not have a transforming effect on the host society? The migrants were certainly numerous and over a short time constituted a reasonably high proportion of the old population, but they were not of one sort; they came from a number of different countries and were notoriously intolerant of each other. If Greeks and Turks, Serbs and Croats, Arabs and Jews live in peace in Australia, it is not because they brought tolerance with them. Let us abandon absurdity and explore a commonsense hypothesis: that the migration scheme has been a success because the roots of the tolerance lay in the society which invited the migrants to join it.

Multiculturalism makes ethnic origin into destiny. So at the last census Australians were asked about their ancestry and encouraged not to answer 'Australian'. Even those whose families have been here for four or six generations were meant to declare a European ancestry. As with individuals, so with society. In the eyes of multiculturalists Australian society of the 1940s, 150 years after first settlement, is adequately described as Anglo-Celtic. At least this acknowledges that the people of Australia were Irish and Scots as well as English, but it has nothing more substantial than a hyphen joining them. In fact a distinct new culture had been formed. English, Scots and Irish had formed a common identity – first of all British and then gradually Australian as well. In the 1930s the historian W. K. Hancock could aptly describe them as Independent Australian Britons.

To say that the Australians were more British than the British carries more of the truth than is usually realised. Britishness was not a very strong identity in Great Britain itself. The heartland of the United Kingdom was England and the English thought of themselves as English and only on the rare occasions when they wanted to be polite to the Scots did they use the term 'British'. In Australia the pressure of the Scots and especially of the Irish forced the abandonment of 'English' as the identity of the colonies in favour of 'British'. The Irish of course could still bridle at a British identity even when it included them as equals. In time, with the passing of the first generation born in Ireland and the growth of a distinctively Australian interpretation of Britishness, they were prepared to accept it. The Irish had done well in Australia and saw the adoption of self-government within the empire as the solution to the Irish problem at home, the system which had worked so well in the colonies.

Multiculturalists pride themselves on their respect for the identity people give themselves. They tell us that if Greeks want to call themselves Greeks, they should be referred to as such and not as Greek-Australians, still less as New Australians. In calling Australians of the 1940s and their descendants 'Anglo-Celts' multiculturalists depart from their own rule. This term has not been used by these people to describe themselves. They were proud that they had constrained particular ethnic identities and subsumed them into the broader terms of British and Australian. The imposition of 'Anglo-Celt' is the tyrannical arm of multiculturalism. I find the term offensive.

The Irish were present in large numbers from the beginning of European settlement in Australia. Hence Australian society as it was forming had to accommodate the antagonism of Catholic and Protestant which had torn Europe apart and still poisoned relations between England and Ireland. If the Church of England, established by law and funded by compulsory contributions from all, was transferred intact to Australia, the old battles would begin again. We owe it to a liberal governor of New South Wales, a Protestant Irishman, that they did not. In 1836 Governor Bourke decided if there were to be established churches, all three of the great divisions of Christianity within Britain should be established. He would allot public funds on the same terms to the Church of England, the Catholic Church and the Presbyterians. This amazing measure was the clearest signal to the Irish that life in Australia was to be truly a new dispensation. A British government was financing the Roman heresy. The system worked well and was expanded to include any who wanted to join it – even Jews. It lasted in New South Wales until 1862, in Victoria until 1870. Those colonies then adopted the more orthodox liberal principle of complete separation of church and state which had been pioneered in this country by South Australia. Under either system the state was strictly neutral on an issue which could and did bitterly divide its people. This neutrality was policed with an eagle eye. All other distinctions between churches having been removed, the colonists argued bitterly over whether the Anglican bishop should take precedence at a government house levee over his Catholic brother.

Unlike in the United States and Canada, the English, Scots and Irish did not form separate enclaves. There was a remarkably even intermingling. This in itself suggests a high degree of toleration which was advanced further by the determination to keep sectarian rivalry out of community organisations. In the nineteenth century, hospitals, charities of all sorts, trade unions, friendly societies, sporting clubs, the mechanics institutes and the schools of arts which ran the libraries and the public halls – all these had Catholics and Protestants on their boards and among their members and clients and worked to keep them together. This was not easy. There was always low-level tension and sometimes spectacular brawls. Separate community organisations for Protestants and Catholics would have avoided this dissension, but threatened much worse.

In society at large public feuding between Protestant and Catholic occurred regularly and was sometimes savage. Historians who search mindlessly for conflict latch on to such episodes as if they have discovered a Belfast or a Beirut. But this public feuding did not lead to polarisation at community level or residential segregation and it encouraged people of goodwill on both sides to redouble their efforts to neutralise the conflict. The commitment to avoid old-world divisions was much stronger than the desire to perpetuate them.

The worst sectarian violence in our history occurred in Melbourne in 1846 when Catholic and Protestant mobs fired on each other on the anniversary of the Battle of the Boyne. But note the response. The colony's mini-parliament immediately passed a law banning processions held to commemorate festivals, anniversaries, or political events related to any religious or political differences between Her Majesty's subjects. Banners and music calculated to provoke animosity were forbidden. The poisonous cycle of demonstration and counter demonstration by which Northern Ireland keeps alive its troubled past was nipped in the bud. But all that colour gone from the streets! A disappointing outcome according to true multiculturalists who appear to believe that no social differences can be damaging, no matter how acute or passionately held they are – so long, of course, as all participating parties have access to a regularly-updated multicultural policy statement.

The liberal hope for education was that children of all religions could come together in schools run by the state. Religion would still be taught. Either the regular teachers would teach a common Christianity – the essentials of the faith to be agreed on by all the churches – or clergymen of the different churches would be allowed to come to the schools to instruct their own children. The opponents of these schemes were the churches, or more precisely the clergy. The laity in general supported them. The only church finally which could sustain its opposition to these schemes was the one where clergy had most power over the laity – the Catholic. Here old world antagonisms could not be kept at bay.

The Catholic bishops and priests were Irish and judging by their Irish experience thought any state scheme of education must be designed to undermine their faith. They could not see that the governments of the British colonies of Australia were different from the Protestant English state which oppressed Ireland. The Catholics were a large minority, but not large enough to stop the liberal schemes of education. The Catholic opposition to these schemes made state education into a Protestant cause. This issue became the most divisive in nineteenth-century Australia. The Catholic clergy set out to build their own schools and demanded that government money be granted to them. This was fiercely resisted. On the other hand the state rejected pressure to adopt some Protestant forms of instruction and worship in its schools. The state schools remained strictly neutral. Some Catholic children continued to attend them.

This battle confirmed the widely held view, stronger probably among Protestants than Catholics, that the clergy were a grave threat to the development of a tolerant society in Australia. They had an interest in exaggerating the virtues of their own faith and the shortcomings of others. In some colonies clergy were prohibited from becoming members of parliament to reduce their opportunities for sowing discord. In community organisations it was impossible to have a single clergyman participating; there had to be representatives of all major denominations. The usual practice was to have none. To isolate the divisive force of religion was relatively easy since no one church had ever established its pre-eminence. Much more than in England, Ireland, Scotland or Wales the clergy were confined to their churches.

Class differences which became significant from the 1880s were accommodated in a similar way to religious differences. At first sight Australia seems an unlikely place for strong class feeling to take root. In the late nineteenth century most of industry was still small-scale, living standards were the highest in the world, and workers did not experience the hauteur of an aristocracy or stigmatisation from a solid bourgeoisie. But doctrines of liberation galvanise best those who are more than half liberated already. Because the working class was better off and more self-confident they adopted more eagerly the new doctrines of socialism and aggressive trade unionism. These did not so much lead working men to concentrate a new hatred on their class enemies – for these seemed inconsequential – as encourage them to think that an improvement in their own lot and the transformation of society could be readily accomplished. This heady optimism was rapidly punctured. The largest employers – ship owners, mine owners and pastoralists – quickly developed their own organisations and when the unions blundered into a national strike in 1890 they were decisively defeated. During this struggle and the more desperate shearers' strikes of 1891 and 1894, employers were totally intransigent, police and troops were deployed by governments, on occasions strikers used or threatened violence, and some strike leaders were gaoled.

There was widespread dismay that social disruption and hatred of an old-world intensity had broken out in the new. This was the mood in which the distinctively Australian response to class conflict emerged – the establishment of an arbitration court which would compulsorily settle industrial disputes. This did not end class conflict, but it institutionalised it at a distance. The new disruption, which threatened so much, was declared to be amenable to the time-honoured procedure for dispute-settling, the law. Trade unionists accepted this regime because they were weakened by strikes and depression and because the rapid success of their new Labor Party gave them some guarantee that the state would not be used against them. The left has criticised them ever since for transferring industrial conflict, which is meant to be the growth point of socialism, to the tribunals of the capitalist state. But it was a capitalist state of a special sort which enhanced the status of workers by treating them as litigants of equal standing with employers and made their wages and conditions a matter of regular official concern.

Class differences were ameliorated in another way. In face-to-face encounters Australians gradually dropped old-world formality and deference and spoke to each other as equals. This is an egalitarianism on which Australians have come to set great store. So far their historians have told them very little about how it came about. We know that complete equality in form of address was first practised on the goldfields when men of all conditions were dressed in working man's clothes and doing hard manual labour. Everyone was 'mate'. We do not know how long it took for this practice to spread to the rest of society. It is hard to imagine it proceeding any further than the point it has now reached where given names are used not only in casual but in formal encounters.

The success of the Labor Party depended on its ability to keep Protestant and Catholic working men together. Since the Irish were overwhelmingly working class, the numbers of Catholics and Protestants in the party were close to being equal, which made it very different from any other public body. From the beginning it committed itself unequivocally against taking sides in any religious matter. Despite the high proportion of Catholics among its members, it refused to take up the Catholic cause of funding for church schools. Following the split in the party over conscription during World War I, the Catholics became even more prominent. The church began to think it could pressure the party to deliver on funding for its schools. The Catholic parliamentarians resisted. A Catholic party contested the New South Wales 1920 election to teach the Labor Party the lesson that it could not have Catholic votes if it ignored Catholic causes – and failed disastrously. Catholic voters and parliamentarians had refused to be diverted from the main cause, the improvement of workers' conditions, and this involved working with people of other faiths or no faith.

The other great Australian institution of the twentieth century, the RSL, had to discipline itself closely if it were to keep the old soldiers together. It had to avoid any party political or religious alignment. It could not take the easy option of ignoring religion altogether since it wanted a religious service to conclude the annual Anzac Day march. This was drawn up as a non-denominational service but the Catholic Church forbade its members to attend it which was its practice regarding any service not conducted according to its own rites. Conscientious Catholics accordingly dropped out from the march toward its end. This always rankled with the RSL whose animating spirit was the desire to retain the camaraderie of war which had made all the differences of civilian life seem irrelevant. In 1938 the Victorian RSL faced up to the problem of bringing the religiously divided together, the theme of so much of our history. It was an extremely tricky issue: to win Catholic participation the service must be completely non-religious, but to drop all references to God at the behest of Catholics would outrage Protestants. The League devised a new civic service, but to show it was not anti-religion it encouraged churches to hold their own services on Anzac Day and the civic service itself was left open for religious use. There was to be a two-minute silence – in which soldiers could pray according to their lights. There was even a hymn, 'Lead Kindly Light', a cunning choice this, written by a Catholic and not actually mentioning God. There were loud complaints from Protestant clergy at these changes, but they don't seem to have affected participation in the service. The Catholic Archbishop, Daniel Mannix, gave the new service his blessing and thanked the RSL for its consideration. For the first time Catholics and Protestants remembered their dead together.

*

It is true that British Australia before World War II was intolerant of non-British migration, but it was expert in the modes of toleration. The old dinner party rule that religion and politics should not be discussed had been the principle on which the formation of civil society had proceeded. Matters which were known to be divisive had to be kept at a distance or subject to strict local quarantine. Civil society should not be shaped by religion or politics, but preserved against them. This explains both the decencies of our private and community life and the vacuousness of our public discourse. The contrast with the United States is complete. There religious and ethnic differences have firmly shaped community life and the commitment to equality and toleration is made in public discourse: the noble words of the Declaration of Independence and the Constitution.

The reasons for the success of the migration program should now be apparent. Migrants had to suffer personal abuse and suspicion, but Australian society, except in its treatment of Aborigines, is uneasy with sustained and systematic social exclusion. Its instincts are inclusive. As one migrant reports, 'Australians did not especially like "foreigners" but they disliked drawing attention to themselves by being nasty to people more than they disliked foreigners.' It should not be forgotten that assimilation, now criticised for its cultural arrogance, was a welcoming attitude. And it demanded less than its latter day critics imagined. There was not a homogeneous society insisting on complete conformity. Migrants were not being asked to abandon everything; rather they were not to make a public display of difference; they were to 'mix in' and live among Australians and not in their own enclaves. That is, these new differences were to be handled like the old Protestant–Catholic differences had been.

The Australian ethos, as I have outlined it, was concerned not to obliterate difference but to overlook it. It is best caught by Henry Lawson:

> They tramp in mateship side by side
>> The Protestant and Roman
> They call no biped Lord or Sir
>> And touch their hat to no man

This is not envisaging a world where there will not be Protestants and Catholics or employers and employees. It insists that person with person, face to face, these differences are not to count. Much ink has been wasted by social scientists 'proving' that Australian society is not egalitarian because it has quite distinct differences of class and status. Our egalitarianism is rather the means by which we live more comfortably with those differences; it makes them less disruptive and demeaning.

Now, to leave differences out of account, as D. H. Lawrence observed in *Kangaroo*, can make for very superficial encounters. I can well understand migrants' complaints that Australians were passionless, offhand, and even when most polite, strangely indifferent to their background and experience. We are not looking for reasons why migrants were comfortable or contented – for migration must always be more or less traumatic – but to the general social circumstances which allowed for the accommodation and melding of peoples to proceed relatively smoothly. The process would have been different if the Australian people had been more divided socially among themselves and less concerned to bridge barriers.

Nearly all migrants entered the Australian economy as workers. It is often said that migrants were exploited because they had to take the lowest paid jobs which Australians thankfully left. But the trade union movement only agreed to the admission of migrants as long as they were to be paid award wages. Unskilled migrants, knowing no English and with no experience of trade unions, came under the protection of the arbitration court. This put a severe limit to their 'exploitation'. The unions' historic opposition to migration had arisen because they feared that migrants, especially those with low expectations and less ability to defend themselves, would drive wages down. They had to be assured that this would not happen before they would support the postwar scheme.

Some Australians were disappointed that migrants did not mix in readily and that they formed, temporarily as it turned out, their own residential enclaves. But the freedoms of a free society are real. Freedom of movement, of residence, of speech and publication, of association, of business enterprise could not be denied the migrants. The commitment to an open society means that we agree to live with what is unusual, distasteful or even threatening. It is a great act of faith and easy enough to think it foolhardy. However, if liberalism has its dangers, it also has it unexpected rewards. Modern Australia is one of them. In the space which an open and tolerant society gave them migrants found security, prosperity and self-confidence and transformed the society in ways which their hosts had not intended. They have made it a much more diverse, lively and exciting place. Because the outcome was unintended, Australians can take no great credit for it, though the commitment to openness and tolerance was theirs. Since liberalism's achievements depend on self-restraint, it is easy to overlook its outstanding practitioners.

The children and grandchildren of southern European peasants are now flocking into Australian universities. If they choose to study sociology, there is a good chance they will be taught that migrants are a badly treated minority. They might well have as their textbook Professor J. S. Western's very popular *Social Inequality in Australian Society* which declares that the history of migration 'has, in many important aspects, been a history of economic deprivation'. This amazing conclusion is reached by surveying the population twenty or thirty years after the migration program has begun and 'discovering' that migrants are over-represented in the ranks of unskilled labour and under-represented in the professions and boardrooms.

How, you might ask, would a just society have treated these migrants? (This is not a question Professor Western asks: enough for him that every difference is an inequality.) Is it seriously being suggested that Australian society should have contrived to have these migrants distributed evenly through the hierarchies of skill and wealth in the first generation, even though so many of them arrived without skill, capital and knowledge of the language? What a piece of social engineering that would have been. The immigration officer at the foot of the gangway as the ship from Italy berths: 'All those from Calabria will be brain surgeons.' Given the mindlessness of these statistical surveys one wonders why they do not examine the migrants at the point of arrival. Then they could 'discover' that *all* migrants were unemployed and owned little or nothing and hence pronounce even more decisively on the inequalities of Australian society. But to remind us that migrants had little or nothing to begin with would spoil the story of 'deprivation'.

We would need to be worried about the position of migrants in Australia if we did not believe that after two or three generations their descendants would be fairly evenly distributed through the economy and society. The signs are looking good. Already the statistical information on the first wave of southern European migrants – the Italians and Greeks – confirm what old Australians have long known: the migrants are doing very well. Italians and Greeks are more likely to own their own home, less likely to be unemployed, and more likely to keep their children on at school than the rest of the population.

Migrants have had to work hard to do well. They have experienced great difficulties in coming to terms with a culture very different from their own. These aspects of the migrant experience are brought forward in Professor Western's account not to lead us to admire the migrants or to understand better their difficulties, but as a further sign of the *inequality* of Australian society. This is the final absurdity. Try to imagine a society in which outsiders, ignorant of its mores and language, would not be handicapped and have to make special efforts to succeed.

In Professor Western's eyes to think of migrants, even the most recent, as outsiders is illegitimate. He criticises us for demanding that migrants become naturalised before they can join the public service, hold certain public offices and practise law. All this is discrimination!

We have reached the heart of the multicultural outlook: the denial of any superior legitimacy to the host culture. Insofar as multicultural-ism makes what it calls 'Anglo-Celts' the equivalent of Italians and Turks, it denies the very notion of a host. We are all immigrants of many cultures, contributing to a multicultural society. This may serve the needs of ethnic politics. As serious historical or sociological analysis it is nonsense. To found policy on it may be perilous.

I say 'may' because there are grounds for believing that multicul-turalism has made little difference to the way migrants and the host culture interact. Migrants face a cruel dilemma – to get on and succeed they must adapt to the host culture (of whose existence they have no doubts); as strangers they are anxious to hold on to the culture they have brought with them. When our policy was assimilation the migrants held onto more of their culture than the policy-makers wished. Now when multiculturalism encourages them to keep their culture they are probably assimilating at the usual rate.

Many Australians appear to have interpreted 'multiculturalism' as a new name for the traditional toleration of difference and the willingness to accept migrants into their lives. When John Howard as leader of the Opposition attacked multiculturalism they thought he was a bigot, planning to close down Italian restaurants or prohibit the speaking of the Italian language. The Prime Minister, Bob Hawke, defended multiculturalism but then launched a citizenship campaign and began to stress what must be the common elements of our culture: the English language, parliamentary democracy, the rule of law, tolerance, the fair-go, – all of course 'Anglo-Celtic' which it seems is *not* to be just one among many cultures.

Multiculturalism interpreted in this way, a diverse society united by core institutions and values, is unexceptionable. But the institutional legacy of a more separatist multiculturalism is still with us: public funding of migrant organisations so they can maintain their culture. This has two dangers. Firstly, the obvious one that migrant cultures contain elements antagonistic to the core values. If you fund Greek schools, will you breed intolerance of Macedonians? If you fund Muslim schools, are you undermining the policy of equality for women? The second, indirect danger is that the support of migrant culture smacks of official favouritism. Nothing could more endanger the standing of migrants in this society; it is offensive to the liberal and egalitarian elements in our culture, the same elements which have been so important hitherto in the success of the migration program. No wonder, as the Fitzgerald Committee reported, the majority of Australians are puzzled and annoyed at multiculturalism. The multiculturalists of course see migrants as a disadvantaged group and so worthy of state assistance. Ordinary people, with a much better nose for these things, know that while new migrants might need help the Italians and Greeks are now a long way from being underdogs.

How could policy-makers be so obtuse as to push the migrant cause against the grain of this society? Perhaps because they have no knowledge of or respect for old Australia, which they label 'Anglo-Celtic, intolerant'. Let them suspend operations until they learn what sort of people we are.

1990

Distance – Was It a Tyrant?

In 1966 Professor Geoffrey Blainey published *The Tyranny of Distance*. The book is subtitled 'How distance shaped Australia's history' and its preface claims that 'Distance is as characteristic of Australia as mountains are of Switzerland'. Blainey is concerned both with the distance of Australia from Britain and distance within Australia. His first theme explores what he terms the 'contradiction' that Australia 'depended intimately and comprehensively on a country which was further away than almost any other in the world'. This is the more satisfying section of the book. It includes an account of the British decision to settle Australia which gives particular emphasis to its potential as a supplier of naval stores. This portion of the book attracted most attention from reviewers and has since been the subject of scholarly dispute. This critique, however, is solely concerned with the second of Blainey's themes: distance *in* Australia.

The chapters relating to this theme are chapter 6, 'Land Barrier', which deals chiefly with the establishment of the pastoral industry, and chapters 9, 10, 11 and 13 in Part Two, 'The Taming of Distance', which deals with the introduction, development and influence of railways, steamships, cars and aeroplanes. With the detailed argument of these chapters there can be very little quarrel. They are vintage Blainey: informative, lively, provocative and wide-ranging. My objections arise when Blainey expects these chapters to sustain an argument which he outlines only very sketchily in his introductory sections: that distances were very great in Australia and that the problem of overcoming distance was particularly obstinate, so much so that its malign effects can be described as tyranny.

*

In the preface to the book Blainey notes that the Australian coast encloses as much land as the United States excluding Alaska. One recalls the school atlas maps which made the same point by fitting all the countries of Europe inside Australia. Yet it is misleading to suggest that the historian of Australian social and economic life is concerned with continental Australia. Portus and Hancock, who in the 1920s and 1930s preceded Blainey in pointing to the special problems of distance and isolation in Australia, were notable offenders in this regard. To estimate the density of population in Australia Portus divided the population by the total area of the continent, two-thirds or more of which was uninhabited. Hancock highlighted the problem of distance in Australia by noting that there was no doctor between Hawker on the northern fringe of the settled areas in South Australia and Darwin, 1300 miles away. Of course there were virtually no people there either. That situation was not typical of the settled areas of rural Australia.

In the body of the book Blainey is much more careful in his analysis. He is at pains to explain why most of Australia's people and its economic activities are concentrated in its south-eastern perimeter, the Boomerang Coast, an area less than one-tenth the size of the continent. In several places Blainey emphasises that in the nineteenth century there was no national economy, but a number of separate economies. This is the crucial factor in his explanation of the development of the three railway gauges. Railways were designed to take the produce of each region to a coastal port; they were not needed to move goods from one region to another. What trade there was between the regions could be carried more cheaply by sea. When the various rail networks were connected, the break of gauge was not felt to be a great drawback, because passengers and mail could move easily from one train to another. Many passengers and goods continued to go by sea. So continental Australia disappears from view. Settlement is confined to the Boomerang Coast and within that area there are a number of separate economies with their own access to the sea. But is not this a different picture from a country having an area as large as the United States? Blainey says distance is a 'manageable problem' in the Boomerang Coast. Is it just, then, to describe it elsewhere as a tyrant?

Even within the settled areas in the south-east of the continent it may be urged that distances were comparatively great and difficult to overcome. In chapter 6, 'Land Barrier', he explains what effect distance had on the nature of settlement in the Boomerang Coast. In this area there were no navigable rivers stretching inland through the mountain ranges, and the terrain made the construction of canals impossible. Hence most of inland Australia could not be served by the cheapest means of transport, water carriage. The cost of land transport was so high that severe limitations were placed upon what could be produced there. The land later proved capable of growing wheat, but for most of the nineteenth century it could not be utilised for this, because wheat is a 'heavy' product, expensive to transport. Grazing solved the problem of distance behind the ranges because wool is a 'light' product – a ton of wool was worth between ten and twenty times a ton of wheat – and so it could be carted long distances to the coast, shipped overseas, and still return a profit.

One can accept this analysis and still question the nature of the tyranny which distance exercised. Is it simply that it forced the production of one commodity rather than another? Blainey's chapter is in fact a celebration of the ease and speed with which the inland plains were settled and integrated into a market economy. It would be difficult to persuade someone acquainted with the slower development of other colonies of settlement that distance here was a difficult problem, let alone a tyrant. In new societies where the problem of distance has really been intractable settlers have been forced to adopt a subsistence economy.

Consider the situation of the settlers beyond the Appalachian Mountains in the United States in the early nineteenth century. They could send some goods down the Mississippi river system, but until the development of the steam river boats they could not receive goods upstream. They were connected to the coastal settlements by roads, but cartage was too expensive for them to send wheat to those markets. With little opportunity for them to sell their produce, they could buy few manufactured or imported goods. In 1815 the two million people west of the mountains were largely self-sufficient and only peripherally connected to the market economy. Their isolation only ended when British capital built canals which connected them to the east and steam boats reached them from the south. Blainey notes the advantage the United States enjoyed over Australia in being able to use water carriage to serve these inland areas. But settlers in these areas had been on the land some time before they could enjoy the benefit of water carriage which eventually made them part of the market economy. Because inland Australia was settled in the nineteenth century when there was a growing demand for wool in Britain, no squatter beyond the Divide ever moved outside the market economy. Wool was carted to the coast and shipped to Britain; stores were carted from the coast, and some of these – tea, sugar, tobacco, and clothing – had themselves been shipped halfway round the world. The immediate integration of the inland plains into a market economy must be considered *prima facie* evidence that the problem of distance was not particularly intractable.

In the old world working people seldom moved far from their own village. Witness the scene in Hardy's *The Mayor of Casterbridge* when a young couple are about to part because the man has to take work elsewhere:

> 'I'm sorry to leave ye, Nelly,' said the young man with emotion. 'But, you see, I can't starve father, and he's out o' work at Lady-day. 'Tis only thirty-five mile.' The girl's lips quivered. 'Thirty-five mile!' she murmured. 'Ah! 'tis enough! I shall never see 'ee again!'

At no stage in its history could such a scene be set in Australia. As Russel Ward has made plain, the labour force up the country was from the earliest times remarkable for its mobility. Bush men moved readily from one job to another and after working some time, they would go on a spending spree – quite frequently to the coastal capitals as these were the only substantial towns. Melbourne, perhaps even more so than Sydney, was the labour centre of its hinterland. Squatters and their overseers rode down to hire men or arranged to have them sent. Such mobility in the workforce was made possible because of the shortage of labour. Fear of unemployment did not tie men to one place or employer. Decent wages also enabled men to save enough to support themselves between jobs, and the hospitality of the bush greatly reduced the expenses of travelling. As Blainey has pointed out elsewhere, when his theme was climate and not distance, men could walk between jobs all the year round because the Australian winter was not severe. So in the pastoral age in Australia, working men moved more freely and over much greater distances than in the old world.

Blainey's claims about distance in Australia are implicitly comparative: Australia has greater distances than most other countries and has suffered more from the 'tyrannies' of distance. But with what is the comparison to be made? If we compare Australia in the 1830s and 1840s with Britain at the same period, it is certainly true that goods moved more readily and cheaply on the British canals and railways than they did by bullock wagon in Australia. But if the comparison is made between the general economic and social development of Australia and that of other countries, then the response must be very different. In Britain, as in the rest of Europe and North America, the unified economy which the canals and railways made possible replaced a series of localised economies and communities. It is to societies constituted in this way that the term 'tyranny of distance' could perhaps be more appropriately applied. Nearly all the needs of the great mass of the population had to be met by what could be produced in the immediate locality. Movement of people was rare. Australia, even before the construction of the railways, had no experience of this localism either in its economy or society. If the 'tyranny of distance' is interpreted in this way, its application to Australia is peculiarly inappropriate. Europe and North America still bear more marks of the 'tyranny of distance' – in the variety of speech and dialect, the institutions of local government, and the distribution of towns and villages – than Australia does.

*

Part Two of the book, 'The Taming of Distance', deals with the introduction of railways, steamships, cars and aeroplanes in the years after 1850. Lest one should think the story of these triumphs is at odds with the book's title, Blamey adds a cryptic final sentence to the brief note which precedes Part Two: 'The long era in which distance was a tyrant seemed suddenly, but mistakenly, to be fading away.' The implications of 'mistakenly' (as it concerns distance within Australia) are not pursued at all in the chapters that follow. In the 1850s when the first of these innovations reached Australia, the settlement at Sydney Cove was seventy years old. That might be a 'long era' in Australian history, but for most of Australia the gap between first white settlement and the arrival of these innovations was much shorter. Thirty years after the squatters took possession of Victoria a railway ran across the colony from Melbourne to the River Murray, and every significant town was connected to the electric telegraph network. That these innovations were available so early in the country's history is a further reason for doubting that distance was a particularly intractable problem in Australia. The benefit which the colonies derived from the technological developments in the old world was, in fact, greater than Blamey allowed. By treating the 'taming of distance' for only the period after 1850 he makes no concentrated study of the innovations which were used before 1850 in roads, bridges and coastal shipping. In the period after 1850 he has given scant attention to the development of the telegraph within Australia.

Australia was first settled by white men at the opening of a great age of road and bridge building in Britain. Large sums were invested in these works and new construction techniques were developed. Metcalfe, the first modern road engineer, began work in the 1760s, Telford and Macadam, whose name was given to his road-building method, early in the nineteenth century. Blamey gives some account of early road building in Australia, but he does not refer to the advantage enjoyed by the Australian settlement in being able to use these new road-building techniques. The roads built through the settled districts of New South Wales in the 1810s and 1820s were constructed on Macadam's principle. Contemporary observers declared they were as good as the highways of Britain. From the 1820s a regular service of stage coaches connect Sydney with Parramatta, Liverpool and Windsor. Stage coaches may now seem a primitive form of transport, but when Australia was settled, they were a comparatively recent innovation in

Britain. Though they had first appeared in the seventeenth century, they remained unimportant until the last half of the eighteenth century when the heyday of coaching began. Before that, most of the travelling had been done on horseback. Peter Cunningham, who reported favourably on the roads and coaches of New South Wales in his *Two Years in New South Wales*, published in 1827, noted that many parts of Europe still did not enjoy such advanced means of transport as New South Wales.

As settlement spread beyond the Cumberland Plain, the same standard of road building could not be maintained. The Surveyor General, Sir Thomas Mitchell, realigned many miles of main roads and devoted his resources to improving the most difficult sections of the routes. His most notable achievement was the Mount Victoria pass in the Blue Mountains on the road to Bathurst. The young Charles Darwin was most impressed with this work. He wrote that in both design and execution it was worthy of any road in England. For his bridge building Mitchell was fortunate to have the services of David Lennox, who had worked with Telford on the Menai suspension bridge and a single-span stone bridge across the Severn near Gloucester. Lennox was Superintendent of Bridges in New South Wales from 1833 to 1844, when he was given the same job for the Port Phillip District. His work is a clear example of how the pioneering colony benefited from skills developed in the first industrialised nation.

From the 1840s fewer convicts were available for road building and the care of main roads passed to a multitude of local authorities which allowed them to fall into disrepair. The next concerted road-making program was undertaken in the new colony of Victoria. The Central Road Board was appointed in 1853 and by 1857 it had macadamised virtually the full length of the two chief roads in the colony: from Melbourne to Bendigo and from Geelong to Ballarat. This rapid improvement in the roads led to a sharp drop in the costs of carriage. Echuca, on the River Murray, forty miles north of Bendigo, had developed a substantial trade with the goldfields since it was less expensive to ship goods up the river from South Australia than to cart them the 100 miles from Melbourne. Once the road had been improved, however, the river trade fell away and Bendigo was linked firmly to Melbourne.

The improvement of the road also led to a quicker passenger service between Melbourne and Bendigo, especially after Cobb and Co. entered the business in January 1854 with their lighter and sturdier coaches and more frequent stages. Cobb and Co.'s coaches left Melbourne at 6 a.m. and reached Castlemaine, eighty miles away, by evening. On the next morning they completed the journey to Bendigo. By January 1856 the road had improved to such an extent that they took only one day for the trip. The Melbourne newspapers were then available in Bendigo on the day of publication. In the winter of 1854 the service had to be suspended, but thereafter the coaches ran right through the year. Cobb and Co.'s Bendigo coaches maintained an average speed of between nine and ten miles an hour. In the eighteenth century in Britain no coach travelled at this speed. In 1750 the average speed was approximately five miles per hour. Regular speeds of nine or ten miles an hour were not achieved until the 1820s. The Bendigo coaches travelled at this rate five years after the city's foundation.

The first steamship in Australian waters came into service in 1831. Blainey dismisses the contribution of steamships before 1850 as insignificant. He rightly says that in 1850 most of the coastal trade was still carried by sailing vessels, but the role of the coastal steamers as carriers of passengers and mail cannot be ignored. The first steamship service on the Australian coast was between Sydney and the towns and settlements along the Hunter River, 100 miles to the north. The Hunter River Valley was separated from Sydney by very difficult country. All the trade between Sydney and the river was carried by sea. Before the 1830s travellers who wanted to avoid a voyage in the small sailing vessels, which by turns could be dangerous or tedious, had the alternative of a three-day journey on horseback. The introduction of the steamships brought a great improvement. By the late 1830s there was a daily steamship service between Sydney and Newcastle and the time for the journey was a mere eight hours. As well as carrying the mail for the Hunter River and the country beyond, the steamers were used by the government to transport soldiers, convicts and stores.

Along the coast north of Newcastle the introduction of steamships coincided with the first settlement of the land. A group of graziers and their agents hired the steamer *King William IV* to inspect the land along the Clarence River. Steamships took away convicts from Moreton Bay and brought some of the first free settlers. Governor Gipps visited the settlement by steamship in 1842 and fixed on Brisbane as its port. A regular steamship service was established between Sydney and Brisbane the following year. At the same time, a service was begun between Sydney and Melbourne, but the seas along the southern coast were more boisterous and the steamer had to seek shelter on every other voyage. The mail between Sydney and Melbourne continued to be taken overland. Within the calm water of Port Phillip Bay a steamer began to ply between Melbourne and Geelong, the second town in the District, in 1841. Within a few months the mail service was transferred to the steamer which was quicker and more reliable than the mail cart. From 1843 there was a daily steamer service each way between the two centres.

The omission of any discussion of the telegraph within Australia is a serious distortion in Blainey's account of the techniques available to conquer distance. The first telegraph line, between Melbourne and Williamstown, was opened in 1854. The telegraph was relatively cheap and could be put up quickly. Within eight years, as the accompanying map shows, it connected the capital cities and every substantial town in south-eastern Australia. There was nothing 'mistaken' about this rapid triumph.

The telegraph was used chiefly for commercial messages. By this means country storekeepers could send urgent orders to the capital cities and wheat buyers receive daily instructions from their principals. Private personal messages were sent by the rich and by the rest of the population in cases of emergency. Its public uses were quite extensive. Information about the weather and the movement of ships was collected and distributed by telegraph both within and between colonies. After the opening of the intercolonial telegraph the newspapers printed each day a few items of news from the other colonial capitals and gradually they added telegraphic dispatches from country centres as well. The telegraph enabled country newspapers to present important news from the capital and up-to-date information on prices and markets. In 1859 the line between Adelaide and Melbourne enabled newspapers for the first time to give on-the-spot reporting from the

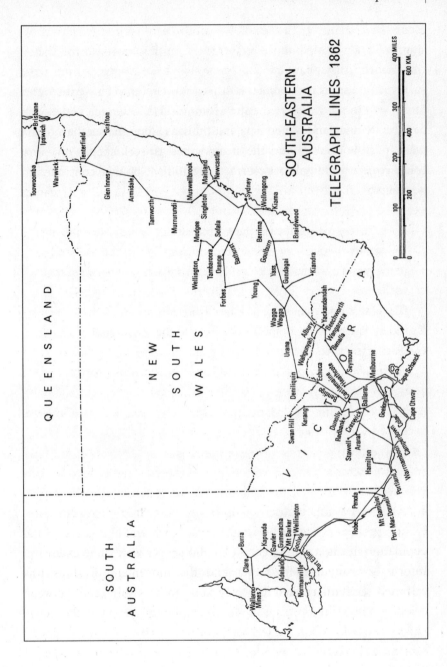

SOUTH-EASTERN
AUSTRALIA

TELEGRAPH LINES 1862

scene of a disaster. On the 6th of August the steamship *Admella* bound from Adelaide to Melbourne was wrecked on the coast near the Victorian–South Australian border. Some of the passengers and crew survived on the aft portion of the ship which remained above the water line. It was five days before the survivors could be taken off, and day by day the newspapers carried accounts of the rescue attempts and estimates of how many were still on the wreck and who they were. The *South Australian Register* described the impact of this new form of journalism:

> Never before, perhaps, were the horrors of a shipwreck so intensely realised by those who were not actual sharers in them. Every sweep of the waves over the wreck, every effort of the brave men who went to the rescue, every shriek of despair from the forlorn sufferers – in fact, almost every emotion, whether of hope or dread, on the part of those engaged in the desperate struggle for life – were flashed along the electric wires to Adelaide, and sympathised in by thousands of anxious beating hearts. The calamity was one which afflicted all.

For the conveying of information, the telegraph had annihilated distance.

The colonial governments were the largest single users of the telegraph. In Victoria, where government messages did not have to be paid for, they constituted in the 1860s about one-quarter of all messages sent. In New South Wales, where departments had to pay for their messages, they constituted a smaller, though increasing share of the total. The telegraph enabled the colonial governments, which in the absence of strong local bodies performed a multitude of functions, to rule their territories more effectively.

*

Two years after *The Tyranny of Distance*, Blainey published *Across a Red World*, which records his impressions of a rail journey through China and Russia. Here he encountered vastness on a new scale. Not only are the territories of these nations immense, they have people distributed right across them. In an interesting chapter entitled 'The

Red Mass' Blainey considers the effects of the huge size of Russia and China on their political history and in particular on the triumph of communism. He assumes that the large area of both countries made them more difficult to govern. So far China and Russia are the only countries for which Blainey has considered the relationship between distance and the forms and functioning of government. If he were now to consider the effective functioning of the highly centralised colonial governments in Australia, could he avoid the conclusion that distance – or more precisely in this case the conveying of information – was not a great problem in the Australian colonies?

The rule of powerful central authorities in the Australian colonies was most severely tested in New South Wales during the 1830s and 1840s when there was a rapid expansion of the pastoral frontier. Part of the new pastoral areas formed a separate economy based on Melbourne, and this was administered by a superintendent under the governor's authority, but the government in Sydney remained directly responsible for all of what is now New South Wales and Queensland. The government's officers in the pastoral areas were the commissioners of Crown lands and their bands of mounted police. The commissioners supervised the licensing of the squatters and all other occupiers of Crown lands – mechanics, doctors, shipwrights, storekeepers and cedar getters. Their constant task was the settling of disputes between the squatters over the boundaries and possession of their runs. They also collected statistics, made assessments for the stock tax, controlled the ticket-of-leave men, held inquests and dealt with the property of deceased persons. They have been described as petty dictators, but their rule was subject to scrutiny from Sydney. Squatters, aggrieved at their decisions, complained to the colonial secretary and commissioners were frequently called on to explain their actions. In a cause célèbre at Deniliquin, 500 miles south-west of Sydney, the big squatter Ben Boyd had a commissioner's ruling overturned. The commissioner had granted a licence to a former employee of Boyd to set up a store on Boyd's run which would have competed with the station store.

In the administration of their office and staff the commissioners were very closely tied to Sydney. All except very minor expenditure had to be approved by the colonial treasurer in advance and explained to the auditor-general at the end of the year. A commissioner could not put new shingles on his hut without asking Sydney first. He had to send a form each month to the auditor-general to receive pay for himself and his men. He had to give a regular account of all the stores and equipment in his possession to the colonial storekeeper. The cooking pots of the commissioners and their men were numbered in Sydney. Red tape seems to have had an effortless conquest over the bush.

The licensing system was also administered from Sydney. The commissioners did not issue licences. They made recommendations about the applicants, but the licence itself was issued by the colonial treasurer after he had received payment in Sydney. The squatter's Sydney agent made the payment and collected the licence for him. The register of licence holders was kept by the treasurer and he had to be informed of all alterations in the ownership of runs. This centralisation of administration mirrored that of the economy. It could be assumed that the squatter would have an agent in Sydney to transact business with the treasurer, because it was from there most of the wool was exported. Sydney's position as both trading and administrative centre was not threatened even though settlement had spread hundreds of miles into the interior.

*

It may be difficult to resolve arguments as to whether distances in Australia were great or not, though it is helpful to define what the relevant distances are. (Of course, there may be arguments about this, but such disputes will be an advance on the simple practice of using the dimensions of the whole continent.) It is a commonplace that distances are relative. The freedom with which goods move in a society is not related primarily to distance, but to the nature of goods that can be produced, the markets for them, and the means and costs of transport. The mobility of population depends on social structures, attitudes and expectations, as well as on personal means and the means of transport. Whatever the distances, the other circumstances of Australian settlement have been such that, from the beginning, goods, people and information have been highly mobile. Blainey's chapters speak of this movement, and it may seem churlish to object to the introductory sections and the title. However, it is my impression that the title of the book has an influence apart from the book itself. It diverts attention from the mobility which has made the Australian experience distinctive.

1975

Women and History

If history accepted a democratic commitment to record the experience of all past lives, nearly all the history books would concern peasants, since that is what most people have been for most recorded history. But ten thousand books on the peasant experience would not explain why two hundred years ago 90 per cent of Europe's people worked the land and now only 10 per cent do so. To explain that transformation the historian deals with forces outside the peasant realm – with the growth of capitalism, industrialisation, urbanisation. The chief human actors in this transformation were men: entrepreneurs, bankers, inventors, engineers, landlords, politicians. When history accounts for change, it inevitably concentrates on people of power and influence. Feminists simultaneously declare that women have been excluded from power and that they must have an equal place in history. Since feminism's claims about the past treatment of women are true, its claims on history cannot be realised.

For the past thirty years feminist historians have been attempting to escape this dilemma. Whatever the answer to the riddle of history, they insist that there must be lots of women in it – for otherwise it will damage women's self-esteem to read history. Having broken down almost every barrier in contemporary society, feminists do not want history to be left as the doings of a male club. Of course it is not just feminists who have elevated the promotion of self-esteem to a prime object of education. Education is no longer to take students out of themselves, but to make their selves the central object of study. So women's studies must be provided for women students, Aboriginal study for Aborigines, and migrant studies for migrants. A Greek migrant who wanted to study Bismarck would be a puzzle. An Aborigine who wanted to study Bismarck would be regarded as a freak. A woman studying Bismarck is thought to be in danger for she might come to believe that only men can be chancellors and conduct foreign policy. That she might learn something about diplomacy and the balance of power is not worthy of consideration.

So whatever the difficulties, a history with equal representation of women, a history which can be safely put in women's hands, must be created. The first step in the feminisation of history was a search for influential women, whom it was assumed male historians would have overlooked. A very thorough search revealed very few, and they only of the second or third rank. However patriarchal male historians have been, they were true to their discipline. When the evidence revealed a powerful woman they recorded the fact with no dissembling. None of them argued that Queen Elizabeth I was the tool of her male courtiers or that Queen Catherine de Medici was overawed by her sons.

That approach having failed, feminists then sought to discover the women who had been involved in broad social movements. They did uncover women who had been active in strikes, demonstrations and protests, but they were usually only subordinate allies to men. To perpetuate that view of women would be dangerous. This was not history useful for the cause. Only rarely were groups of women important actors in their own right. When they were – as in the march to Versailles in the French Revolution – male historians had already noticed them.

Then feminists struck gold. They joined their concern to the broader interest in social history, no longer defined as history with the politics left out, but as the social order considered as a whole. Every social order embodies a relationship between men and women; how that relationship is fixed and contested is one of its key constituents. To study this relationship and its changes means that women and men must be given equal attention. The way to bring women into history was to focus attention not on women, but on gender, how the sexes are given their identity and place.

On this theme feminist historians have done valuable work which

no historian can ignore. It is a true discovery, a widening of our understanding. However, feminist historians claim too much for it; they
insist that historians who ignore gender can't be doing their job. But it
is clear that gender relations change very slowly. The gender order can
remain the same and a nation can be conquered or liberated or fall into
civil war or be convulsed by revolution. Historians of these events don't
have to give too much attention to gender; they might choose to notice
the differential effects of these events on men and women which in
turn might affect gender relations. Changes occur in gender relations
as a consequence of broad changes in society at large; they are not self-
generating – or at least not until modern times. To understand these
broader changes which have affected gender relations we must return
to mainstream history, what feminists choose to call 'men's history',
patriarchal history or phallocentric knowledge, that is, the study of
economics, politics, wars, revolutions, ideology and religion.

Feminist historians denigrate the scholarship of their male predecessors and regularly draw on it for their own work. 'Men's history'
turns out to concern more than men. A feminist historian is dealing
with women in the middle ages. She wants to explain how both free
people and slaves moved to the intermediary status of serfs, so she
reaches for the classic work on feudalism by Marc Bloch. When she
deals with women in the towns in the early modern period she sets the
scene by referring to Fernand Braudel on capitalism. A new five-volume
History of Women in the West (eds Georges Duby and Michelle Perrot)
rather shamefacedly announces that each volume deals with a standard
period in European history (as established by men): the classical age,
the middle ages, Renaissance and Enlightenment, from French Revolution to World War I, the twentieth century. That is, 'men's history' even
when not particularly interested in women's experience, has dealt with
the broad economic, social and ideological formations which have set
the bounds for the lives of both men and women.

Feminist historians have disputed whether the great transformations in European history have had similar consequences for men and
women. The Renaissance promoted new learning and education,
including education for women – but was this advantage offset by a
constriction of women's opportunities? In the new centralised states

they could not exercise the power they had had as the wives of semi-independent feudal magnates or experience the pleasure of being courted by lovelorn knights. The Protestant Reformation and the French Revolution in their early stages gave women new freedom and opportunities, but did they then provide new means for restricting them? Whatever part these transformations played in the lives of women, whether they brought advantage or disadvantage, feminists acknowledge their significance. The transformations in the first instance were the works of men, and feminists have little to offer in explanation of why they occurred. Again they are dealing with effects, not prime causes.

There is a grand feminist claim, larger even than Marx's on class struggle as the motor of history, to the effect that what we call human history is a working-out of maleness. The development of hierarchical society, the elaboration of religions, the growth of economies, the rise and fall of civilisations, the fighting of wars – certainly, the wars – should be viewed as boys' games. When we examine male actors in history, it is their maleness and all that it implies which should first concern us. Gender is thus always relevant. This is so large a claim that it is well nigh useless for normal purposes. It is difficult to assess in the absence of societies without male dominance. Its power as propaganda is obvious. History is a record of 'crimes, follies and misfortunes' because it is the history of *man*kind. The claim may well be true – as Camille Paglia has observed, if women had been in charge we might all still be living in grass huts. But if all history so far constitutes one era, that of male domination, it must be admitted that there has been a huge variety within it. It is interesting and profitable to consider why. Just because male domination has been so complete, gender, which is what feminists want to talk about, will not be an important factor in explaining variety and change in the past.

*

These reflections are prompted by the appearance of the first feminist history of the Australian nation (*Creating a Nation*, by Patricia Grimshaw, Marilyn Lake, Ann McGrath and Marian Quartly, McPhee Gribble, 1994). This is the long-awaited new interpretation of our history by those who have complained so loudly about the old. Its authors declare in their introduction that the nation has not been exclusively created by men; women, too, have been 'major actors in the colonial and national dramas'. Three of the authors deal with the history since European settlement: Marian Quartly to 1860, Pat Grimshaw to 1912, Marilyn Lake to the present; Ann McGrath discusses Aboriginal society and its experience of the European invasion and occupation in three separate chapters interspersed through the rest. The authors are all able historians who have made notable contributions to the history of women and of gender relations and to Australian history generally.

A nation-state is a public thing – a polity and a people's shared view of themselves. Defining the nation, ruling the nation and defending the nation have been done mostly by men. *Prima facie* it is unlikely that women, generally excluded from the public realm, would have exercised the influence claimed for them here. I am pleased that the authors attempting this task are so able, because their failure is the more instructive. No matter how able the historian, it is impossible to write an intelligible history of the nation and sustain this feminist claim for female influence. Insofar as this book does provide a history of the Australian nation, it is not noticeably new.

Marian Quartly opts for intelligibility and ignores the claim made for female influence in the introduction; indeed she explicitly rejects it. She was perhaps less likely to be drawn into feminist excess, since her first task is to deal with a convict colony planned by British officials and run by officers, civil and military, all male. That the few hundred women among the convicts could be presented as major actors in this enterprise is inherently implausible. That the women were present at all is of course highly significant, and this gives Quartly her cue. The shaping forces in her narrative are male, British planners and officials, the early governors, and later the British policy-makers who stopped the transportation of convicts and replaced them with free labour. In all their plans and decisions on the shape of the colony they were, among other things, determining a gender order, explicitly or implicitly. Quartly moves between official action and what this meant for the lives of ordinary people, men and women, and their relations with each other. She is of the 'normalising school' in her depiction of convict society – that is, New South Wales approached a normal community rather than a hell-hole, and she conveys a good sense of the opportunity it offered by following the lives of named people and their families. Her chapters are a fine display of the breadth and particularity which the best of the new social history offers.

Quartly is as interested in men as in women and compares their lot open-mindedly, something which her co-authors are not prepared to do. She notes for instance that women convicts had much easier work than the men and also the opportunity to escape official tasks by becoming married. She gives particular attention to marriage because, in deciding whether to marry and if so whom, convict women had the chance to exercise some influence over the shape of their lives. It was at this point only that women were independent actors.

Decisions about marriage, like the allocation of resources necessary to create farms and businesses, depended on official favour: 'the government's marriage policy put the personal decisions of convict women and men into the hands of magistrates and clergymen and ultimately governors … ordinary couples got so used to a public ordering of their private lives that ex-convicts and even the native-born asked the governor's permission to marry'. So far is Quartly unembarrassed in depicting official male authority as the shaping force in early Australian society.

With the opening of Pat Grimshaw's chapters a new approach emerges. Here on in there is a determination to put women on centre stage even if the male bit players finally determine the action. Marian Quartly opened her chapters with James Matra's 1783 plan for a settlement in New South Wales. Pat Grimshaw begins hers with Caroline Chisholm's 1860 lecture in support of the campaign for breaking up squatters' land into smallholdings. Chisholm had not initiated this campaign and she contributed very little to it. Her lecture nevertheless gets a page and a half while the mass demonstrations and meetings by which men actually secured access to the land are not treated at all. Nevertheless, Pat Grimshaw is an honest historian and she reports: 'The territorial and economic expansion of the colonies in the decades from the 1860s to the 1890s continued to be spearheaded by white men, certainly. But it is important to capture at the same time the place allotted to white women, who may have played a less obvious, though still significant, part in these transformations.' So women were something less than the 'major actors' of the introduction.

*

From the late 1880s women entered public life for the first time in campaigns for the vote, greater equality in civil rights and against the liquor trade. At the same time men in trade unions and the Labor Party organised to mitigate or remove the oppressions of capitalist society. Grimshaw treats this class movement sympathetically and as a dynamic in itself. She is interested in how far the men's plan for social change complemented or conflicted with the women's. For instance, was the threat posed by low female wages to be met by paying men more so that women would not have to work or by equal pay for men and women? Grimshaw concedes that the labour movement was stronger than the 'smaller, dispersed, but energised, women's movement'. The women's movement did achieve the vote, but generally women had worked for the improvement of women's status in marriage and the home, not outside. So: 'the route they negotiated for themselves kept women marginal to mainstream politics ... the women's vote split, as did men's, on the basis of economic interest and party political divisions'. Male historians have treated the women's movement in less detail, but it appears they were correct in their emphasis on economic interests, class and party.

In Pat Grimshaw's chapters, unlike Marian Quartly's, there are occasional strident claims for the importance of gender which are not sustained. For instance, the Arbitration Act must be understood, she says, as a gendered settlement in that it provided a family wage for male workers and a much lower wage for women. But was this its chief significance? Women's wages had previously been lower than men's as they were everywhere else. The Arbitration Court certainly institutionalised this, but the chief effect of this was that when opinion changed on women's entitlements the Arbitration Court could quite rapidly ensure that equal pay for equal work became the general rule. The chief significance of the Arbitration Court was that in Australia a state instrumentality set the level of wages and the conditions of work for men and women. The first obligation of any history of Australia is to offer an explanation of why this extraordinary system was inaugurated. This history does not.

Generally in Grimshaw's chapters there is a loss of intelligibility in that obviously important things are happening off stage with little or no explanation. Grimshaw refers to Australia as democratic, egalitarian, possessing a less rigid class structure than Britain and a benevolent state. We are not too fazed by the lack of explanation of these characteristics because we recognise this Australia. It is the one identified, described and analysed at length by male historians.

Marilyn Lake is the most ambitious of the three. She is chiefly concerned with women's movements, the forms of women's participation in the public realm, the growth of women's paid employment and the arguments it engendered, changing views on sexuality, birth control and the birthrate – all part of a project of making the differences between men and women an essential dynamic of history. There is no doubt that changes in gender relations in this period constituted a major transformation in Australian society and Lake's account is lively and revealing. I think her the most original and arresting of the feminist historians. Her weakness is a tendency to push men and women further apart than they really were in order to create her gender dynamic. For instance, she describes men and women forming very different visions in response to the trauma of the 1930s Depression. Men wanted policies of full employment and a social security safety net. Women wanted fewer babies as a way to self-possession and freedom. In fact women had been having fewer babies since the late nineteenth century and it is well known that until recently the birthrate only fell when men co-operated with women in birth control. Men's co-operation was essential when the condom and withdrawal were among the chief measures used. Married men shared women's desire to limit the birthrate (Grimshaw acknowledges that it was *couples* who limited births). And where is the evidence that married women were not interested in full employment for married men? The stigma against a married woman who worked and so threatened men's employment was maintained as fiercely by married women at home as by trade unionists in the workplace.

It is instructive to compare the conclusion of Lake's chapter on the Depression with that of Stuart Macintyre's in the *Oxford History of Australia*, volume four. Macintyre uses the oral testimony of survivors to report that when asked who suffered most in the Depression husbands answer their wives, and wives their husbands. This bespeaks a mutual understanding and respect between husband and wife in these marriages where women were in charge of the house and men worked or looked for work outside it. Mutual understanding is not what Marilyn Lake looks for.

A history of gender relations, which constitutes the chief theme of Lake's chapters, is something less than the history of the nation. Lake herself is aware of this and her chapters include a mini-history of the economy and politics. Every government and prime minister is treated or at least mentioned. I detect little novelty in this: it summarises the standard left-liberal view of our history. It is deftly interwoven with the gender theme, but the influence of gender on the economy and politics is not substantial. Lake makes a connection between women's reluctance to have babies and the migration program after World War II. So were women responsible for multicultural Australia? Not altogether, since men co-operated in the decline in the birthrate and it required the imagination of male politicians – or of one politician, Arthur Calwell – to solve the population problem in the way we did. Rather than transforming the national history, Lake has added the gender theme to it. Of course it did not require a feminist history to identify changes in gender relations as a major development of the last thirty years.

*

It falls to Marilyn Lake to deal with a key episode in the development of the Australian nation, World War I and in particular the Gallipoli campaign. Her approach to the war is to discuss women's activities as much as possible and summarise men's. So the campaign by women against price rises is treated and no mention is made of the victories of Monash and the AIF in the closing campaign against Germany. It may be said that this only redresses a long imbalance, since women's activities have usually been entirely ignored. But this won't do. The Australian victories were a more significant national event than the women's campaign against prices because they greatly increased national pride and self-confidence.

Gallipoli is the great test for this book. This was the occasion when by common consent Australians threw off their colonial self-doubt and believed themselves to be a nation. What can a feminist do with this foundation legend of male warriors? Give it a grudging treatment and then declare that the soldiers not only attacked the Turks, they became attackers of Australian women! The soldiers were hailed as those who gave birth to the nation, when everyone knows it is women, facing great danger, who give birth. Women's function had been usurped by men!

What are we to make of this extraordinary claim? No evidence is offered that in fact attitudes to women as mothers changed as a result of this metaphorical appropriation of 'birth' by men. Lake should not need to be told that women giving birth is a most unlikely process to be celebrated as a national symbol, since childbirth is a natural process not varying from nation to nation or between tribe, empire and nation. No evidence is offered that Australian women of the time felt this alleged appropriation of their function; the truth, of course, is that women were as great admirers of the Anzacs as were men. This passage does not constitute feminist history; it is not history of any sort – it is a feminist wail.

All the authors share the post-modern view that the development of national symbols is a process of exclusion, since people not represented in the symbols feel their identity is denied. Post-modern feminists may feel excluded by male symbols but they should not assume that all women in the past – or indeed the present – feel so. The teenage school-girl opens her folder covered with photos of pop stars and footballers and inscribes at her teacher's dictation that Australian women felt excluded by the maleness of the digger legend! People don't look for representativeness in their heroes and heroines. Otherwise Ned Kelly would not be famous, since few people are cattle thieves and bank robbers. And 'Waltzing Matilda' would never have been heard of except in the lore of suicidal swagmen. People are stirred into hero worship by daring, recklessness, self-sacrifice, grace, a master player or a master spirit. For obvious reasons it has been mostly men who have been able to achieve heroic status, but not exclusively so. Britannia has stirred many male British hearts. Joan of Arc has inspired French men. There have been a number of Australian women heroes and stereotypes little considered in this volume. An heroic figure of the opposite sex can be more attractive – a thing undreamt of in post-modern, feminist philosophy.

On the formation of the national polity itself the book has almost nothing to say. Federation is treated in a couple of paragraphs. To treat it more extensively would prolong the recognition that women were not major actors in it. There is no discussion of the complex processes by which six colonies within the British empire became self-governing within the empire and then a nation within a commonwealth. Nor of the parallel shift in identity from British to British–Australian to Australian. There may be a feminist perspective on these matters, but in this book – silence.

The great puzzlement of the book is that four authors determined to find female influence should have overlooked the one area where it was greatest – in the home. The influence was strong because the common form of Australian marriage was companionate, not patriarchal. The companionate marriage, in which husband and wife were partners, emerged in Britain from the late eighteenth century. The man earned the income and the woman was in charge of home and children, and both took decisions which affected the family as a whole. This form of marriage came to Australia and became more widespread than in Britain. A man who wanted to assert his headship in all things could still do so, since that is what the law allowed, but there is no doubt of the cultural pressures on men to accept the enhanced status of women which the companionate marriage provided. One sign of this is the widespread practice in the working class of husbands giving over their pay to their wives. The women were in charge of the household budget: the provision of food and clothing, the payment of rent, and the arrangement of credit. Feminists, looking only to externals, consider that the family wage, institutionalised by the Arbitration Court, gave men economic power over women. They overlook the fact that many men abdicated this power to their wives. When the Arbitration Court first set the level of wages it consulted not trade unionists but five of their wives who spent their husbands' earnings. Working-class wives at home were working managers; it was their husbands who were workers under orders – a point lost on those feminists who consider all work outside the home as a form of liberation. Many married women well understood what their men endured at work in order to provide them and their children with continuing support. Married men had to be more reliable and compliant at work, which was why employers often preferred them.

Quite unaccountably the authors of *Creating a Nation* refuse to recognise the existence of companionate marriage. They insist on male headship and control: 'the domestic government exercised by the male head of the household'; 'the power of individual men to govern individual women in private'; 'man's paramount position as head of household'; 'the husband's right of domestic government'. Our patriarchal history is summarised on the last page of the book: the lives of Aborigines, women and ethnic minorities 'have been largely ruled by white men of British descent'. What little information the authors provide on particular marriages suggests that they were not patriarchal, but on this point the book is not interested in evidence, not even its own; patriarchy is axiomatic. Marian Quartly briefly strays from this position. She records the new idea which took hold from the 1830s that in marriage women could make men good. Of course they could not do that if they were totally subordinate to men. Women's superior goodness was part of the thinking that led to the companionate marriage: it gave women moral authority and made them the parent better suited to control the children. But having noticed the first signs of the arrival of the companionate marriage in Australia, Quartly reverts to the standard line and asserts, on the authority of a feminist theorist, that men had absolute rights to govern their family.

The evidence that women were not ruled by men, that indeed within the household many women ruled their men, is abundant. There are living witnesses to what women pre-liberation were like. Tim Winton is one:

> I grew up in an extended family where the matriarchs made all the running. Perhaps it was a genetic hiccup, but the women made all the plays and the men followed. The women had more drive about

them, they had more of a hardness. They were stronger-willed and altogether more fierce as personalities. Their children feared them into middle age and beyond. I was always more fearful (or at the very least, watchful) of my grandmothers and aunts than their men. Most of them had the tempers and the tongues; they were more vengeful than their men and they were always the final authority. My grandmothers ran their families by sheer force of character, by brilliant organisation and hard work or by mean-spirited sabotage and humiliation. Their husbands, by comparison, were mild and ineffectual.
—*Good Weekend*, 27 August 1994

Winton, hearing what modern feminists say, thinks his experience of matriarchs was unusual. Consider then what Janet McCalman in *Struggletown* writes on the women of working-class Richmond:

The working-class family was most commonly a matriarchy where women bore the major responsibility for the expenditure of the family income, the care of the children, the quality of family life. Women sometimes regarded their husbands as one of the children except that they slunk out to play at the pub or with the SP bookie. Battling against poverty bred often formidable middle-aged women who towered over their feckless and immature husbands. The vast majority of men regarded it as a matter of pride that their wives did not have to go to work, and their wives agreed with them: a working wife signalled masculine failure. None the less, men could resent their role as compliant and barely tolerated providers.

Female domination could sour a marriage as profoundly as male dominance, but true companions did exist. Listen to two men talking about their marriage. Notice that these men, contrary to what feminists allege, respected their wives for the work that they did in the house. The first is Albert Facey in *A Fortunate Life*:

my wages averaged four pounds per week and our budget was very tight. My wife managed quite well and I often wondered how, but I always got plenty to eat and the children were all well looked after and content. Evelyn was wonderful – she knew all the things required for making good palatable meals, and what she knew about making children's clothes was something you would have to see to believe.

The second is a gold digger returning from Western Australia to Sydney because his wife had died, as depicted by Henry Lawson in 'They Wait on the Wharf in Black':

More'n twenty years she stuck to me and struggled along by my side. She never give in. I'll swear she was on her feet till the last, with her sleeves tucked up – bustlin' round ... And just when things were brightening and I saw a chance of giving her a bit of a rest and comfort for the rest of her life ... I thought of it all only t'other week when things was clearing up ahead; and the last [money] 'order' I sent over I set to work and wrote her a long letter, putting all the good news and encouragement I could think of into it. I thought how that letter would brighten up things at home, and how she'd read it round. I thought of lots of things that a man never gets time to think of while his nose is kept to the grindstone. And she was dead and in her grave, and I never knowed it.

These four quotations tell you more about Australian marriage than the 314 pages of *Creating a Nation*.

*

The insistence that women were subject to the government of men leads the authors into contradiction and absurdity. Patriarchy is their theme: men were in charge of the public realm, from which women were excluded, and they were in charge of women in the home, to which women were confined – and yet women were major actors in Australian history! How did they escape the patriarchs to initiate anything? And why should these nineteenth-century patriarchs legislate to provide education for women, more equitable divorce for women and votes for women? Isn't it more credible that women began to enjoy equality in companionate marriage, that some women then became active in public to ensure that the law recognised women's equality and that male legislators responded positively, not inaugurating a new order but endorsing and promoting one already in existence?

This point was first made sixteen years ago by one of the authors of this volume, Pat Grimshaw (in *Historical Studies*, No. 72, April 1979). She criticised an early feminist work which claimed that Australian women were the doormats of the Western world by asking why, then, did Australian women gain the vote so early? Now it is Pat Grimshaw who is embarrassed by the enfranchisement of women. Since it will scarcely be believed that a feminist history of Australia would be reluctant to discuss why women were enfranchised I reproduce in full the book's treatment of the subject:

> the women's movement in the 1890s turned its attention to the enfranchisement of women in the colonies and in the coming federal state. There was a victory for suffragists in South Australia in 1894, and in Western Australia in 1899. Although in both colonies the suffrage passed the legislatures with a combination of unexpected manoeuvrings by male politicians anxious to reap the benefit of the women's vote, the success was nevertheless heartening. Still more exciting, however, was the passage in 1902 of the act allowing women to vote in the federal elections.

That's it! The whole issue is reduced to parliamentary manoeuvre and vote-seeking. To look more widely into women's place in society, to understand why women's franchise was not rejected out of hand, would be to blow the whole game.

I am not suggesting that women's standing was extraordinarily high in Australia because the vote was granted to them early. The key precursor to the granting of the franchise was companionate marriage, which was common to the United Kingdom, the United States and Australia. One reason why the vote was granted earlier in Australia was that there were fewer women wanting to exercise their rights *outside* the home. That's what scared the male politicians in the east coast of the United States and in London. This is a point made by Audrey Oldfield in her very useful study *Woman Suffrage in Australia: A Gift or a Struggle?*

Why Pat Grimshaw has changed her mind, why these authors jointly offer a degraded view of women in the home, she and they will have to explain. On this matter the book does not seek to explain. My guess is that since feminists are so committed to getting women out of the house, they are reluctant to acknowledge that while remaining at home women did achieve an enhancement of their status and an opportunity to share with men in the governance of home and family. Furthermore, feminists, with reason, do not want to celebrate this gain too much because the wife's position as partner was not guaranteed: a drunken or brutal man could make her life hell. Nevertheless, the change was real, widespread and vastly influential.

To govern the home in Australia was to govern a significant realm, since homes and home life were highly valued. In the cities, where a high proportion of people lived, homes were separate from work places and hence it was impossible for men to supervise them continuously. They stood on their own ground in extensive suburbs. When virtually all married women stayed at home the suburbs in daylight were women's territory in contest with their children. Again – can it be credited – home life in the suburbs is not discussed in a book on Australia and women's influence upon it. Marilyn Lake is blind to this female realm: she thinks married women at home were in 'solitary confinement'.

Creating a Nation attempts to establish female influence by depicting women as high flyers – 'major actors in the colonial and national dramas' – and by talking about women a lot. The better way is to consider what influence women had on Australian culture in the broad sense. *Creating a Nation* announces its interest in this, but does not pursue it. There are three impressive histories which do, all of which take the home seriously and don't see men as dominant in it. Janet McCalman's *Struggletown* has already been mentioned. Alan Atkinson in his fine study *Camden* makes a large claim for female influence on the emergence of nineteenth-century liberal political culture which included ordinary people if they were clean, literate, and independent:

This far-sighted authority which women now assumed, and their newly perceived moral power – as 'grand wielders of the moral pruning knife' – were both allied to the invading virtues of Liberalism.

Women, more than men, were really the makers of Liberal culture. They provided its sharp edge in local and family life where the work of application began.

John Rickard, in *Australia: A Cultural History*, discusses the distinctive qualities of Australian culture and on every point is concerned to trace the different experience and activity of women and how they were accommodated in the culture. Like the feminists, Rickard wants to treat men and women separately and not pursue a unitary history, but he is more interested in the terms and conditions on which they met. None of these books flies feminist banners, but they give women a more secure place in our history than *Creating a Nation* because, paradoxically, their first care is to characterise the whole society, the whole culture. That approach gives men more space than *Creating a Nation* wants to allow them.

Aborigines receive special treatment in *Creating a Nation*. I refer not to the three separate chapters devoted to them but to those chapters' relative freedom from feminist ideology. Ann McGrath in tracing Aboriginal relations is interested in gender: European men and Aboriginal women met on very different terms from European women and Aboriginal men. But McGrath is not very interested in the changing gender relations within Aboriginal society since 1788, and she explains that for Aborigines their oppression as a race was the chief determining factor in their lives, for both men and women. This allowance of the subsidiary importance of gender – indeed its relative unimportance – would never be proclaimed in the rest of the book. But of many working-class women it could well be said that the inequalities and shocks of a capitalist economy affected them much more than relations with their husbands. If we could summon up all the Australian dead, wouldn't most of them say that what McGrath reports of Aborigines was true of their own lives: 'No matter what power struggles occurred between men and women, these paled in comparison with the impact of outside forces on their family and private lives'? Consider, for starters, the effects of three depressions and two world wars.

McGrath does give close attention to gender relations within Aboriginal society before 1788. This forms part of an elegant and moving account of Aboriginal life around Sydney at the time of the European arrival. This is blessedly free from noble savagery. The only point which jarred with me was a ritual condemnation of European cultural arrogance, which sits rather oddly in a chapter which could only have been written because of the close and sympathetic attention paid to the Aborigines by the officers of the First Fleet. In her account McGrath does not hide the fact that Aboriginal men beat their wives. You might think this was patriarchy, pure and simple, but no. Gender relations are complex. Aboriginal women could hit back; they had their own ceremonies and activities; they could feed themselves without male aid. It is hard to work out the power balance between Aboriginal men and women.

If only relations between Australian men and women could have been approached so open-mindedly, if only gender had not been considered so central to Australian society, we would have had a much better history, but then it would not have been feminist enough.

1995

Australian History and European Civilisation

The study and teaching of Australian history have their own history. The chroniclers identify a long dark age when there was little or no study and teaching of the subject. At schools and universities British history was what students had to know; if Australian history was taught it was not as a separate subject but as part of the history of the British empire.

The dark ages ended in 1946 when the University of Melbourne offered the first full course in Australian history. Since then Australian history has made up for its long neglect. In many schools virtually the only history taught is Australian; in the universities the subject is widely offered and students can major in history without having to study the history of anything else.

Could there be a narrower education than this? Yes. In a New Zealand university you can major in history by studying only New Zealand history, though admittedly this narrowness is offset by the opportunity to take a complementary major in New Zealand literature.

These are more truly the dark ages, for students are cut off from the knowledge of British and European history without which their own society is unintelligible. In the 1920s and 1930s primary school children knew something of the origins of civic and political rights in Britain, of Parliament's victory over the King, and the law's struggle for independence. University students can now complete their historical studies without knowing anything of this. If the rationale for studying Australian history is to understand one's own society, then these students do not understand the origins of our legal and political institutions. And how can they understand the history of religion in Australia if they do not study the Protestant Reformation in Europe in the sixteenth century? And how can they understand secular liberalism and radicalism in Australia if they do not understand the eighteenth-century Enlightenment? When Australian history was first taught, the students had already studied British and European history. The University of Sydney still follows the practice of the 1920s and 1930s. Believing that Australia is a derivative society, it will not let students study Australian history until they have studied British and European history. For this it was rapped over the knuckles in 1986 by the government committee charged with Australianising the curriculum.

The teacher of that first Australian history course at the University of Melbourne was Manning Clark. No-one could quarrel with the breadth of his conception of his subject – the arrival of European civilisation and its fate in this country. But before the Europeans other civilisations – the Hindu, the Chinese, the Muslim – had come close to Australia without ever settling it. So the beginning point for Clark's Australia was the simple comparison between barbarism within (Aboriginal culture) and civilisation without.

The first questions to be addressed were why the Europeans rather than other civilisations discovered and settled Australia, and of the Europeans why the English and not the Dutch, the Portuguese or the Spanish. The English were a Protestant people, but among the officers and gentlemen of the convict colony in New South Wales were men of the Enlightenment who believed in reason and progress and who saw religion as useful merely to keep the lower orders in check. Among the convicts were a substantial minority of Irish who kept the Catholic faith alive in a Protestant world. At the foundation of European settlement, then, were followers of the three great faiths – Catholicism, Protestantism and the Enlightenment. Clark saw his task to be the exploration of how they developed in reaction to each other and in response to the new strange environment. The key development occurred in the second half of the nineteenth century when Protestants, because of their deep hostility to Catholics, allied themselves with secularists of the Enlightenment to keep religion out of schools and public ceremony. Australians created 'a society unique in the history of mankind, a society of men holding no firm beliefs on the existence of God or survival after death'.

Clark took great pains to prepare himself for writing his *History*, which ran finally to six volumes, the first appearing in 1962 and the last in 1987. In the 1950s he published short articles sketching out his approach and two volumes of documents whose annotations and introductions were so full that they are reference books and interpretative essays as well as documentary collections. In the introduction to Volume II of the documents, which covers the period 1850–1900, Clark challenged the prevailing radical interpretation of Australian history which posited a radical hegemony running from the gold rushes of the 1850s to the strike camps and Labor Party of the 1890s. Clark knew that whatever the consequences of the democratic reforms of the 1850s, they had not prevented the establishment of a solid bourgeois society whose monuments of churches, town halls, schools and banks still dominated the Melbourne of his youth. The radical interpretation was not merely wrong about radical strength; it was crass in accepting the radicals' own measure of success, solidarity and better material conditions. Clark concluded his introduction with these words: 'So we leave them, dumbfounded at their optimism, astounded that belief in material progress and mateship could be their only comforters against earth and sky, man and beast.'

Clark was to break the narrow bounds of Australian history by bringing it under the gaze of a mind steeped in the great literature of Europe. Manning Clark in his springtime was courted by Peter Coleman of the *Quadrant* circle which insisted that culture in Australia must take its standards from Europe.

His early essays and the introductions to the documents are the best history Clark wrote. They are fair-minded, accurate, subtle in their understanding of social and economic process, clear and fresh in their interpretation – all qualities which become increasingly difficult to discern in the six volumes of the *History* which follow. In the early work the dramatist and the prophet were under the discipline of the social scientist; in the *History* he broke free and if he succeeded as dramatist or prophet it was at the expense of rendering a clear account of the history of Australian society. The books are loosely organised chronicles with the events linked to each other on no firmer ground than that they were happening at the same time. The evidence on any point never accumulates, so the author's judgments carry no authority; they are *obiter dicta* of a rather wayward and impressionable judge. Clark was increasingly preoccupied with individual lives, not merely with their public influence but with their private selves. He was a frustrated biographer masquerading as a general historian. His was a tragic vision and he was adept at finding fatal flaws in his characters. To have uncovered and convincingly depicted two or three tragic heroes among Australia's public figures would have been an achievement; in making Hamlets of them all, he went dangerously close to bringing himself into derision.

Meanwhile, what had happened to the theme of European civilisation in Australia? It had become attenuated and debased. Let us look at the final volume of the *History, The Old Dead Tree and the Young Tree Green*, which covers the years 1916 to 1935 and whose chief theme is the relationship of Australia with Britain. The demands of drama require that there be a simple opposition between those who were loyal to Britain and those loyal to Australia, and the interest in individuals leads to Menzies being cast as the representative of one position and Curtin the other. Needless to say the truth was much more complex than this. For the majority of Australians loyalty to both Britain and Australia co-existed without undue strain. But in Clark's eyes, because Menzies looked for an empire defence of Australia he was a 'groveller' to Britain; Curtin was to find the way to escape this dependence. Fortunately the volume ends in 1935 before Curtin's method of doing so had to be discussed, for he became a 'groveller' to the United States, and when towards the end of the war he feared its influence he ran back to Britain and appointed a duke as governor-general.

Upon these crudities Clark built the great antithesis of the title: was Australia to be part of the old dead tree, Europe, or was it to be the young tree green? Certainly from the 1920s to the 1940s the argument over literary and artistic culture in Australia was polarised in this way. The Europeanists upheld the highest standards and doubted whether Australians could ever reach them; the nationalists wanted Australians to stop reading European literature and develop their own. The argument ended with the defeat of both sides and the emergence of a mature Australian literary culture within the European tradition. Such a process is of central interest to someone studying the fate of European civilisation in Australia. Clark rightly discussed it. The puzzle is that he accepts the antithesis, Europe or Australia, and endorses the nationalists' position – this from a man who took his inspiration from European literature and his comfort from European music! So in the end Clark became the sort of historian he had set out to supersede – a barracker for the 'progressive' side who accepted uncritically its view of the world. The whole game escaped him.

I am a critic of Clark's practice and admirer of his original vision. His theme of European civilisation in Australia must be the basis for any intelligible history of this country. My concern is that his vision is now being undermined. I identify three forces which are antagonistic to it. Clark himself succumbed to them in varying degrees. They are (1) the claim for Aboriginal priority in Australian history; (2) the conception of Australia as a collection of ethnic groups; (3) the nationalist concern for Australian distinctiveness.

The Claim for Aboriginal Priority

If Clark were to announce today as he did in the opening of his first volume that he was to treat the mighty theme of the coming of civilisation to Australia, he would be told that a civilisation was already here and that the arrival of another was a crime. If he were to proceed to discuss the European discoverers of this continent he would be told that the Aborigines had discovered Australia many thousands of years before.

These objections would be made by Aborigines and their sympathisers or by those anxious not to offend Aborigines. It is offensive to say that a human society is uncivilised because it suggests a debased or degraded form of life. It is totally inappropriate for a culture as rich as we now know Aboriginal culture to have been. But if we agree that the Aborigines were not uncivilised, there is still point in saying that they did not constitute a civilisation. I too have no wish to give offence, but we are in danger today of being so anxious not to give offence that we are unable to explain how anything happens in human affairs. Much of what now passes for social science is concerned not to explain human differences but to explain them away.

The short reason for classifying Aboriginal society as not a civilisation is that it did not have cities. The word *civilisation* has at its core the word for city and to understand what cities entail is to understand the chief features of civilisation. Cities emerge in societies of large populations; they are made possible when producers of food are willing or are forced to feed others besides themselves; this distribution is organised by government which supports itself by taxation; the working of government requires record-keeping and writing; writing is used to inscribe the law which controls the large populations; the ultimate enforcers of the law are soldiers paid by the government. These key features of civilisation are absent from the small, undifferentiated, face-to-face society of hunter-gatherers such as the Aborigines were before the arrival of Europeans.

For most of civilisation the group enjoying its full benefits has been very narrow and its exploitation of the rest has been gross. The equality of condition among the Aborigines may well seem a more just social order. But with its harsh yoking of people together civilisation greatly increased human capacity – for warfare which was what civilised governments were mostly concerned with; for the exercise of power over large areas which usually meant little more than heavy-handed extraction of taxes, but sometimes as in the Roman Empire the establishment of order and law; and of thought, for thinking was not under such rigid social control as it was in tribal life, what Professor Stanner described, in reference to Aboriginal society, as 'the one possibility thing'.

European civilisation in the modern period acquired capacities unmatched by any other. Through science, which it invented, it was able to control and harness natural forces far beyond anything previously achieved and to cure or prevent much human disease. Through the industrial revolution it was able to generate such economic growth that eventually brought all its people to undreamt-of levels of prosperity and comfort. And directly or indirectly it brought all other civilisations and societies under its thrall.

The expansion of Europe was the transforming force in human history of the last 500 years, and yet the modern academy looks for reasons not to study it. In the era of decolonisation the new nations want to stress their indigenous roots and sympathetic scholars explain that European influence was not overwhelming, but that it was used and subverted by locals for local purposes. To concentrate on Europe is criticised as 'Eurocentric'. But to ignore Europe makes the history of any part of the globe unintelligible. Granted all that can be said for indigenous continuity, no-one can claim that European influence has been transient, certainly not while the new nations, themselves modelled on European originals, struggle to extend their Western technology and industry and the provision of Western medicine. Even the most ferocious critics of European civilisation, the Islamic mullahs, issue their *fatwas* on television and when they fall ill travel by jumbo jet to Boston hospitals.

*

The Australian mode of downplaying the European effect is to query the claim that Europeans discovered Australia. If the word *discovery* survives it is in quotation marks, the fig leaves by which the modern generation covers unwelcome but undeniable phenomena. Certainly the Aborigines were the first people to settle in Australia but they lived in separate tribes and did not have a notion of the continent as a whole or of their relation to the rest of the inhabited globe. They came originally from Asia but by the time the Europeans arrived they believed, as some still do, that they had been created here. Their discovery of Australia was lost in a philosophy which insisted that there was nothing new. The European discoveries were the process by which Europeans explored and mapped the whole globe so that they were the first to know where everything stood in relation to everything else, which was, of course, part of the reason for their success as conquerors and colonisers.

The European discovery rather than Aboriginal occupation constitutes Australia's pre-history. Australia – its economy, society and polity – is a construction of European civilisation. Australia did not exist when traditional Aborigines occupied the continent. Aborigines have been participants in Australian history, but that story begins with all the others in 1788.

The Aboriginal and European ways of life were incompatible in almost every respect and the displacement of one form of life by another was abrupt and complete. In recent years Australian historians have highlighted how violent and bloody this displacement was, yet they have sought in other ways to soften this disjunction. They have recast their subject as the human occupation of the continent. If they write the history of any particular aspect of European civilisation in Australia, say education or law, they include a first chapter on Aboriginal law or education. In the Bicentennial history issued by the Australian Academy of Science even science was treated in this way. General histories of Australia now begin, as Clark's did not, with a chapter describing Aboriginal society and culture. These approaches are a primitivist way of acknowledging the priority of Aboriginal occupation, but they do not make for intelligible history, for there is and can be virtually no connection between the first chapters of these books and the rest. The one subject which demands that the whole human occupation of the continent be considered is a history of the land itself. But whatever the influences of people on the land, the land has not had a determining influence on the nature of human society which has existed upon it. The same land and resources which sustained scattered bands of hunter-gatherers were made to support within one generation of European settlement a much larger population settled in cities, towns and farms.

Before the Europeans arrived, there were 500 to 600 tribes in the continent speaking different languages. They did not have a common name or share an identity; they regarded each other as enemies. The Aborigines as we know them today, a national group with a common identity, did not exist before European contact; they are a product of the European invasion which destroyed traditional culture, brought people of different tribes together and gave them a common experience of oppression and marginalisation. They are not an ancient people, but a very modern one. Only in the lands which Europeans did not want or settled very sparsely did traditional groups and something like traditional culture survive. The more substantial the traditional culture is, the less likely are its possessors to think of themselves as Aborigines. They are Gurindji or Walbiri. The majority of Aborigines possess only traces of traditional culture – a few words, the strong, mutual support among kin. Overall they are as far from the bands of hunter-gatherers as Europeans in Australia are from the medieval village.

In recent years governments have been making a determined effort to ensure that Aborigines enjoy the full benefits of European society of which they are a part. The seeming stolidity of Aborigines in the face of these offers leads perplexed ministers of Aboriginal affairs to claim that Aborigines are still deterred and blocked by white prejudice. They denounce racism and plan education campaigns. Would that things were so simple! In fact the prejudice against Aborigines is weakening and the institutional support for bypassing it is enormous. A more serious inhibitor is that at the core of the Aboriginal identity is a great negative: the determination not to be like the Europeans who have controlled them and in whose shadow they have lived. To get on, to live fully in the European way, particularly to exercise authority, is a form of betrayal.

Many of those well disposed towards Aborigines regard the original invasion as the irreversible wrong which mocks all efforts at a better deal for Aborigines. But if the European invasion is cancelled, the Aborigines, as we know them today, disappear. The intractability we face, the great burden of our history, is not that tribespeople were over-whelmed by European civilisation, but that Aborigines took their origin as an underclass within it.

The expansion of Europe was a phenomenon of such magnitude with such a profound and irreversible effect on humankind that it might be thought that our moralising tendency would be silenced in the face of it. But as we saw on the 500th anniversary of Columbus's voyage in 1992, there are those who think that its disastrous conse-quences for indigenous people make it quite definitely a bad thing which should not have happened. Unprovoked invasion of the terri-tory of another society is immoral by our standards and breaches current international law, but if these be the standards we apply to history there will be no end to our condemning. Conquest and the obliteration of peoples pre-date the expansion of Europe; they are part of human history everywhere including the Aboriginal occupation of this continent.

By the eighteenth century the British had become more scrupulous conquerors. If native people lived a settled life the British accepted that land should only be taken from them by treaty or purchase. Before the plan to send convicts to Australia was adopted they were to be sent to the west coast of Africa. The plans for this settlement included a provision for the acquisition of land from the native owners. When the convict plan shifted to Australia, the British assumed that they did not have to negotiate for the land because Aborigines were not settled permanently upon it. They had a very poor understanding of the connection between Aborigines and the land, but by their own lights they acted correctly.

Australians owe a moral debt to the Aborigines. It is determined by the standards we set ourselves today and the current position of the Aborigines. It does not depend on a condemnation of the first Europeans who settled the country, just as our compensatory action cannot be directed to restoring the *status quo ante*.

*

If the European invasion of Aboriginal territory was a wrong, it would be so no matter what the nature of Aboriginal society. But in recent times there has been a tendency to compound the Europeans' fault by making them disrupters of a paradise of human harmony and co-operation. It is enough to expose this absurdity to point to the regular warfare and vendettas between Aboriginal groups. Europeans did not introduce fighting to this continent; in fact Aborigines were less effective in resisting Europeans because at first they did not hold them responsible for their deeds of violence but ascribed them to the sorcery of their traditional enemies. When they did recognise the Europeans as masters of violence they sometimes urged them to attack their traditional enemies. In recruiting for the native police forces Europeans exploited the indifference and hostility which Aborigines showed to people of other tribes.

We have been living recently with a re-run of the noble savage ideal and as in the first time round much of the admiration for traditional society is opportunistic. This is evident from what the admirers of Aboriginal life choose to focus on – in the 1960s Aborigines were deeply spiritual, in the 1970s they practised equality of the sexes, in the 1980s they were conservationists. It is somewhat odd that those who are most opposed to tradition and fixed roles in European society hold up as a model Aboriginal society with its pre-programmed roles sanctioned by an unquestionable tradition. The admirers denounce national service and embrace the initiation of Aboriginal warriors. They delight in Aboriginal women being hunter-gatherers like the men and overlook young women being given to old men in marriage.

Anyone with a thorough understanding of Aboriginal society would hesitate to draw lessons or models from it for our own. Its otherness is almost complete; we can admire but not copy. Understanding just how different Aboriginal society was has been one of the great challenges of scholarship in this country. The first observers declared that Aborigines had no religion. Now we know how deeply religious they were and how far religion affected all of life – to such an extent that perhaps our term *religion* is not appropriate since it is one of the labels by which we distinguish different aspects of life which in Aboriginal society were all intimately interconnected. When the terms of life are so different our language is strained to make adequate description. What makes W. E. Stanner, in my view, the best of the great anthropologists is that he recognised this problem and had the ability to overcome it. Listen: 'The Dreaming is many things in one. Among them, a kind of narrative of things that once happened; a kind of charter of things that still happen; and a kind of *logos* or principle of order transcending everything significant for Aboriginal man.' And when the resources of language are exhausted he invents a word: 'One cannot fix The Dreaming *in* time: it was, and is everywhen.' If I were asked to nominate the finest achievement of European civilisation in Australia I would point to the fifteen pages of Stanner's essay 'The Dreaming'.

The work of the anthropologists after reaching such sophistication is now being censored. The Australian government has recently published a bowdlerised edition of the booklet *Australian Aboriginal Culture* which it has been issuing since the early 1950s and which has sold over 100,000 copies. The first two editions were written by anthropologists; the most recent edition has been produced by a project co-ordinator. She and her associates have removed the section on 'Fighting'. This was the first paragraph of that section; all knowledge of these matters is now being kept from the reader:

> A strict system of punishment upheld the social and religious struc-ture of Aboriginal society. Feuding occurred mainly between clans or local groups, but camp fights were a common event. Vendettas were carried on for years between clans and could result in many deaths. The main purpose of warfare was to avenge an insult or crime or to capture women, but not to take the land or other possessions of an enemy. The most serious crimes were murder, the stealing of women, incest and ritual offences.

The section on 'Magic and Medicine' has been renamed 'Healing' and instead of the difference of the Aboriginal worldview from our own being stressed, the concern is to find similarities. The first para-graph of the old edition read:

> Supernatural forces were blamed for almost every mishap or disaster known to the Aboriginals. The only corrective measures possible were through magic and ritual.

The first paragraph of the new edition reads:

> As in Western societies there are doctors who diagnose and treat the sick, so too in Aboriginal society there are men and women who perform these roles. These are the traditional healers.

The section on 'Growing up' in the new edition refers to spiritual ini-tiation but omits references to circumcision, subincision, tooth evulsion and fire ordeals which were reported in the earlier editions.

A similar tendency is evident in the book *The Aborigines*, directed like *Australian Aboriginal Culture* to general readers and school chil-dren. It too has gone through three editions, but the author, R. M. Gibbs, has remained the same. In the most recent edition he has cen-sored himself. The detailing of the physical operations of initiation has been removed in favour of a vague reference to 'various tests and ordeals'. A reference to infanticide has been removed completely, though it was carefully explained in early editions as occurring 'usually because of the effects of harsh seasons and lack of food, or because the baby was seriously deformed'. In making these revisions the author acknowledges the assistance of the Aboriginal Curriculum Unit of the South Australian Education Department. I understand that these organisations, which operate in a number of states, are committed to suppressions of this sort.

With the disguising of the Aboriginal worldview and the removal of practices which offend modern sensibilities, Aboriginal culture is becoming only what is accessible and good: Dreamtime stories, inventiveness in food gathering, caring and sharing, close ties with the land, a rich art and craft. Should we object to these distortions? In the main they are created for worthy motives – to raise the self-esteem of those Aborigines who have little or no traditional culture and to encourage more positive attitudes towards Aborigines (our educators seem unaware that perfection can be galling). But these depictions are also used historically to foster the view that Europeans were disrupters of a Garden of Eden. If this fantasy has any plausibility, it is only because Aboriginal culture has been reshaped to meet the standards and preoccupations of the civilisation we are told should not be here.

Australia as a Collection of Ethnic Groups

In its continuing search for legitimacy multiculturalism has declared itself ancient. Australia, it is claimed, has always been multicultural. Its population has always been diverse. It has always been composed of migrants and the children of migrants. Its society is the summation of the 'contributions' made by the various ethnic groups which have constituted its population. This view of our past is common in public rhetoric, has been widely adopted in the schools and is being urged on the universities.

In the mid-1980s there was an officially sponsored effort to get all Australians to adopt this view of themselves. Various ethnic organisations requested the Bureau of Statistics to ask an ethnic question in the census. The questions on place of birth and place of birth of parents identify migrants of the first and second generation, but subsequent generations officially disappear. This is of concern to the ageing ethnic communities which want to keep their numbers and their funding up.

The plan was to induce all Australians to declare an ethnic attachment of some sort. An Ethnicity Committee was set up by the Bureau to develop an appropriate question. It noted the common Australian understanding that ethnics are minority groups speaking a language other than English, but it continued, 'This usage ignores the fact that the term is derived from the Greek word *ethnos*, meaning "nation" or "people". Accordingly *all* persons living in Australia are ethnic ...' Some people might consider that they are ethnically Australian but it would be much better if old Australians could be induced to identify as English, Scots or Irish.

When the Ethnicity Committee developed trial questions and put them to samples of the population it ran into difficulties. If asked to identify with an ethnic group large numbers of Australian-born people would consider the question did not apply to them and skip it. If they were given the option of saying 'none' or 'Australian' two-thirds would take it – but this defeated the purpose of the exercise. After trying seven questions with different meanings and explanatory preambles the Committee resolved that an ethnic question could not yield useful results: a question on ancestry should be asked instead. Its final word on the difficulties of framing an ethnic question was 'that the root of the problem lies with the concept itself'. Indeed! The ethnic conception of Australia's present has a great weight of history against it.

That Australians are all migrants or the children of migrants, the first premise of multicultural history, is at best a misleading half-truth. The Aborigines were at first migrants but when they enter Australian history they were – if the term is to have any meaning at all – an indigenous people. Of all the people who have lived in Australia only their culture has no reference to cultures beyond our shores. If we make one category of those who were genuinely migrants, we lump together the founding population, who came to a country run by their own government and speaking their own language, and the non-English-speaking migrants who came to a well-established society after World War II. Their role and experience were vastly different. The children of migrants are added to migrants as if they are a sub-group of this category, but to be born in a country is to be a non-migrant. The vast majority of the Australian-born, whose origins date back to 1788, have regarded this place quite unambiguously as their home. Since the 1870s they have constituted the majority of the population. They have not thought of themselves as ethnic, as the Ethnicity Committee discovered, nor do they think of themselves as Anglo-Celt, the term multiculturalists impose on them.

That Australia has always been a diverse society is the second multicultural premise. This is true. In the nineteenth century there were (to name the largest groups) Aborigines, English, Scots, Irish, Chinese and Pacific Islanders as well as the native-born. However, those who controlled the society considered that the process of nation-building required ethnic identities to be limited and superseded. The English, Scots and Irish were traditional enemies bound together in one state, the United Kingdom. In Australia there was a conscious, determined effort to avoid old-world enmities and to bring these three peoples to think of themselves as one – British, or Australian–British, or Australian. By the time of the second generation this single identity had been firmly established, even amongst the Catholic Irish and their descendants despite Ireland's grievance against England and the local battles between Catholics and Protestants. In Australia the Irish enjoyed full civil and religious equality and Australia, unlike Ireland, was allowed to govern itself.

As this new nation took shape, it acted to eliminate what it saw as the threat from other ethnic groups. The Chinese were forbidden entry and the Pacific Islanders who had worked on the canefields were sent home. This was done in the pursuit of racial purity and because of a reluctance to constitute the state on any other basis than equality of civil and political rights. Where the minority was indigenous civil and political rights were removed: henceforth the Aborigines lived under a sort of apartheid regime. Fortunately in recent times we have been able to remove this without major upheaval, though we will live with the consequences for a long time yet.

Multiculturalists either overlook this process of nationbuilding and make diversity and contribution the unchanging principle of Australian history or they acknowledge it only to condemn it. The weakness of multiculturalism as a social philosophy is not its opposition to this form of nationbuilding but to any form. It concentrates on 'contributions' and gives too little attention to the creation of the core institutions and values which are necessary if multiculturalism is to be a credible policy. The institutional and social framework which made post-World War II migration a success – and which led in turn to the elaboration of multiculturalism – was a liberal, secular democracy with an easy-going, egalitarian style and a strong predilection for social harmony (don't discuss politics or religion). All this was established when Australia was a diverse society, but when its people were highly conscious of diversity's destructive power.

The 'contributions' which multiculturalists are most anxious to highlight are those of the post-World War II migrants. Since in the schools building self-esteem is a primary aim, migrant children must see themselves reflected when they study Australian history. It would be an affront if they were introduced only to English, Scots and Irish and their descendants. History is a means 'to encourage children to take pride in membership of their own ethnic group' declares Michael Cigler, one of the chief proponents of a multicultural Australian history. Cigler is the general editor of *The Australian Ethnic Heritage Series*, a collection of histories of the various ethnic groups. When these volumes deal with the 'contribution' to Australian society of the ethnic group under study they celebrate the lives of those who have done well in business, the arts or politics. They do not say how business, the arts or politics have been significantly altered by their participation. They cannot do so, for the effect of post-World War II migrants on Australian society is not to be gauged by looking at migrant groups *seriatim*. The multiplicity of migrant groups makes it unlikely that any one will leave an enduring mark. (Our history would have been very different if all the non-British migrants had belonged to the one ethnic group.) The effect of the migration program is to be judged in the broad: it has created a more diverse, interesting and vibrant society, ended more rapidly and decisively Australia's British identity, added to the size of the population and the economy and hence to the nation's strength, and made our foreign policy more difficult to conduct since for many nations with which we deal there is a local constituency.

Multiculturalists encourage vagueness about 'contributions' to give the impression of equal participation, as in the 'new age' school sports where every player in the team must handle the ball before a goal can be scored. If one were to compose a more precise ethnic history it would read something like this: The English, Irish and Scots were the founding population; they and their children established the Australian nation. Of these the English were pre-eminent. They were the largest group and were supported by the imperial power which transferred to the new society English institutions of government and law. The contribution of the Scots and particularly the Irish was to ensure that the identity of the new nation was British, not English, and that the English held no privileged place within it. This nation was joined after World War II by numerous groups of non-English speaking migrants who collectively had the effects outlined above, but none of them individually exercised an influence similar to that of the founding minorities of the Irish and Scots. The new migrants did not form regional enclaves, they inter-married with each other and the old Australians, and are broadly assimilating to the predominant culture.

Assimilation is of course no longer official policy, but we should not be surprised to find that governments do not determine the dynamics of cultural interaction. We can now begin to see that government policy did not so much control developments as provide reassurance to those who feared them. The assimilation policy reassured the old Australian population that the new migrants would change nothing, when plainly they would; multiculturalism reassures migrants that their culture will not die, when plainly it does. The volume *Czechs in Australia* in the Ethnic Heritage Series records the steady disappear-ance of the community through intermarriage and the absence of new migrants from the homeland. It is a paradox, says the author, that in the era of Anglo-conformity Czech community life was rich and now in the multicultural era it is virtually at a standstill.

An ethnic history of Australia which gave the determining influence to the English would be an improvement on multicultural vagueness, but would still be very poor history. It would be accepting the multi-cultural fallacy that everything has an ethnic origin. The English brought much more than themselves, their language and their institutions; in art, literature, religion and science they carried what belonged to European civilisation, which is not an ethnic entity.

The Nationalist Concern for Distinctiveness

Nationalists seek independence for their nation and believe in the distinctiveness of its people. A nationalist will baulk at the notion that our history should be an account of European civilisation in Australia. The other forces working against Clark's vision are new. This is a perennial. Historians writing histories of nation-states are hard put to avoid nationalist preoccupations.

The standard metaphor for the history of a colony is of a child growing up and leaving home. This makes sense for our political history, and the changing relationship between the colonies and mother country was commonly understood on both sides in this way. At first Britain ruled the Australian colonies; then it allowed internal self-government and reserved defence and foreign policy for itself; finally it granted full sovereignty and independence. To claim and discharge these responsibilities successfully the colonists had to acquire new competencies and greater self-confidence just as children do before they can successfully live away from home. But even there, where it appears most apt, the metaphor is misleading. It would be less so if it were applied more comprehensively. Children who have left home carry much of their parents, in their genes and nurturing, with them. When the colonies came to exercise their independence, they did so through the British instruments of government, parliament, cabinet and the rule of law. At the moment Australia cast off British control, it became more like Britain.

Confused thinking about heritage and political independence is evident today in some of the opposition to Australia becoming a republic. To become a republic, it is alleged, is a denial of our heritage. But where did the idea of a republic come from? And where the parliamentary system which it would retain?

'Leaving home' is a completely misleading image for understanding the history of literary and artistic culture in Australia. Historians of

literature or art know that they cannot explain the development
of their subject from within Australia. There cannot be an Australian
history of Australian art. In the 1880s and 1890s Roberts, Streeton and
others, taking their inspiration from the French impressionists, formed
the first national school of Australian painting. In the 1940s Drysdale
and Tucker and others formed a new imagery of Australia under the
influence of European surrealism and expressionism. The paintings of
both groups are accepted now as quintessentially Australian, but why
Australian artists saw their country in one way in the 1880s and in
another in the 1940s cannot be understood apart from changes in
European imagination and sensibility.

When Australian writers struggled against local disdain, some of
them looked forward to the development of a truly indigenous literature as the only means of countering the richness of the British
imports. An Australian literature would grow from the new land, the
new forms of life, perhaps from Aboriginal culture, and its preoccupations would be totally different from those of the old world. This was
the nationalist impulse to separation and distinctiveness. In the event
good Australian writers emerged and found an audience here and
abroad, not by turning their back on the wider world of letters, but by
practising confidently within it. There was a process of maturing but
the imagery of movement has to be reversed – it was not a movement
to separation but to integration.

It was the first generation of colonial writers who were the outsiders, fearful outsiders, conscious of their isolation from the metropolitan culture and unsure how to handle Australian subjects, and
hence driven to imitation and apology. The next generation were
defiant outsiders like Furphy whose bias was to be 'offensively Australian'. And then Australian writers, with unexpected ease, became
insiders not in the sense that they moved to Europe, though visits
there were important, and not by ignoring the Australian locale; they
were insiders because within Australia there were growing numbers of
people and institutions who knew and valued English literary culture
and at the same time believed – and here nationalism plays its part –
that Australian authors and subjects should hold no inferior place
in it.

Forget children leaving home and consider the history of dictionaries in Australia as a model for the maturing of our literary culture. With new objects and experiences to be named colonists coin new words. They are collected in dictionaries of Australian slang, or Australian language; the dictionaries proper remain unaltered. Then Australianisms, but identified as such, are allowed into the dictionaries. Finally a dictionary of Australian English – the *Macquarie* – is produced which includes Australian words and expressions, but does not distinguish them from the other words in the lexicon. We write English, but we are becoming unselfconscious about what parts of it are Australian. The process of the local being integrated into the metropolitan is complete. Because the integration occurs on Australian soil, it should not be mistaken for independence and separation.

*

The second stock way of understanding a colony is that it is a *new* society. But new has two meanings – of recent origin or novel. Certainly colonial society was of recent origin, but was it novel? Some colonists thought it ought to be: they wanted to seize the opportunity to make Australia a very different society from Britain. They capitalised on the ambiguity of 'new'. But other colonists considered that because colonial society was new it should follow old and trusted ways in order to escape the danger of degeneration.

Australian historians, looking for what is distinctive in Australian society, tend to transform the ambiguity of *new* into a law of social science: new societies will be novel. They regard any conservative efforts in colonies as foredoomed to failure because they will be undone by this law. To sustain this view they have to overlook the conservative, not to say reactionary, regimes established in other parts of the new world – in French Canada, the American South, and Latin America. In politics in Australia the conservatives were defeated, but in other areas of life – the professions, the universities, the schools and the churches – British standards and practices were followed, frequently with the assistance of British-trained personnel. In time Australian nationalists objected to the recruitment of professors and archbishops from Britain, and this supersession by the Australian-born properly forms a part of the nationalist accounts of our development. But the quality of civilisation in Australia was enhanced by this adherence to British standards until Australians could maintain them themselves. There is a danger that the novelty of a new society will be the largeness of the realm given over to Mickey Mouse.

In politics Australia took a radical course. Manhood suffrage and the secret ballot were introduced long before they operated in Britain. But these were not strictly innovations – they were part of the radical program in Britain itself. The first large-scale free migration to Australia occurred when the old political order in Britain was under sustained attack and the first reforms had been wrenched from it. The migrant reformers in Australia had an easy victory, not because conservatism does not travel well, but because the old order in Britain was losing its legitimacy when Australia was taking shape. With manhood suffrage and the ballot the colonists created a new political order, but not an un-British one; their aim was to make Australia a better Britain.

We would put a break on our search for novelty in colonial society if we remembered that though the society was new its people were not. Their culture was as old as those who remained in the mother country. D. H. Lawrence was driven to assert this point during his stay in Australia. Against the notion that this was a new country he quoted a saying of the archaeologist Flinders Petrie: 'A colony is no younger than the parent country.'

The Australian historian who best understands this is David Denholm, the author of *The Colonial Australians*, a modest and much underrated work which explores the nature of colonial society by examining its physical remains. The chapter 'People Building' has at its core an examination and celebration of St Matthew's church at Windsor, north-west of Sydney, designed by the convict architect Francis Greenway. This is how Denholm describes it:

> not at all grand, not at all ordinary … the church that rose on the knoll at Windsor came from the ancient Greeks and their command of straight-line geometry; from the fifteenth-century Italian Renaissance which recaptured the Greek feeling for proportion in the shaping of

things; from the seventeenth-century civilisation of Holland (brought into England by William of Orange) with its Flemish technique of securing bricks one upon another; from eighteenth-century Georgian England's love of functional simplicity, order, symmetry and restraint; and from the early nineteenth-century provincial training of the ex-convict who put it all together ... St Matthew's came, through Greenway's mind, from all the ages of the West.

None of this is to deny that Australia was a distinct society, different from Britain, and with a growing sense of its own identity. Accounting for its distinctiveness and identity is one part of the historian's work. However, the historian should be alert to the nationalists' exaggeration of distinctiveness and wary of their explanations for it. Nationalists tend to overemphasise the influence of the new locale – as in the claim that social hierarchy broke down in Australia because gentlemen beset by flies lost the dignity necessary to sustain their superiority. The effects of colonial circumstances, however novel, do not act directly on the colonists. They make their social and cultural life in new circumstances; the circumstances do not make them. Let us suppose that flies did play a part in the downfall of the colonial gentlemen. This would have been the outcome only if the gentlemen's underlings were looking to assert themselves. That desire did not begin in Australia: we see it in the swagger and the clamour made about rights by the English common people in the eighteenth century. The different circumstances of Australia – the shortage of labour rather than the flies – allowed this freer expression.

*

The days when historians saw the frontier and the bush determining the character of colonial societies are gone. Everyone acknowledges the importance of the culture migrants brought with them, though the terms in which they do so are rather grudging. The migrants' culture is referred to as 'British background', as if it merely sets the scene for the colonial drama, or as 'cultural baggage', which does bring culture closer to its bearers but as something external to them, as impedimenta, which can be readily put down or lost. These terms are very poor metaphors for the process of migrants perceiving the new environment, interacting with each other and interpreting their experiences according to understandings which were set before they sailed.

But even after giving that acknowledgment to the metropolitan culture, we have not finished with its influence. It is not central merely to the plantation of a new society. In a colonial society the parent culture retains its authority and has an ongoing significance. Changes in this realm will resonate in colonial life. In the later nineteenth century in Britain trade unions grew in strength and labour representation in parliament was initiated, with the result that these causes became worthy and legitimate in the Australian colonies and flourished there, even though the class relations out of which they grew in Britain had no parallel in the colonies. We need to escape from the view that, once founded, colonies developed according to an internal dynamic, albeit subject occasionally to 'overseas influences'. The colonial organism lives and grows within the broader culture, and this remains so even when it develops distinctive features and proclaims independence.

If nationalists find this unpalatable they can take comfort from the fact that the great nation-states of Europe are not self-sufficient entities either. At the beginning of his *Study of History* Arnold Toynbee asked whether English history of itself was an intelligible field of study. He decided that it was not, because England's history was so interconnected with that of other European countries, and with theirs had been fundamentally shaped by supra-national forces. England, he decided, could only be understood as part of Western Christendom which had its origin in Charlemagne's empire of the eight and ninth centuries which was in turn an offspring of the Roman Empire. This Western civilisation is the intelligible field of study.

Since Australia is an outgrowth of England, European civilisation is also the field of study for an intelligible history of Australia. This does not mean that every history of Australia has to begin with Charlemagne. It does mean that Australian history not set within European civilisation will convey a very poor understanding of Australian society.

I was appointed to La Trobe University to teach Australian history. I now teach a course on European civilisation beginning with classical Athens. I am still fulfilling my brief – I am introducing Australian students to their history.

1993

How Sorry Can We Be?

In 1897 John Farrell, editor of the Sydney *Daily Telegraph*, wrote a poem to mark Queen Victoria's jubilee and sent it to Rudyard Kipling, hoping for praise and endorsement. Kipling lighted on the passage in which Farrell regretted the bloody excesses of the empire's conquests and took Farrell to task for his easy moralism. He declared:

> A man might just as well accuse his father of a taste in fornication (citing his own birth as an instance) as a white man mourn over his land's savagery in the past.

The critic only exists because of the deed he criticises. Let us call this the hard realist view of Australia's origins. It avers that it is morally impossible for settler Australians to regret or apologise for the conquest on which colonial Australia was built. It is the view that I share.

No-one has been putting this view publicly in the recent history wars over the extent of frontier violence. Keith Windschuttle, rightly sensing that accounts of violence towards the Aborigines have been used to question the legitimacy of the nation, argued not that violence was inevitable but that its extent had been grossly exaggerated. In the case of Tasmania, on which he has produced the first of a promised series of books, he concludes that only 118 Aborigines were killed (later increased to 120). To his mind, with this low figure, he has rescued the reputation of the British empire and its successor settler nation from their detractors. Compared with the Spanish in the new world, the British in Australia, he says, were restrained by Christian and Enlightenment values in their dealings with the indigenous inhabitants. Tasmania 'was the least violent of all European encounters in the New World'.

With his other critics, I believe that Windschuttle has a misplaced faith in the documents he uses as giving a complete account of what was happening on the frontier. The documents from which he draws the figure of 118 dead themselves speak of terrible deeds being committed in the woods, which by design were leaving no records. But even if Windschuttle were right about the number of those killed by direct violence, he cannot deny that forty years after the European settlement, all the Tasmanian Aborigines had either perished or had been removed to offshore islands. Empires even good empires believe in conquest and by any standards this was a complete and rapid expropriation. A people and their way of life had been destroyed. Compared to the starkness of that fact, how many had been directly killed by settler violence seems a matter of lesser consequence.

Again with his other critics (and one or two supporters) I am surprised at Windschuttle's lack of sympathy for the plight of the dispossessed Aborigines. A position of hard realism about the nation resting on conquest certainly does not require that we abandon sympathy for Aborigines as fellow humans. We must understand what Aborigines have experienced since 1788 if any policy-making in Aboriginal affairs is to be effective.

In the course of his argument Windschuttle claimed that Aborigines had no attachment to the land and that in attacking the settlers they were not defending their territory, still less conducting a war; they were simply wanting to acquire the settlers' goods. This was plunder and murder merely. Windschuttle's critics suspected that he was intent on demolishing the claim that present-day Aborigines had to the land or to compensation. So they thought it important not only to destroy Windschuttle's claims about land and resistance but also the symbolic heart of the book: the fewness of the deliberate deaths. There was much argument about the numbers.

At the Melbourne Writers Festival in August 2003 Windschuttle agreed to a debate with Robert Manne, who had edited a book of essays designed to demolish Windschuttle's Tasmanian book. I was in the chair. Among his other criticisms, Manne pressed Windschuttle hard on the numbers: even given his own methodology, could he be sure that Aborigines injured in a battle did not later die of their wounds? Windschuttle did concede that this was possible.

In question time one woman in the audience declared that she was sick of the argument about numbers. Even one death, she said, was one too many. This remark was met with spontaneous applause, which though not universal was nevertheless revealing. The woman and those who applauded believe that it was possible to dispossess the Aborigines without bloodshed. The woman did not speak of dispossession but she and her supporters were located in the Malthouse Theatre which stands on land that formerly belonged to Wurundjeri. Let us label this the liberal fantasy view of our origins. It avers that the conquest could have been done nicely. This view is quite widespread and influential and warrants close examination.

Liberal fantasy is prominent in the judgments given in the *Mabo* case in the High Court. The Court found that since 1788 the common law had not been properly interpreted: it should have respected the Aborigines' rights in their land. The Court did not rule that the invasion itself was illegitimate. On the contrary, it legitimised the invasion by declaring that the British Crown's proclamation of sovereignty over Australia could not be questioned in an Australian court. The error of the Crown and the courts was to assume that sovereignty meant that Aborigines could be summarily dispossessed of their lands. Justices Deane and Gaudron in a famous passage said this:

> The acts and events by which that dispossession in legal theory was carried into practical effect constitute the darkest aspect of the history of this nation. The nation as a whole must remain diminished unless and until there is an acknowledgment of, and retreat from, those past injustices.

This envisages that the nation could have come into being without a dark past. The darkness is only an 'aspect' of our history; there could have been a nation without it. But even if the law had been as the High Court now declares it should have been, the desire of the white invaders for Aboriginal lands would have been no less. The clash between Aboriginal hunting and gathering and European pastoral pursuits would have been as stark. What would have happened if the Aborigines on being fully appraised of the invaders' intentions had refused to negotiate any of their land away? – they would have been *forced* to negotiate. Even if each tribe had been persuaded to yield half their land, Aborigines would still have regarded the invaders' sheep as fair game and white shepherds would have misunderstood what was involved in their acceptance of Aboriginal women – two potent sources of conflict in the world as it really happened. It is very hard to envisage a settlement history without violence. It is a great conceit on the part of these two judges to think that a difference in the law could have tamed the force of European colonialism and given us a history with no dark aspects. From all that we now know of what the land meant to the Aborigines, they would not have yielded it without a fight. The judges insult them by thinking that it could have all happened peacefully.

From 1823 the law in the United States on Indian land was as the High Court says it should have been in regard to Aboriginal land in Australia. The United States had sovereign control over the whole landmass, but the Indians had the right of occupancy over their lands until it was extinguished. Indian land could officially only be yielded up by treaty. But the Indians were not free to make or not make treaties. They were pressured into treaty-making after they had been defeated in battle or in an attempt to save some of their lands from the onrush of the settlers, who did not wait for official sanction before pressing into Indian country. Under these treaties Indians in the east had to agree to be moved westward and the Indians in the west were confined to reservations. The treaties provided that on the reservations they should be supported in money or goods, but the Indian agents frequently robbed them of their due. Their reservations were always subject to incursions by settlers. If the Indians fought back, this was an 'uprising' that the US army would savagely suppress. The area of the reservations was regularly reduced and from 1887 reduced even further by the policy of allotting farm-size plots to each Indian family and opening the rest to the settlers. The process of Americanisation of the Indians required that children be forcibly removed from their parents and placed in boarding houses. The recognition of an Indian right in land did not save the United States from a 'dark aspect' of its history.

One might have thought that Henry Reynolds, the author of the classic work on Aboriginal resistance, *The Other Side of the Frontier*, would be proof against the liberal fantasy. Yet it sustains one of his later books *This whispering in our hearts*, which deals with those few colonists who opposed the disruption and destruction of Aboriginal society. One or two of these dissenters thought the Aborigines could be saved only if the colonists left. Most thought that colonisation could and should proceed by 'purchase, treaty and negotiation'. This view Reynolds endorses without considering how this process would have been implemented and what difference it would have made. The dissenters were all opposed to punitive expeditions. Reynolds himself is very definite that punitive expeditions were 'indiscriminate and disproportionate violence'. So the historian who celebrated Aboriginal resistance and wanted their battles to protect their lands honoured in the War Memorial now thinks that milder measures – a bit of deft police work, perhaps – would have been enough to make the Aborigines give up the fight.

The liberal fantasy has a strong hold on Kate Grenville, one of the best of our fiction writers. Her latest book *The Secret River* deals with the European settlement along the Hawkesbury River north of Sydney. The chief character is loosely based on one of her ancestors, a waterman on the Thames who was transported for thieving. In the modern way she has talked and written a lot about her project and hence revealed the impulses that drive her. She told the ABC:

> You want to go back 200 years and say to the settlers, 'Look, this is how the Aborigines are,' and to the Aborigines, 'Look, this is why settlers are behaving the way they are. Let's understand this. There's no need for all this brutality.'

Here is the liberal faith that conflict comes from misunderstanding. Actually, if Aborigines had earlier understood the settlers' intentions there would have been more violence and sooner. The settlers were fortunate in that the Aborigines at first welcomed them or avoided them or attempted to accommodate them.

Grenville wants there to have been peace, but she knows why there was war. In the book she gives a good account of the dynamics of conflict. Her character is a good man who does not want to do the Aborigines harm, but in his dealings with them on his Hawkesbury farm he is perplexed, fearful and finally angry and desperate. He is a very good man, amazingly sensitive for an illiterate waterman brought up in a hard world. He also appears to have read the modern textbook accounts on Aboriginal society. So he realises that 'the blacks were farmers no less than the white men' and that hunting and gathering allowed plenty of time for 'sitting by their fires and laughing and stroking the chubby limbs of their babies'. On one occasion he beats his son for avoiding work and playing with the Aborigines. When the son remains defiant, he says, 'Do I got to get the belt out again, lad?' But his anger soon leaves him. On the transport ship he had learnt that repeated floggings did not work. He says to the boy 'Just joking, lad. I beat you once that were enough.' *Just joking?* At what date did a parent first say that after threatening to discipline a child?: try the 1950s in the United States.

Kate Grenville ponders what she would have done on the frontier and what sort of person that would have made her. The leading character in her novel is not an eighteenth-century waterman at all; it is herself. And so it is no surprise that the waterman, having joined in a massacre of the Aborigines that ends their harassment of the settlers, finds that the land he has possessed gives him no comfort. This is clearly meant as a parable of the nation.

Worrying over the conquest; wishing it were peaceful; feeling that somehow it has to be rectified if settler Australia is to be at peace with itself: these are the products of the liberal imagination. Its decency knows no bounds or thought. *Even one death is one too many.* This mindset has perverted Aboriginal policy over the last thirty years so that it has not been dealing with Aborigines as they are or may be and it raises expectations that cannot be met. The *Mabo* judgment was a great offender in this. Having denounced settler atrocity and called for a retreat from past injustices, it then proceeded to legitimise the invasion and declared that native title had been extinguished on all freehold and leasehold land.

Kate Grenville thinks that novelists, better than historians, can get into the heart and mind of past people. Depends on the novelist – and the historian. Between Kate Grenville and the historian Inga Clendinnen there is no contest. In her study of the first years at Sydney Cove, Clendinnen is not projecting herself back into the past; she knows that these people, settlers and Aborigines, are very different from herself. You need to work hard to understand them. One of the several novelties of *Dancing with Strangers* is Clendinnen's characterisation of the Aborigines as warriors and her cool appraisal of how violence worked in their society. When Governor Phillip orders the first punitive expedition against the Aborigines, she does not hasten to condemn him; she thinks he has correctly divined the sort of retribution Aborigines will understand. The expedition failed to find any Aborigines – which Clendinnen, not altogether convincingly, claims is what Phillip intended, reckoning that the threat of retribution would be enough.

Grenville is appalled by the plans for this punitive expedition. Aboriginal heads were to be cut off and brought back in bags. Her modern sensibility reels at this hacking at bone and muscle. Her historical enquiries into violence have obviously not been extensive. Europeans were still hanging, drawing and quartering their own when Sydney was founded. Grenville is rather coy about Aboriginal violence. We see the results as visited on the settlers but not Aborigines performing it. The settlers on the Hawkesbury follow what Aborigines are doing elsewhere through the pages of the *Sydney Gazette* and we are encouraged to think that Aboriginal violence is to some extent a media beat-up. However, the climactic European massacre of the Aborigines is rendered in close-up grisly detail.

The liberal imagination, appalled at European violence on the frontier, tends to cast the Aborigines as victims merely and not fine practitioners of violence themselves. Violence was more central to their society since its practice was not allotted to a professional caste of soldiers; all adult males were warriors. Aboriginal warfare was endemic, usually with a small number of deaths, but occasionally Aborigines massacred each other. This is an account based on reports by the perpetrators:

Spears and boomerangs flew with deadly aim. Within a matter of minutes Ltjabakuk and his men were lying lifeless in their blood at their brush shelters. Then the warriors turned their murderous attention to the women and older children, and either speared or clubbed them to death. Finally ... they broke the limbs of the infants, leaving them to die 'natural deaths'.

The writer is T. G. H. Strehlow, who grew up with the Aranda of the Centre. His life work was to record and translate their songs. Of their warrior songs he wrote that the 'unbridled expression of blood-lust was relished by old and young'.

Kate Grenville cannot imagine how she would have behaved on the Hawkesbury frontier because, unlike the Hawkesbury settlers, she does not believe in savagery, European superiority and conquest. The pioneer settlers are not ourselves. Nor are the Aborigines whom the pioneers encountered the Aborigines of today. Settler Australians no longer hang and flog offenders or colonise other countries. Aboriginal Australians no longer abandon their old, kill their superfluous young and levy war against their neighbours. We are all a long way from 1788.

There is literally no place for settler Australians to stand to decry the conquest of this country. It all belonged to the Aborigines. The only honest approach is to recognise the conquest as conquest and not to give any utilitarian defence of it – like that the land under European control was able to provide food and fibre to the rest of the world, a view which Geoffrey Blainey advances. In the European world of the late eighteenth century acquiring new territory was perfectly legitimate; what dispute there was concerned the treatment of the people already there. An heroic moralist of today may say that the European conquests were wrong and attempt the impossibility of imagining world history without conquest. Better, if you must speak of right and wrong, to say that according to their lights the settlers were right to invade and the Aborigines were right to resist them. It is our common fate to live with the consequences of that conjunction.

*

The consequences were more varied than is commonly imagined. Here is a thumb-nail sketch of race relations since 1788, the work of an Aboriginal radical which would be assented to – except perhaps for the Nazi comparison – by many progressively-minded settler Australians.

> When white men arrived in this country, they shot the blacks, poisoned their waterholes, murdered them, left, right and centre. Those that were left were rounded up like dogs and cattle and stuck in these places called Aboriginal reserves, which were nothing less than concentration camps. And there they stayed until very recently.

It is correct that there were two attacks on the Aborigines, but wrong to imply that the second followed hard on the first. After the first attack – the taking of the land and the crushing of resistance – the Aborigines were more or less left alone. The time between the two attacks was as much as a hundred years in the lands settled first in New South Wales.

The Aborigines, depleted in numbers more by disease than violence, remained on their own land. Unlike the American Indians they did not have to be put on reserves to stop their resistance. Many took work in the pastoral industry, which until 1900 was much more important than farming and sat more lightly on the land. The boss who hired them might well a few years previously have been shooting at them. The more remote the property, the more reliant was the pastoralist on Aboriginal labour and the less likely the Aborigines were to be paid wages. But where the white presence was slight Aborigines could retain more of their traditional life. As Ann McGrath wrote in *Born in the Cattle*, we can exaggerate the significance of the settlers to the Aborigines, ruthless and exploitative though the settlers were. As well as doing the regular work on the pastoral stations, Aborigines became drovers and shearers. The Shearers Union (later the AWU) was fanatical in its opposition to Chinese labour but allowed Aborigines (and Maoris) to be members. There were some reserves and missions, more important as refuges to the Aborigines where settlement was denser, but Aborigines were not confined to them; they were free to come and go.

Across the countryside Aborigines remained a presence. Some were ruined by drink and survived by begging and scrounging. Most made their own living and the good workers gained reputation and respect. On the missions Aborigines could be living in cottages as good or better than those of the working class. On the pastoral stations and near the towns they lived in humpies from which they might emerge in suits and hats. Aborigines were local notables and the giving of King plates to 'chiefs' continued and the deaths of the last of the tribe were commemorated. The tide of general opinion was becoming more hostile towards the Aborigines as an inferior race, but settlers on the land had their experience of particular people to temper their attitudes.

Aborigines of the first generation after contact have consistently been described as a mild, uncomplaining, generous people. This seems a puzzle: why would defeated warriors display these characteristics? In his Boyer Lectures W. E. H. Stanner, the great anthropologist, thought the mildness was a sort of anomie induced by homelessness, powerlessness, poverty and confusion. I think his essay on 'The Dreaming' provides a better explanation: the cosmology of the Aborigines cannot be destroyed by any disruptions in their life here and now. It is beyond time and circumstance. This attachment to what is unchanging meant that Aborigines were less inclined to quarrel with pain, sorrow and sadness. Their stoicism we may take to be an aspect of character, but as with the original Stoics it had its basis in philosophy.

After their homelands were taken from them, the Aborigines were, in the terms of the society that had overwhelmed them, a marginalised people, but in their own understanding they were, in a double sense, not a displaced people: they were on their own territory and what gave ultimate meaning to their life still continued. Their 'sense of oneness with Eternity', in Strehlow's words, 'made them more kindly, tolerant and helpful towards their human fellows everywhere'.

In this way we can understand the lack of resentment towards the settlers and the willingness to be of service to them. This is celebrated in the many stories of Aboriginal trackers finding lost children in the bush. Someone rides for the tracker who briefly becomes the leader and instructor of the settlers before returning to the humpy from which he was fetched. The stories having become legendary are a continuing reminder of the laissez-faire times between the first and second attack on the Aborigines.

The second attack began in the decades around 1900. The Aborigines presented no new problem to white society except that they continued to exist. By processes that had little to do with the Aborigines, the new nation had formed its ideals in and through the slogan White Australia. Once the nation had given itself that racial identity, the Aborigines became an anomaly. Much indulgence had been shown to the Aborigines in the nineteenth century because they were expected to die out; now there were growing numbers of mixed-blood people. The white nation seemed likely to have a permanent group of people of 'inferior' blood. Two solutions were adopted. In the more closely settled areas part-Aborigines were to be separated from their full-blood kin and encouraged to disappear into the wider community. This involved the shrinking and destruction of the Aboriginal communities on the reserves and missions and the removal of children from their parents. Where Aboriginal populations were larger they were to be confined on reserves (as far as was compatible with the need for their labour) and their interbreeding with whites forbidden. To control, confine and manage Aborigines in this way their civil rights had to be removed.

The second attack on the Aborigines disturbs me much more than the first. I am not shocked at a settler riding out to shoot Aborigines. He acted in hot blood to protect what was close to him, the lives of himself and his workers and the survival of his highly risky enterprise. Nor am I shocked that settlers and their men sometimes rode out together hoping to kill enough Aborigines to give themselves finally the security they craved. But I cannot be calm at police arriving at settled communities to drag children away from their mothers. This was cold-blooded cruelty planned by a distant Bureau in pursuit of the ideal of racial purity. Humankind has been very inventive in its cruelty, but cruelty of this sort did not appear until the early twentieth century. We are still struggling to come to terms with it.

Concern for racial purity was then general in European civilisation; it had a peculiar intensity here because Australia happened to form its national ideal when racism was at its peak and it had experienced and disliked migration from Asia. Its ideals of a progressive, egalitarian and harmonious society became fully mixed with the racial poison. Now that they have been untangled the nation should apologise to those that suffered – particularly to children forcibly taken from caring parents. I believe that more settler Australians would be ready to acknowledge this wrong and apologise for it if the proponents of apology did not urge apologies for everything.

So why does the second attack on the Aborigines warrant an apology and the first one not? Though the High Court judges in *Mabo* spoke of the Australian nation expropriating the Aborigines, this is not so. The settlers were English, Irish and Scots who invaded Aboriginal lands with the sanction of the British state. Only subsequently was the Australian nation formed by those settlers and their children. It is true that the nation was only made possible by this expropriation, which is why I consider it cannot be apologised for. Some might be tempted to point the finger at the British, but settler Australians are the beneficiaries of their deeds. The second attack on the Aborigines was an attack by the Australian nation (though the agents were the various state governments) in pursuit of a national ideal. I accept what Rai Gaita has argued that if a nation can feel pride at its past achievements it can properly feel shame (though not guilt) for its past misdeeds. Forcibly removing Aboriginal children was undoubtedly a misdeed. What finally makes the case for apology compelling in this instance is that some of the victims are still alive.

*

Civil and political rights were rapidly restored to Aborigines from the 1950s. Settler Australians showed their willingness to see Aborigines become equal citizens by the overwhelming assent they gave to the 1967 constitutional amendment. But just at this point Aboriginal policy took a new separatist turn. The new policy proposals were for self-determination, land rights, a treaty, even Aboriginal sovereignty. These were the fruits of liberal fantasy conjoined with Aboriginal radicalism, which fed on each other.

The liberal fantasy is that the conquest would have been acceptable had there been recognition of the land rights of traditional owners and negotiation with them. Hence the most urgent need of policy is to rectify these omissions which are the source of all our ills. But a treaty with the Aborigines would not be with a traditional grouping. The traditional groups numbered about 500 tribes, only a few of which survive. The Aborigines are a group formed since the conquest from those tribespeople and their descendants who had the common experience of oppression and exclusion at the hand of Europeans. The failure of 1788 is to be rectified by dealing with a group that did not exist in 1788.

In the 1950s and 1960s, when assimilation and integration was the policy, differences between Aborigines were acknowledged. Some Aborigines, chiefly of mixed blood, were already part of the wider society. Their problems were not that different from those of the white underclass with whom they frequently intermarried. In remote Australia there were Aborigines living something like a traditional life who were to be induced or encouraged over time to move into settler society. But with the new policies of separatism, the Aborigines were regarded as a single group and whatever characteristics were ascribed to traditional Aborigines, were true for them all. That is, Aborigines wherever located and however distant from a full-blood ancestor, were considered to possess, and may well have come to believe that they did possess, traditional ties to land and a deep spirituality.

William Cooper, the pioneer leader of Aboriginal protest in the 1930s, referred to himself and his supporters as 'the *descendants* of the original owners of the land'. Now all Aborigines were simply the original owners of the land. The politics of identity eroded history.

The High Court in *Mabo* encouraged all Aborigines to think that they had been deprived of their land rights, but it indicated that traditional ties would have to be demonstrated still to exist for a claim to land under native title to be established. Many non-traditional groups attempted to present themselves as having traditional ties to land. An early indication that these claims were spurious was the ferocious battles between Aborigines over who constituted the groups and over what land they had a claim. After millions of dollars of public money had been spent on lawyers' fees, the Federal Court and then the High Court ruled that the Yorta Yorta in Victoria no longer had traditional ties to their land; they had been washed away in the tide of history. No other decision could have been reached, but the Yorta Yorta now have a grievance that they did not have before policy departed from need and all Aborigines were encouraged to think of themselves as traditional.

The *Mabo* decision and the *Native Title Act* which followed might be considered a treaty with Aborigines who still have traditional ties with the land. But proponents of a treaty do not regard it as such and the demand for a treaty with 'the Aborigines' continues. There are suggestions that a treaty should confer particular rights and privileges on Aborigines and provide them with compensation. The immediate difficulty with such a proposal would be to define who the Aborigines are.

An official definition already exists. It has three parts. An Aborigine has (1) to be a person of Aboriginal descent, with no particular proportion of this ancestry stipulated (2) to identify as an Aborigine, and (3) to be accepted by other Aborigines as an Aborigine. This definition is appropriately loose. Aboriginal communities in the more settled parts of the country have been very open and accepting.

But this looseness is now being exploited. People are claiming to be Aborigines partly in order to qualify for the benefits and opportunities specially provided for Aborigines. Tasmania is the state in which the number of Aborigines is rising most rapidly. Dr Cassandra Pybus, who knows the state and its records well, estimates that three-quarters of the people now identifying as Aborigines do not have an Aboriginal ancestor.

In 1997 Michael Mansell, the Aboriginal leader in Tasmania, brought an action in the federal court to challenge the right of eleven people to stand as candidates for the now defunct national Aboriginal parliament, ATSIC. He claimed they were not Aborigines. The judge was plainly unhappy at having to examine lines of descent; he was prepared to give the benefit of the doubt to people who had a strong family tradition that there was an Aboriginal ancestor. He excluded only two of the eleven. He said that today identity is much more social than genetic. In effect he relaxed an already loose definition. This might not matter too much when the issue is standing for ATSIC, but if under a treaty a class of people with special legal rights was being defined, this looseness would be unacceptable.

Cassandra Pybus, who gave evidence in this case, is sure that some people accepted by the judge have no Aboriginal ancestor. All their ancestors were settlers. The descendants of those who shot the Aborigines and took their land are now receiving benefits earmarked for Aborigines.

Many people do not recognise how well integrated many Aborigines are. When they think of Aborigines they think of tribal people in the outback, not people who have been living in the suburbs for three generations. In their partnering the Aborigines of the cities and towns are a less cohesive group than the Greeks in Australia or the Jews. A majority of Aborigines have partners who are not Aborigines.

Consider this household. The husband is an Aborigine of mixed descent; one of his four grandparents was Aboriginal. His wife is of English, Scots, Irish and Italian descent. Their oldest daughter in her late teens becomes interested in her Aboriginal heritage. Her siblings show no interest. She declares that she is an Aborigine and seeks out other Aborigines. There can be no objection to this; it is a free country. But is it seriously proposed that by treaty she should officially be declared indigenous, that she acquire special rights, and that she be given compensation for the loss of her ancestral land, language and culture? That this notion is entertained shows how far policy has departed from an assessment of need.

A treaty has been criticised as divisive. It certainly would be and in a more profound sense than is commonly realised. The division and the bitterness would begin with the act of defining who the Aborigines are. It would give members of the same family a different status.

In the 1980s the Hawke Labor government contemplated and then abandoned the idea of a treaty. Instead it proposed a process of Reconciliation which would begin in 1991 and be completed in time for the centenary of federation in 2001. Liberal fantasy was again at work. The premise of Reconciliation was that nothing significant had so far been done to right past wrongs and yet complete harmony was within close reach.

Reconciliation as a process was borrowed from societies where two groups had been at loggerheads if not at war. In Australia Aborigines had regained their civil and political rights thirty years previously; they enjoyed a large measure of goodwill from the settler Australians and huge sums of public money had been spent on their welfare and advancement. Aboriginal art and dance were widely appreciated; Aboriginal sportspeople were honoured. Traditional Aborigines had acquired the rights over their land. Assimilation and integration of other Aborigines – though those names could not be breathed – were proceeding rapidly. Intermarriage was high and increasing. And yet Reconciliation presented Australia as a fundamentally divided society. We were compared to South Africa or the Middle-Eastern conflict between Jews and Palestinians.

The naming of the groups presented them as being a long way apart. There were indigenous Australians and non-indigenous Australians. This is an amazing formulation; 98% of the population is defined by what it is not. The use of the term indigenous for Aborigines had innocent enough origins. The Torres Strait Islanders do not want to be mistaken for Aborigines, though they want to share their status. Hence the mouthful term 'Aborigines and Torres Strait Islanders' had to be used. Indigenous was a simpler portmanteau term and simultaneously it was coming into use at the United Nations which also needed a generic term. But only in Australia was the settler population then defined as non-indigenous – there are not non-indigenous Americans or non-indigenous New Zealanders. 'Non-indigenous' implies a people without roots in this place; it elides the fact that settlers have been here for eight generations, that they have formed a distinctive polity and are not indigenous to anywhere else; they regard Australia as their home. On the other side it elides the fact that most Aborigines are descendants of settlers and the original indigenous population. The formulation in fact casts modern Australia as if it were 1788: one group has just stepped off the boat and confronts the traditional owners of the country. That's where the liberal imagination is fixated.

The process of Reconciliation enjoyed bipartisan support in the federal parliament. The Liberal and National parties had opposed Labor's dalliance with land rights and a treaty; it supported Reconciliation with the proviso that the Reconciliation Council was to consult widely before it committed itself to any document of reconciliation. The Council did produce a Declaration of Reconciliation, elegantly drafted by David Malouf and Jackie Huggins, which acknowledged Aborigines as original owners and custodians and that the land was colonised without their consent. It also offered an apology in these terms: 'as one part of the nation expresses its sorrow and profoundly regrets the injustices of the past, so the other part accepts the apology and forgives.'

To discover what the Australian people thought of the Declaration, the Council commissioned a poll and organised focus groups. On the issue of an apology, people were asked to agree or disagree with the proposition that 'On behalf of the community, governments should apologise to Aboriginal people for what's happened in the past.' This was a more comprehensive apology than envisaged by the draft where the apology was for 'injustices'. Fifty-seven per cent of people disagreed with the proposition; 40 per cent agreed. This was the strongest dissent that the pollsters encountered. The advantage of defining closely what should be apologised for was obviously not recognised. 'What's happened in the past' includes the European settlement of the country. Only hypocrites can apologise for that.

The apology survived in the final document, which was presented to Australian leaders at the Sydney Opera House in May 2000. Prime Minister John Howard produced a revised version of the document without an apology. He had always made clear his opposition to an apology of any sort. The government was prepared to express 'profound regrets' that past injustices had occurred but not to apologise for them. The government very firmly rejected the Reconciliation Council's plan to continue working on a treaty after 2001, which had passed without the spectacular results hoped for it.

The acute social problem that Australia faces is not the division between Aborigines and settler Australians. It is that many Aborigines in remote Australia live in communities which have appalling records on health, housing, employment and rates of imprisonment. These are Aboriginal communities; the few settler Australians who live there provide services to them. Decent liberal-minded people worry enormously about this social malaise, but they keep mistaking its cure; they think that the moment of reconciliation which they desperately seek is necessary to fix this problem. In fact their attitudes have been making it worse.

The Reconciliation Council which was formed to heal a social divide had added to its brief the addressing of what was called Aboriginal disadvantage. The Liberal and National parties supported Reconciliation on the basis that practical measures would be taken to improve Aboriginal communities, which they saw as more pressing than symbolic acts, still less a treaty. This is the approach that Prime Minister Howard later termed 'practical reconciliation'. Those who believed in the symbolism of a declaration of reconciliation or a treaty then argued in response that Aborigines cannot be whole people until past hurts are acknowledged. The difficulty with this argument is that among the most troubled communities are those that exist on their own land and, comparatively, have experienced little disturbance from settlers. Their health and life expectancy are appalling but they may still be initiating their young men.

The social situation in these communities has got worse over the past thirty years not better. Welfare without the usual work tests replaced employment at low wages; schools were built without ensuring that students attended them; health declined because of alcohol and drug abuse. Huge sums were spent on buildings and equipment that were trashed or never used. The situation was allowed to continue because of the commitment to supporting traditional life on Aboriginal lands, though there were few worthwhile jobs there. Generosity and respect in this generation have done more damage to Aboriginal communities than the indifference and neglect of the past.

Now in Cape York the erstwhile radical leader Noel Pearson is steering a new course. He has attacked welfare dependency; he wants to create real jobs for his people; and he plans to send the young away to get a decent education. He has identified as part of the problem the progressively-minded people in Sydney and Melbourne who walked across bridges as one of the symbolic acts sponsored by the Reconciliation Council. He complains that their soft-headness about social problems has been too influential on policy: the treatment of welfare as a right; of alcohol abuse as a symptom of malaise rather than something to be attacked in itself; and the willingness to excuse anti-social behaviour as the result of poor treatment in the past. Perhaps soon the progressively-minded people will be asked to apologise.

*

What does Australian history look like if we assume a close interaction between settler Australians and Aborigines and not distance? Here are some Notes Towards the Definition of an Integrated Australia.

The explorer Matthew Flinders, knowing the Aboriginal love of ceremony, put on a special display when he left King George's Sound after spending a month there in 1801. He ordered his marines ashore and put them through their drill. The Aborigines were delighted with the men in their red coats and white crossed belts; these 'red-and-white men', said Flinders, had 'some resemblance to their own manner of ornamenting themselves'. They followed their drill closely and one old man put himself at the end of the rank and using a stick imitated the soldiers' movements as they shouldered and grounded their weapons. When the anthropologist Daisy Bates visited King George's Sound over a hundred years later she found an old man who could still do the drill. He covered his torso in red and put white pipe-clay across the red and performed the movements as his father and grandfathers had taught him. The Aborigines had made of the drill a sacred ceremony with Flinders and his men being spirits returning from the dead. John Mulvaney in *Encounters in Place* writes, 'This Aboriginal application of ritual exchange, of formal ceremonial involving hierarchy, persons with special functions, particular dress, and display of regalia, has application to later developments' – like the enlistment of Aborigines into the Native Police and their enthusiasm for organised sport, especially cricket.

Aborigines were attracted to European food and tobacco – and this before their own society had broken down. Stanner witnessed this process in the Northern Territory in the 1930s. He reports in 'Continuity and Change' how one group of Aborigines tried to get tobacco and tea through another which had a supply because they had settled with Europeans: 'The encroachers used every claim of right they had – kinship, affinity, friendship, name-sake relationship, trade partnership – to get and keep a toehold.' This movement towards settler society was not intended as a break with their own, though that could be the consequence. Aborigines saw immediately the superiority of iron axes to their own stone ones. In a famous 1952 article, 'Steel axes for Stone-Age Australians', Lauriston Sharp argued that the new axes threatened the stability of Aboriginal society since the making and distribution of stone axes was intimately linked to the maintenance of kin relationships and no explanation of the new axes was provided in the Aboriginal cosmology. This view of Aboriginal society as a fragile structure is now discredited. The axes were not so disturbing – axes occur because of white man's Dreaming.

However, Aboriginal society had its points of tension. Older men took the young women as wives and the young men were left with none or with the older women. Young men and women wanting to escape this regime were attracted to settler society, which could not always protect them from the retribution of the old men. On Bathurst Island the Catholic missionary Bishop smoothed matters over by buying the young girls from the older men and then marrying them to young men. He became known, as his book telling of his exploits has it, as *The Bishop with 150 Wives*.

Henry Reynolds in *With the White People* tells of how much Aborigines contributed to the European exploration and development of the country. The explorers were not 'discovering'; they were following their Aboriginal guides. Bushman learnt their bushcaft from the Aborigines. Much of the work in the outback was done by Aborigines. Today, choose at random six white Australians and six Aborigines and examine their family history. Of the whites, two would be postwar migrants or their children, two could trace descent from late nineteenth-century colonists mostly in the cities, perhaps two would have ancestors who had done pioneering work on the land. But of the Aborigines all six would have ancestors who were stock-workers, shepherds, trackers, troopers, pearl-divers. Much of this was forced or semi-forced labour. However the priority for Aborigines was not good working conditions but a proper relation with the boss. Reynolds writes,

> Aborigines worked out of a sense of obligation – as a favour to particular individuals, not because they felt they should be 'industrious'. Work was not a matter of an unequal exchange between master and servant but merely one aspect of a reciprocal relationship. Long-term bosses were not seen as masters so much as *de facto* kin – as classificatory uncles or brothers.

Most modern Aborigines have Aborigines and settler Australians as their ancestors. The sexual congress between Aborigines and settlers ranged from rape to settled unions, though seldom to marriage. The attractiveness of Aboriginal women to European men, both the lure of 'black velvet', and the stigma of acknowledging it, are the themes of Xavier Herbert's novel of the Northern Territory, *Capricornia* (1938). It honours the lack of hypocrisy of Tim O'Cannon, a railway ganger who lived openly with an Aboriginal wife and acknowledged his children. There is a similar character in *Coonardoo* (1929), Katherine Susannah Prichard's novel set in the north of Western Australia. Sam Geary has several wives and many children and cites the patriarchs of the Old Testament in support of his behaviour. Hugh Watt, his neighbour and the central character in the book, despises Geary and will not give himself to the Aboriginal girl Coonardoo whom he loves. She waits patiently, puzzled, wanting to give herself to him. Hugh's refusal leads to their mutual ruin and that of his station. The novel caused a scandal when it was published for allowing that a decent man could love an Aboriginal woman; it is still in print carrying the message that 'You had to keep in the life flow of the country – its land and its original people – to survive.'

The pioneer anthropologists Spencer and Gillen, who studied the Arunta in Central Australia, coined the term Dreamtime. It was not a translation of an Arunta word; it combined two words that seemed to have a similar root: the word for what is eternal and the word for dreaming. Hence Dreamtime. Stanner took out 'time' altogether, for this cosmology is every-when. Hence The Dreaming. Some traditional Aborigines did not recognise it as appropriate for themselves, but it has become now the term used by modern Aborigines to discuss Aboriginal culture. It has also been used by settler Australians for their own world, as in John Carroll's *The Western Dreaming*.

T. G. H. Strehlow published his *Songs of Central Australia* in 1971. Barry Hill in his *Broken Song* defines its status and its double origin:

> Strehlow designed his book to sing and elucidate the soul of the first inhabitants and it does so with the lyricism of the *Song of Songs* and the gravity of the *Torah*. There have been other renderings of

Aboriginal poetry, and they have been splendid reminders of the depth of the culture that has pulsed here so long, but no other book has been as embracing as Strehlow's, or more honorifically committed to placing the 'first songs' of the 'first people' in the context of world poetry. In *Songs*, Aboriginal life breathes in the company of Greek and Anglo-Saxon, Norse and Hebraic utterance.

In the 1930s Margaret Preston studied Aboriginal design closely and urged that it be the basis of a truly Australian art. She was in touch with the Jindyworobak movement, which wanted to use Aboriginal words and concepts to make a truly Australian literature. These were both awkward appropriations. In the renaissance of Australian art in the 1940s and 1950s Drysdale, Nolan, Boyd and others regularly treated Aboriginal subjects. Geoffrey Dutton in *White on Black* reports that this unparalleled preoccupation went 'beyond national problems to the roots of human existence on earth, and what humans have left on earth'. In the 1970s when Geoffrey Bardon at Papunya gave the Aboriginal elders canvas, boards and paints, the wondrous designs and patterns that had previously been rendered in sand and on flesh could hang on gallery walls here and overseas.

Aborigines today are more devoted to Christianity than settler Australians. Christianity gave new meaning and purpose to part-Aborigines and was frequently the basis of community morale. When traditional Aborigines embrace Christianity, its key figures and episodes take on strange forms within The Dreaming. Tony Swain in *Aboriginal Australians and Christian Missions* found that the Warlpiri at Yeundumu thought that Adam, Moses and Jesus all lived on the one day, a likely outcome when a faith that is historically based enters a cosmology without time. But Christians too need timelessness for some purposes and Swain suggests that The Dreaming is a good rendering of Augustine's understanding that 'eternity is the "now" of God.'

Aboriginal protest is not located outside settler society. To speak their grievance Aborigines have to use the language of their conquerors and manipulate their concepts and values. They have always received help in this from settler Australians.

The Gurindji at Wave Hill struck for equal wages in 1966, a cause that Australians could understand and which was advanced by the presence at Wave Hill of Frank Hardy, the communist, who knew something about how to run a strike. I had always believed, on the basis of Hardy's own account in *Unlucky Australians*, that it was the Aborigines who gradually revealed to him that they were more concerned with pushing their rights to the land. But as Bain Attwood shows in *Rights for Aborigines*, land rights had long been the policy of the Communist Party. So this crucial new turn in Aboriginal protest cannot be set down solely as an Aboriginal initiative.

Tim Flannery in *The Future Eaters* argues that Aborigines and European settlers both mistook the land they came to. Both discovered that it was not as abundant as it appeared and had to make fundamental adjustments to their way of life. He considers the European adjustment has only just begun. I think the contrariness of the country – the droughts and flooding rains – was recognised by settler Australians sooner than Flannery allows. I remember my father saying when some disaster struck, 'We should give the country back to the blacks,' a sentiment which I know did not arise from a recognition of Aboriginal land rights. I could find no other reference to this saying and thought, as was possible, that my father had coined it. Then in Richard Broome's *Aboriginal Victorians* I found this Aboriginal song of the Depression years:

> White boy he now pays all taxes
> Keeps Jacky Jacky in clothes and food
> He don't care what becomes of the country
> White boy's tucker him pretty good
>
> *Chorus*
> Clicketa Boobilah wildy maah
> Billying etcha gingerry wah
>
> Now the country's short of money
> Jacky sits and laughs all day
> White boy wants to give it back to Jacky
> No fear, Jacky won't have it that way

Germaine Greer in *Whitefella Jump Up* and Inga Clendinnen in *Dancing with Strangers* have claimed that there is a similarity in Aboriginal and settler Australian humour. Perhaps this is so. How could it be so? Has it something to do with this bugger of a country?

When David Malouf was working on the Declaration for Reconciliation, he was for the most part improving on the standard talk about Aborigines and settler Australians. He had one novel idea that quickly disappeared because his clients could not understand it. His draft began with 'The people of Australia, of many origins, recognising the gift of one another's presence ...' That's not being sorry or forgiving at all.

2006

WHAT SORT OF NATION?

Convict Society

Australia began life as a jail. Many books refer in this or a similar way to the first European settlement in New South Wales and in so doing emphasise its degraded and unheroic character. But in many ways such statements are seriously misleading. To the modern mind, a jail is a closed, well-ordered institution, rigidly divided into warders and prisoners. Society in early New South Wales was not at all like this.

It would not be so misleading to describe this society as a jail if the jails of the eighteenth century were being referred to. In these there was no bar to the mixing of the sexes. The rations were meagre, but friends and relations could send food into the prison and those prisoners with money could send out for it. Debtors usually brought their wives and families into the jail. Those with more money could pay the jailer for superior bedding and accommodation and a gentleman might be given a room in the jailer's own home. To the eighteenth-century mind, an institution which treated people with no reference to their rank and means and cut them off from family and friends and their influence was almost inconceivable. The penal reformers planned institutions in the modern sense, but when New South Wales was formed theirs was still a small voice.

Some historians now argue that the British government founded New South Wales for strategic or commercial reasons and not merely as a dumping ground for convicts: the government planned a colony and not a jail. But even if we assume the narrowest intentions for the colony, by the ordinary standards of the day, the sending of convicts to

Botany Bay would be unlikely to produce a jail-like society. Look at the human cargo on the first fleet. As was customary with troops on foreign service, a proportion of the marines had been allowed to bring their wives and children with them. Respect for family connection meant that the convict women had been allowed to bring their children. The fact that there were convict women as well as men on board was the clearest sign that the fleet carried the seeds of something more than a jail. In the eighteenth century men were hanged and flogged without qualm, but our practice of locking men up together for years on end and depriving them of all female companionship would have been thought unnatural and cruel.

In the planning of the colony, considerable thought had been given to providing convicts with sexual partners. Since there were considerably fewer convict women than men, Governor Phillip was instructed to make up the deficiency by bringing women from the Pacific Islands. Phillip in his own plans for the settlement considered that at certain times the convicts should have access to the most abandoned convict women and that they should be encouraged to marry the better sort. In time other marriages might be made between convicts and Aboriginal women. The women in the Pacific Islands he envisaged as marriage partners for the soldiers. On the ships convict men and women were segregated from each other, but the officers, marines and seamen had access to the convict women and from these liaisons, some of which survived in the colony, New South Wales gained its first 'native' children. When the convict men finally met the women on Australian soil Phillip's plan of classifying the women and controlling access went by the board. All that remained after the drunken orgy of the first night was a policy of encouraging convicts to marry. Phillip also abandoned the plan to bring Pacific Island women to Sydney where he thought in the colony's straightened circumstances they would simply pine away. He asked for more women to be sent out from England instead.

Far from experiencing a regimentation in their 'jail', the convicts enjoyed a new freedom in their sexual relationships. No attempt was made in New South Wales to enforce the laws relating to bastardry. In England women could still be punished for giving birth to a bastard and the fathers of the children were required to support them according to their means. Convict women were exempt from work while they were suckling children and when the children were weaned they were supplied with a ration. The first government institutions in the colony were the orphan homes to accommodate these children deserted by their parents. When the Female Factory was opened at Parramatta one of its functions was the provision of accommodation for convict women who became pregnant. They remained there, supported by the government and not the fathers of their children, until the children were weaned.

The encouragement to marriage which Phillip began remained a continuing concern in the administration of the colony. More marriages would make the colony more 'moral', which meant in part they would create new centres of order and responsibility: wives would obey their husbands and husbands would provide for children. To those who contracted marriages or at least maintained settled households and raised children, governors were more willing to grant tickets-of-leave, pardons and other indulgences. When the power to give these became restricted, special arrangements were still made to encourage and support marriage. After the opening of the Sydney convict barracks married men were allowed to sleep with their wives in the town and were given Friday as well as Saturday to themselves so that they would have a better chance of supporting their families. From 1816 well-behaved convicts whose wives were in Britain were eligible to have them and their children brought to the colony free of expense. If the husband was not eligible for a ticket-of-leave, he was united with his family by a bold administrative device which ranks above the ticket-of-leave itself as the colony's most notable humane innovation in penal practice – the convict was assigned to his wife. In law she was the master: in practice, of course, he was. Since the labour of convict women was in less demand and they were more troublesome they were more readily given their freedom if they received an offer of marriage. In encouraging convicts to marry governors were urging them to accept new restraints and responsibilities, not those of a jail, but of civil society. Having admitted women to the colony, the authorities could scarcely operate on any other standard especially as encouraging marriage and restricting licentiousness was the special concern of the evangelical lobby in London. But whatever the relations between the sexes, their intermingling made a thoroughgoing penal regime impossible.

When New South Wales is described as a jail, its people are depicted as belonging to two categories only, prisoners and their guards. As a statement about the composition of the population this is true enough, but it gives a misleading impression about the functioning of the society. The military – the so-called guards – had in fact little to do with the day-to-day management of the convicts. The officers saw their duties as strictly military – to protect the colony against attack and insurrection. The officers took a close interest in the convicts only after Phillip's departure when they acquired assigned servants to work their own land. They were employers, not guards. It was the sea and the bush which confined the convicts to the settlement and it was the convicts themselves who served as overseers and policemen and filled other positions of responsibility. Some of these soon became free men as reward for their good service. In 1790 the first pardon was obtained by John Irving who had assisted the surgeons, and the second by James Bloodsworth who had been in charge of the brickmakers.

In the second year at Sydney Cove convicts began to acquire their freedom because their sentences had expired. These men had served most of their time on the hulks before being shipped to New South Wales. Those ex-convicts who wanted to settle on the land were granted thirty acres – more if they had wives and children to support – and convicts, supported by the store, to help them work it. These provisions for the settlement of ex-convicts had been drawn up in London and included in Phillip's instructions since the British government wanted to discourage the ex-convicts as far as possible from returning home. Similar offers of land and servants were made to marines and seamen who decided to stay in the colony rather than return home. So by as early as 1791 a substantial new social grouping, the settlers, had emerged. The ex-convicts who formed the majority of them were always referred to simply as settlers without discriminating them from those who had always been free. They came as one group to the regular musters where the details of the colony's people and their possessions

were recorded. Whatever their reputation for slovenliness and drunkenness, the settlers were part of the settled interest of the country; they
were masters of servants and suppliers of grain.

The early colony's shopkeepers and small traders were almost
exclusively ex-convicts, some of them starting their careers while they
were still technically in bondage. From these humble beginnings a few
expanded their activities into every aspect of the economy and amassed
fortunes which equalled or exceeded those of the wealthiest free emi-
grants. By the end of Macquarie's governorship the ex-convicts held
well over half the wealth of the colony and were masters of the same
proportion of the convicts. Far from being one group in a simple two-
caste society, convicts quickly came to occupy positions throughout
the hierarchy of wealth.

The critics of transportation in the 1830s described the convicts as
slaves and the society of New South Wales as a slave society. These
terms still powerfully affect the way people think about early New
South Wales. The critics and later commentators admitted of course
that convicts were different from slaves in that the term of their servitude was fixed and that their children were not born into bondage, but
while they were in servitude, it is asserted, they were like slaves.
Certainly a convict had to do his master's bidding, and was liable to be
flogged if he did not, but in New South Wales the convict was much less
the creature of his master than a slave. The convict was still a subject of
the Crown and he retained important political and legal rights. He had
the right to petition the governor. Hundreds of petitions were received
each year from convicts requesting tickets-of-leave, pardons and other
indulgences and making special cases for the relaxation of the usual
rules. No convict could be punished except by due process of the law
and in the colony convicts exercised more legal rights than if they had
been kept in Britain. In the criminal courts of the colony convicts were
admitted from the first as witnesses. When the civil court opened in
Sydney in July 1788, the first case was brought by a convict and his wife
to recover damages from the captain of the ship which had brought
them to the colony. Their friends had given them a parcel of clothes and
other articles on their departure and these had been either lost or
stolen on the voyage. They were awarded £20 damages. The court

ignored the English laws under which convicts were unable to be witnesses, to bring actions or to own property. That a convict could be a witness allowed him to give evidence in court against his master, something which no slave in the Americas was able to do.

These differences make the comparison of a convict with a slave dubious: what is even more doubtful is the likening of New South Wales to a slave society. The differences which everyone allows – that convicts served for a limited term and their children were free – are enough to invalidate the comparison, for it was the maintenance of perpetual bondage from generation to generation which characterised the slave societies and gave them their peculiar and acute problems of controlling a subject people. The rulers of New South Wales never faced problems of this order and there was no parallel in the colony to the ideologies which justified the oppression of the slaves. Slave societies varied in the ease with which they allowed slaves to become free. In New South Wales nearly all the convicts became free, for even those sentenced to life could eventually be rescued by tickets-of-leave and pardons. Slave societies varied, too, in the position they offered the ex-slaves, but in none of them was there the equivalent to the New South Wales practice, begun under Phillip and continued for thirty years, of offering to ex-'slaves' immediately on their release a farm and bond-labour to work it. In no slave society were the ex-'slaves' so prominent in the master class. For this unique social formation, the term 'slave society' is as inappropriate as 'jail'.

When early New South Wales is described as a jail or a slave society, the question naturally arises as to how it transformed itself or was transformed into a free society. This is a false issue since at no stage had the society erected any barriers to freedom. While convicts were sent to the colony, the British government maintained a system of auto-cratic rule there, but political arrangements are a different matter from the composition of society itself. No-one had a vote in New South Wales until transportation ended, but the making of a free society had been going on almost since the day it began. Free children had been born to convict parents. Convicts had been gaining their freedom: no bar was placed on their economic activities and they enjoyed the same legal rights as those who had come free. Employers of all sorts had become used to a mixed labour force, part convict, part ex-convict and later native-born and free emigrant as well. When transportation ended, no legal or institutional changes were required. The convicts still in bondage gradually progressed to freedom. The proportion of convicts in the labour force declined to zero. Slave societies do not have such quiet endings.

1983

Transformation on the Land

In 1850 nearly all the good land in Australia's fertile crescent – the strip of land 200 miles wide along the eastern and south-eastern coast of the continent – was occupied by pastoralists who grew wool for the British market and supplied meat to the local market. The pastoral holdings were huge, the labour employed small, and throughout the huge pastoral domain there was only a thin scattering of townships. A pastoralist carted his wool to the coastal ports, and from there frequently he obtained his stores – flour, tea, sugar, tobacco. During the next eighty years this landscape was transformed. Wheat had joined wool as a major product of the region. In many areas the large pastoral holdings had disappeared completely and been replaced by wheat farms and other small holdings; in others, portion of a few large holdings survived; in some places most of the land was still held in large holdings, and the small holders were few. At the beginning of this period the small man grew wheat and the large man ran sheep. By the early twentieth century this distinction had almost disappeared. On their much reduced holdings pastoralists frequently planted some land to wheat, and the farmers, who were increasing the size of their holdings, spread their risks and rested their land by running some sheep. In this period the coastal cities had continued to grow – they now handled wheat as well as wool – but third-order service towns of one or two thousand people, occasionally more, were now spread throughout the wheat and sheep belt and between them smaller villages and hamlets.

The concerted campaign against the pastoralists' monopoly of the land began in the early 1850s in Victoria and New South Wales, the two best-endowed and the two most populous colonies, and achieved its first legislative success in the early 1860s with the passage of the Selection Acts. These provided that anyone could select a farm on the pastoralists' holdings – in Victoria, certain areas were set aside and surveyed for selection, and in New South Wales the selector could select anywhere, even before the land was surveyed. A relatively high price for the land was maintained – at least £1 per acre – but the selector was able to pay this off over a number of years. He was obliged to reside on his selection, cultivate it and improve it. These first attempts to break up the pastoral holdings and settle an industrious yeomanry on the land were in the short term at least dismal failures. The pastoralists were able to secure their holdings, or key sections of them, by employing mediums – known as dummies – who selected land on their behalf, and then transferred it to them; and because cash sales at auctions continued at which the pastoralists met no competition from small men.

The early historians of this period ascribed the failure to develop small holdings and agriculture to the power of the pastoralists to out-bid other buyers, and their willingness to subvert the intention of the selection legislation.

Subsequently, economic historians who considered the technology, markets and transport available to small holders in the 1860s, declared the conditions were not favourable for agriculture, and that no legislation could have guaranteed success to small holders. Only patchy success was possible in areas where farmers could supply local markets. In the 1870s and 1880s, however, the railways reached further inland, and so gave farmers access to wider markets and improved technology was available from the long-established farming areas in South Australia. Then the wheat belt could develop across northern Victoria and through western New South Wales. The early failure, and the later success, could thus be explained with little reference to the land laws at all. This conclusion was held to the more firmly, I suspect, because it freed the historian from the tedium of actually examining the land laws, which are very complex, and in Victoria at least were frequently amended.

Appropriate markets, technology and transport were necessary conditions for the establishment of the wheat belt, but they won't explain why most of the farmers in the wheat belt were owners rather than tenants. Why didn't the pastoral runs turn into landed estates, to be rented out to farmers when wheat-growing became possible? That is what happened in Argentina when pastoralism gave way to wheat-growing. To explain the triumph of the family farm in Australia we are driven back to politics and to the land laws.

Some writers who have noticed the similarity of the pastoral economies of Australia and Argentina in the middle years of the nineteenth century have made the mistake of attributing the same power and position to the pastoral land holders in the two countries. It is very important to understand that in Australia in 1850 the pastoralists did not own their land, they only leased it; and that their political power in the matters they cared about most was severely limited. Let me explain this further.

When the pastoralists first moved out beyond the older settled districts around Sydney they were occupying Crown lands illegally – hence the origin of the term 'squatter' by which they were known. The British government's policy in the 1830s was to restrict the spread of settlement to maintain order and civilisation and reduce the costs of administration. Within the settled districts they sold land for relatively high prices (it reached £1 an acre in 1842) and used some of the proceeds to pay for the immigration of free labourers. Wool-growing wouldn't pay on land acquired at such prices, and so the pastoralists took their sheep out on to the unoccupied land, and within fifteen years they had taken up most of the best land in south-eastern Australia. Having failed to stop this movement, the government was nevertheless determined to control it, and it obliged squatters to take out annual licences, and insisted they had acquired no permanent right to the land. The squatters of course wanted security. They demanded that they be able to buy their land at much-reduced prices – 2/6d. or less an acre (one-eighth of the ruling price), or that their occupancy of the land which had transferred a barren waste into a valuable possession should be sufficient to give them a freehold title without further payment. In Argentina the right to take a certain number of cattle on the pampas became a right to own the land on which the cattle grazed. But the British government refused to yield to such demands. It insisted that the Crown lands should be held in trust for the whole empire, and in particular for the immigrants who would subsequently go to Australia. Land should not be given away to the lucky first-comers. It recognised that pastoral land was not then worth £1 an acre, but its value would rise as settlement spread, and access to markets improved. It refused to believe the squatters' claim that the land would only ever be suitable for sheep.

However, in 1846 and 1847 the British government did make substantial concessions to the squatters. This followed a spirited campaign mounted by them in Sydney and London after they had been angered by the local government's proposals to raise more revenue from them in return for some security, and after they had been made desperate by the crippling depression which hit the industry in the 1840s. In 1847 the British government gave the squatters leases instead of annual licences, to run for eight to fourteen years depending on the locality of their holdings. During the lease they could purchase the land, but at the standard rate of £1 per acre. They had no right to a renewal of their lease, but they were to be compensated for improvements at its expiry. Contemporary opponents of the squatters, and many historians, have claimed that this was a great victory for the squatters and they declared that the leases on these terms gave the squatters a virtual freehold to their property. This was far from the truth. How the squatters would fare in the future would depend in part on who held political power and hence the right to interpret the terms of the leases, and how their leaseholds would be treated when they expired.

The three major colonies – New South Wales, Victoria and South Australia – did not obtain the full right to self-government until the mid-1850s. Before then landowners and squatters dominated the local legislature, but those bodies had limited power. Executive authority rested with the British appointed governor and his officials. The limitation which the pastoralists felt most keenly was their inability to control land legislation. That matter, as we have seen, was in the hands of the British government. It was the eagerness of the pastoralists to gain control of the land which had fuelled their demands for self-government in the 1840s. After the squatters had obtained their leases in 1847 they became less concerned to gain self-government, but if any became complacent they were rudely awakened by the social and economic transformation brought about by the discovery of gold in 1851 and 1852. The population, particularly in Victoria, rose spectacularly; the thousands of gold diggers who rushed from find to find in the interior, were turning over the soil in the heart of the pastoral domain.

Business in the coastal capitals boomed, merchants and importers were no longer chiefly reliant on the fortunes of the pastoral industry. For the next two decades exports of gold were as valuable as exports of wool. Opposition to the pastoralists' monopoly of the land became intense. Those who had made money in the towns or on the diggings wanted to invest in land, and those immigrants who hadn't made their fortunes – and these were the majority – wanted the chance to settle on the land. The middle class led the attack against the squatters, and they had an enthusiastic following among the workers and gold-miners.

In Victoria, the pressure against the squatters was overwhelming, and many squatters soon saw how little security they had. To appease the land hunger the governor, with the support of his superiors in London, used a loophole in the lease – the power to reserve land for 'public purposes' such as townships or roads or 'for otherwise facilitating the improvement and settlement of the colony' – to withdraw thousands of acres from the squatters' holdings around the new goldfields, and to offer them for sale. The squatters were furious, but when their representatives in London failed to persuade the British government to disallow the governor's measure, there was nothing more for them to do. Competition for the land was keen, and it fetched high prices. Lots of it went to speculators. More land would have to be opened up and special facilities given to the poor man before the land cry would disappear.

Self-government was established in 1856–57. The new constitutions provided for two houses of parliament on the Westminster model – an Assembly and a Council – with the government being formed in the Assembly. Landowners and pastoralists dominated the new Councils – in New South Wales the Council was a nominated body, and in Victoria it was elected on a narrow property franchise – but the Assemblies were, from the beginning, in the hands of their enemies, the

Liberals and Democrats from the towns and the goldfields. The Assemblies were initially elected on a very wide franchise, and very quickly this was extended to adult male suffrage; the secret ballot was introduced and electorates redrawn to reduce the weighting in favour of rural areas. Land reform was the issue which sustained the Liberal/Democratic advance, and after a short struggle the first measures for land reform were carried in the early 1860s. In political life at least the pastoralists had been overwhelmed. They remained a significant political force, particularly in the Council, where they could thwart or distort popular measures, but they never controlled governments or set the agenda of politics.

Notwithstanding this, for a time they won the battle for the land. Large areas of their leaseholds were being transferred into freehold. The loopholes and vagueness in the selection legislation which the squatters exploited were partly there because of their influence in the Legislative Councils.

Their economic resources were of course much greater than potential small holders, and their local influence in rural areas meant that land officials were sometimes working in their interest. But governments and the popular Assemblies did not give up the battle. At the outset land reform had been a crusade which had rallied thousands in the towns and goldfields with the hope that the pastoralists would be turned off their land and every man would gain his farm. The issue never reached the same intensity again – most of the diggers and immigrants found jobs in the towns rather than on the land – but land reform was kept alive by the constant and continuing interest of those small holders who were on the land – tenants in the original farming districts near the coast still wanted to escape landlords and own their own properties, those selectors who had managed to find a farm wanted to move to larger holdings, or better land, or to induce governments to allow them more generous terms for the purchase of their holdings. Farmers of all sorts wanted to get more land for their sons. Farmers and Selectors Associations were developed. The squatters' lack of political power finally told against them.

Briefly the measures which were adopted to give the small man a better chance to acquire land were these:

1. The abolition or limitation of open sales at auction. The Selection Acts had been designed because small men couldn't hope to compete against the pastoralists at auction sales, but Liberal and Democratic governments continued them because it was an easy way of raising money.

2. Dummying – that is, the employment by squatters of men who selected on their behalf – was made more difficult by the insistence that a selector couldn't obtain a title to the land unless he had resided on it and improved it over a considerable number of years. The early Victorian legislation allowed a selector to obtain title immediately if he had the funds. That meant a dummy only had to be employed by the squatter for a few days. He'd select the land, pay for it, and transfer it to the squatter. It was a much riskier and expensive business for the squatter if his dummy had to be employed for years before the title could be obtained.

3. The terms of repayment for the selector were made more generous and eventually a system of leasing at low rental was introduced. This meant that the selector could afford to take more land and he could spend more of his capital on improvements and machinery.

4. More effective and flexible administrative procedures were developed. Land Boards were set up to examine all applications for land. This helped to screen out dummies and to reduce the squatter's influence in the local administration of the law. Ministers of Lands gained more power. They could cancel selections if they considered they were not bona fide. This proved much more effective than taking offenders through the courts.

Those writers who downgrade the importance of the land laws in Australia usually overlook these improvements in the law. In Victoria the improvements were most marked in the 1860s, in New South Wales in the 1880s and 1890s. After these measures had been adopted there was in these colonies a great expansion in the area planted to wheat. These were also the years when conditions became more favourable for wheat-growing, but I believe that the more favourable laws were in themselves a stimulus. With more confidence we can assert that the amended land laws and the political weakness of the pastoralists ensured that the new wheat belt would be worked by men who owned their farms and not by tenants of those who originally held the land.

In the 1890s Australian politics was transformed. The Labor Party and a new radical liberalism emerged which supported a more interventionist government and were prepared to carry the program of land reform a stage further. Labor men and radical Liberals were interested in land reform partly because the huge estates established in the early years of settlement and during the first years of the Selection Acts were the clearest examples of monopoly in Australia, and also because both groups had significant support from small farmers and labourers in the country. They proposed that progressive taxes should be levied on large estates, and that the government should repurchase them, compulsorily if necessary, for sub-division to small holders. They favoured the establishment of state banks to lend money on favourable terms to small holders, and state assistance for the marketing of primary produce. The conservative groupings which formed in reaction to the emergence of the Labor Party and the radical Liberals, originally opposed measures of this sort – but to survive electorally they had eventually to support or acquiesce in their adoption. The re-purchase of large estates was carried on extensively in the early twentieth century, and after World War I for soldier settlement, and this meant that there were very few areas left where large estates predominated. Some of the large holders, under pressure from the Land Tax, and wishing to realise on the increased value of the land, sold out voluntarily to small holders. Once small holding predominated, there was much less prestige or power to be had from the ownership of a large estate. In Australia, landed estates were the most vulnerable form of property. Even the anti-Labor parties would not, or could not, defend them. Those parties increasingly represented the interest of business, manufacturing and mining enterprises.

One of the leading issues in politics for the eighty years after 1850 was the settlement of small holders on the land. In this sense politics determined the nature of rural society, rather than the other way about. This process of small-scale settlement of owner-occupiers was made possible by the political defeat of the squatters in the 1850s and 1860s. It is important to realise that, though pastoral activities were, for the most of the nineteenth century, the basis of the economy, the pastoral-ists themselves were never a ruling class. Before self-government they occupied a pre-eminent place in the local political institutions, but these bodies had limited powers and executive authority was vested in a British-appointed governor and his officials; after self-government Liberals and Democrats ruled. This explains why a landed oligarchy could not establish itself and become a constant threat to a democratic polity as happened in Argentina.

1979

Colonial Society

Our task as Australian historians is to understand a dependent culture. Two forces continue to distract us. As nationalists we want to establish what is distinctive about our society so we seek out those aspects which are as un-English as possible. The bushman, the digger, the pioneer have done noble service. That British institutions, habits or ideas may have been distinctively modified in substance or import in Australia may seem a tame theme by comparison. We are also distracted because in our desire to have a mature historiography we look to Europe to guide us in theme and method. So we practise family history, psycho-biography, the new social history. But the Europeans cannot help us with our central problem. They are not historians of dependent cultures. Our independence as historians will be achieved when we have developed the methods to cope with the dependence of our culture.

We have already a stock of ideas to deal with the relationship of the colonial and metropolitan culture. There is the British 'background'; there is colonial improvisation, usually limited to the material culture – stringy-bark and greenhide; there is British society in Australia deprived of its top and bottom elements (the aristocracy and gentry and the poor mostly did not come); there is the copying of British models, sometimes ahead of their implementation in Britain because of there being fewer obstacles to change in a new society, sometimes behind because of 'cultural lag'. There is, at another level, W. K. Hancock's *Australia*, Douglas Pike's *Paradise of Dissent*, Michael Roe's *Quest for Authority in Eastern Australia*, which all take seriously the dependent nature of our culture.

My aim in this paper is to explore the Australian careers of some British institutions in the hope that I can extend the stock of our ideas for the interpretation of a dependent culture. The first part of the paper refers to an institution which was not transported to Australia – the English poor law. The dependent relationship is of course as evident in what a colonial society rejects as in what it adopts from the mother culture. I am particularly interested in the consequences of the absence of the poor law for the treatment of the unemployed. The second part of this paper examines three institutions which were transferred to Australia – the mechanics institutes, the friendly societies, and the labour party – and flourished wondrously here.

In exploring the nature of a dependent culture we are fortunately not alone – we can borrow from the historians of other dependent cultures. The work of the grand theorist of dependence, the American Louis Hartz, is now well known here, though *The Founding of New Societies* has generally been regarded as not very helpful. Hartz's central idea is that Europe's colonies of settlement are fragments of Europe whose nature and course are determined by the ideology which prevailed at the time they left the mother culture. So Latin America is a feudal fragment, the United States is a liberal, bourgeois fragment, and Australia is variously a radical, proletarian, or collectivist fragment. In the new world the fragment ideology is nationalised so that its European references are lost and it comes to be regarded as a distinctive indigenous ethos. The liberal ideology becomes Americanisation; the radical and collectivist ideology becomes mateship. Europe remains a dynamic society with ideologies in contention and new ideologies forming, but the fragment societies become conservative, their development limited and controlled by their founding ideology. In the twentieth century, however, the isolated and inwardly-looking fragments have to face those European developments which they have hitherto escaped. A new generation knows more of the wider world and realises that the fragment is not a whole universe, that it has been impoverished by its isolation.

What follows will reveal me as a poor man's Hartz. *The Founding of New Societies* has been criticised as theory on altogether too grand a scale which passes sometimes into metaphor. When the facts are not wrong, there are no facts at all. The processes discussed below are, I hope, sufficiently plain and concrete. To the extent that they can be interpreted in Hartzian terms they take on added significance and if they redirect attention to Hartz's work they will have done very good service indeed.

*

The time at which the Australian colonies were founded was certainly crucial to their determination not to reproduce the English poor law. The American colonies, some of them critical of much in England, adopted poor laws as a matter of course. However, during the period of the founding of the Australian colonies – from the late eighteenth century to the 1830s – the poor law ceased to be an accepted part of English life. It was subjected to concerted criticism and after its amendment in 1834 became a matter of savage contention. The poor law provided a complete service for those in need or distress. It was administered on a parish basis by the magistrates and financed by a rate on the occupiers of land. Under the old poor law parishes ran poor houses or work houses, but the chief relief afforded was out-of-doors in the form of doles, pensions, fuel and assistance with rent. The able-bodied poor in work received a supplement to their wages or an allowance for their children if their family was large; out of work they received a money payment or were put to work with the ratepayers and occasionally given jobs on some local public work. From the late eighteenth century onwards the cost of poor relief rose dramatically, for which during war and rapid industrial growth there were many reasons, but at the time the chief was thought to be the practice of supplementing wages. This had long been a part of the poor law but from 1795 the practice became widespread and permanent in the southern counties. Farmers had every incentive to keep their wages low knowing that their workers could be kept alive by payments contributed to by all the landholders in the parish. The reforming Whig government, which took office in 1830, came to the rescue of the ratepayers. Under the new poor law which it passed in 1834 no able-bodied person was to receive relief unless he entered a workhouse where work was to be arduous and the standard of provisions lower than what the worst paid labourer could secure outside. For him, there were to be no more supplements to his wage, family allowances, or money payments. The new system was introduced without trouble in the southern counties at a time of prosperity. When it was introduced in the north, unemployment was rife and there was determined and sometimes violent opposition to the new workhouses from the working classes. They felt that the traditional right of an Englishman to a living in his own country was being taken from them. The terms on which relief was to be offered were totally repugnant. They called the workhouses with their studied harshness, bastilles, engines of tyranny. In fact the principle of the new poor law could never be fully implemented. In some areas outdoor relief to the able-bodied had to be allowed, but in return the unemployed had to come daily to the workhouse and break stones or pick oakum.

Nineteenth-century Australians formed their notion of the poor law from these experiences. The nightmare increase in the poor rates so that industry and enterprise were crippled to pay them was a powerful folk memory. Australian landowners did not want to pay a tax on land and in particular a poor rate whose incidence was so unpredictable and so likely to increase. Those who might need assistance were equally unwilling to be subjected to the meanness and cruelty of the new-style workhouses which were the institutions most likely to be recreated if poor relief was made a charge on landowners. Generally, Australians regarded the poor law as symbolising what they wanted to escape in the old world: potential ratepayers and potential inmates were united in the belief that there should be opportunity for all and no need for a poor law. Working men should have work, and those who had property should not be hindered in their pursuit of more.

The determination not to have a poor law or anything like it was very clear, but Australians had no firm ideas as to what was to replace it. Though they refused to have a poor law they had to cope with the situations which the poor law was designed to meet. Even in a new country where labour was generally scarce unemployment was sometimes acute; there were still the aged and invalid poor, the unemployables and deserted wives. The colonial governments themselves took on some of the responsibilities met by the poor law guardians, but nowhere did they provide a complete service and particularly in the larger colonies of New South Wales and Victoria the reliance on another English method of relieving distress – charity – became greater than in the mother country itself.

Charity in England was an optional extra; the poor law guardians provided for all those in distress and incapable of looking after themselves. Charity took care of those who were thought worthy of more generous and less humiliating treatment. It operated on the principle of the deserving and undeserving poor, the deserving being those whose misfortune was not caused by any failing in their moral character. The undeserving missed out on charity but they were left not to starve but to whatever the penny-pinching poor law guardians were prepared to provide. In Australia when charitable bodies were running institutions or providing outdoor relief, they frequently had to deal with the undeserving as well as the deserving, which put a strain not only on their resources but also their philosophy for they were reluctant to give up the English distinctions. Shurlee Swain, who has made a thorough study of the charity network in Melbourne in the late nineteenth century, reports that the people dispensing outdoor relief were well aware that the greatest distress occurred amongst the less deserving and that reluctantly they had to give aid in these cases, though less than to the deserving. Nothing else stood between these people and starvation. Since charity was a vital institution its own inadequate funds had to be supported by government money. It might look as if Australia by this arrangement had acquired a poor law. The charitable bodies maintained institutions for the aged poor, orphans and 'fallen' women; they distributed outdoor relief to people whose distress arose from a variety of causes; and the taxpayer met a large part of the bill. No-one at the time considered these arrangements were remotely like a poor law, though the inmates of the various asylums and refuges might have had difficulty distinguishing these places from workhouses. The arrangements were indirect in more ways than one. Until the late nineteenth century no colonial government imposed a direct tax on land, income or wealth. The governments survived by selling off their capital assets – land – and by regressive taxes on imports. The government-supported charities did not involve a tax on land; it was that which was the distinguishing mark of the poor law.

The independence of the charities from government control meant that they could not be directed to take everyone. In New South Wales the hospitals run by charities were reluctant to accept the invalid aged. In Victoria the benevolent asylums did not have accommodation for all the aged poor who needed it. Police and magistrates presented with an invalid or destitute old person who was refused admission to a hospital or an asylum had to improvise. The nearest thing the state had to a network of caring institutions were its jails. To these the sick and aged poor were occasionally committed. In England the workhouses were condemned as prisons; in Australia the anxiety to avoid the cruelty of the workhouses meant prisons were actually being used in their place. As the population aged in the late nineteenth century the problems of finding accommodation for all who needed it became more acute. The agitation for the introduction of the old age pension in Victoria in the 1890s was greatly strengthened by revelations about the practice of committing the old to jail. The reluctance to have the English method of dealing with the aged poor pushed the society into accepting, before England did, the alternative of pensions, for which there were already distinguished English advocates.

The absence of a poor law led to innovation as well as improvisation. In England when a wife was deserted by her husband, she was given support by the poor law guardians who had the power through the courts to get the husband to pay maintenance. In Australia the need to get husbands to support their wives was met in a novel way. From 1840 in New South Wales a deserted wife herself was allowed to sue her husband in the courts for maintenance, a right not granted in England until 1886. So long as the husband could be found – and this was often a difficulty – the wife by this means had a cheap and ready way of getting some assistance for herself and her children without the aid of government or charity. It was, as Margaret James writes in her work on divorce and marital breakdown, 'a significant addition to the rights of women'.

In the absence of a poor law the unemployed in Australia were able to demand with a good deal of success that governments provide work for them. In times of unemployment the charitable bodies gave aid, chiefly food, but the men always insisted that they wanted work not charity. When this demand was first made the men were recent immigrants who had been brought out on assisted passages. They claimed they had been lured to the colony with promises of abundant work at good wages and that the government must provide work to keep faith with them. The founders of South Australia had indeed gone so far as to promise government work to the immigrant working men if private employers did not take them all. Since governments wanted to continue recruiting labour they were to a certain extent at the mercy of the unemployed, for their future recruiting efforts would be undermined if immigrants sent home damaging stories. Once the principle of giving work had been conceded – in Sydney in 1843, in Melbourne in 1842 by the corporation and in 1855 by the government, in Adelaide in 1837 – it became easier to make the demand at the next recession. In the second half of the century as governments became builders and constructors on a large scale, they had greater opportunities to adjust their works program to provide relief for the unemployed. Developing the resources of the country was truly the consensus program of nineteenth-century politics, supported as enthusiastically by working men who wanted employment kept up as by merchants, farmers and land speculators.

The methods by which the unemployed made their demands for work soon fell into a regular pattern. They met in the open, marched around the city, and assembled regularly at parliament house or the government offices to seek an interview with the premier or minister of public works. Invariably the ministers agreed to receive a deputation. Reporters were present to record the interview. The men spoke first detailing the numbers who were out of work, the rebuffs they had encountered, the distress which was being felt, and frequently they suggested specific projects which the government should undertake. The minister in reply said that in every large city there was always a number of men out of work and he hoped that the present distress, which he felt sure was not as great as had been represented, would soon pass. There was plenty of work, he was informed, available in the country and he offered free railway passes to any who wanted to seek it.

Railway contractors in the country could also offer jobs and in a few weeks new contracts for a variety of works would be let. The men then had to explain as they did a hundred times that jobs in the country were of no use to married men. The minister's claims about the availability of work might be contradicted by the deputation which could point to men who had already tried and failed to find work at the places he had mentioned. But for the moment the minister would offer nothing more than railway passes, though he might promise to send telegrams to the country to check on what work was available. The deputation reported back to another meeting of the unemployed and further meetings and marches were planned. The unemployed frequently met daily and agitations could last for several weeks. Considerable ingenuity was needed to devise ways to occupy the men and increase the pressure on government. The unemployed marched to government house, to the chambers of the leader of the opposition, to the bishops' residences and sought interviews with their distinguished occupants to put their case, with the press always in attendance. Deputations were sent to sympathetic members of the House and particular attention was given to the city members in whose constituencies some of the unemployed had votes. On one occasion the unemployed marched up Collins Street in Melbourne with shovels to show that they were ready for work. If the agitation did continue the minister would receive more deputations and agree to accept a list of names of those who claimed to be unemployed. The list, when completed, was passed over to the police for the authenticity of the names and claims to be checked. The police invariably could not find a good number of those who claimed to be unemployed, which allowed the minister to prove that distress was not as extensive as had been claimed, but he agreed to create a special work project for the genuine unemployed (these were known as relief works) or to bring forward or expand some regular public works project. As soon as this had been conceded there were further meetings and deputations about pay and conditions, the men insisting that the work be performed by day labour and not contract. Ministers always hoped that the unemployed would disappear and an alternative tactic to stalling was to give in at once and offer some not very attractive work, for which the number of applicants could usually be depended upon to be much fewer than the number claimed to be unemployed. This might settle the matter for a time.

The politics of the unemployed were simple – they wanted governments to give them work. They were sometimes led by men who sought to teach them the true origin of their discontents and to use them to achieve those reforms which would eliminate unemployment for the future. Land reformers, protectionists, free traders, socialists and in the twentieth century, communists, offered their services to the unemployed. Other leaders were more idiosyncratic stump orators, well-known characters at the traditional Sunday meeting places. Leaders were usually already known to the reporters but occasionally a man would emerge from the ranks and would be recorded among the speakers or deputation members as 'a young man called West' or 'a strong young man named Richard Elliott, who stated that he was a baker'. The unemployed were regularly warned that their cause was imperilled by 'agitators'. There were instances of them disowning their leaders – asking them to stay away from their meetings and assuring a minister that the genuine unemployed were perfectly satisfied with his proposals – and of them passing votes of confidence in their leaders after ministers indicated they would do better without them. The skills of the leaders who were already involved in public life, even if only at the fringes, were clearly important for the launching of an unemployed agitation. However, the unemployed were poor materials for the wider influence which these leaders sought. Whatever the message preached, meetings always ended with a deputation to the minister. If the deputation succeeded, the leaders lost their constituency as the men went off to their new jobs. Ministers no doubt were more ready to offer work knowing that the leaders had bigger barrows to push. The only cause apart from work to which the unemployed themselves were enthusiastically committed was the cessation of further immigration.

Work was regularly provided for the unemployed, but reluctantly and with due care. Real and widespread distress had to be proved. In the 1890s when unemployment was most acute and funds at their lowest, governments could do little and the chief relief to unemployment in the east was migration to the west. Officialdom never acceded to the *rights* which the unemployed claimed: 'the first and great primary right of all others – the right to live by their labour and support their wives and families in moderate comfort and decent respectability'; or (from a hostile source) 'the monstrous doctrine ... that because a man had served seven years to a trade he had a right to have work found for him, and he could not be expected to take any other employment than that to which he had been accustomed'. Harassed ministers would sometimes declare against all the evidence of their predecessors' actions that it was no business of the government to find work for the unemployed and lecture deputations on the need for savings and greater initiative, or a willingness to accept lower wages. A good leader of the unemployed could cope with that:

> He did not say that it was the duty of the Government to find work
> for people out of employment, but he did say that when there was
> a large body of men who could not get work, it was the duty of the
> government to step in and give that relief which they could not get
> elsewhere.

And ministers were finally responsible or why else did they agree to admit the deputations?

I have gone into the unemployed agitations and the responses to them in some detail because frequently in our history we forget the scale of the societies with which we are dealing. To say that central governments gave jobs to the unemployed on public works in Australia whereas in England local poor law guardians ran workhouses would miss so much. What could be more 'local' than the face-to-face encounters between ministers and the unemployed, the discussion and argument about particular job sites and wage rates, the invitations to deputations to call back tomorrow when the results of telegrams sent to contractors in the country would be known? Australian ministers dealing with the unemployed were not unlike the English magistrates who ran the old poor law, who had to deal with crowds complaining about the price of bread, who supplemented wages, and occasionally provided public works for the unemployed. The similarity is not fortuitous. In the special circumstances of Australia's founding, working men were able to maintain those rights to a decent living in their own land which the English poor lost in 1834.

With the advent to parliament in the late nineteenth century of Labor and radical Liberal members, governments came under more pressure to provide work and be model employers. Labor men and radical Liberals had their critiques of capitalism to justify such a positive role for government and what had been done for the unemployed under the lap, as it were, when self-help was the prevailing ideology, was now forthrightly proclaimed as sound policy. These members insisted that in all government work and in any special relief schemes for the unemployed a living wage must be paid. The formula of 'living wage', applied first to government work, was transformed into the ruling principle of the nation when the federal Liberal government led by Deakin with Labor support made the payment of a 'fair and reasonable' wage a condition of manufacturers enjoying tariff protection. Justice Higgins in his Harvester Judgment in the Arbitration Court in 1907 laid down what that wage should be and the figure he adopted for the basic wage, seven shillings a day, was the amount which had been fixed on by radical Liberals and Labor representatives as the 'living wage' for government work. The Higgins decision became the basis for all the courts' awards.

A 'living wage' established on a needs basis and enforced by legal tribunal was a great contribution to social welfare. If men were in work they could be assumed to be adequately provided for. Men out of work could be employed by the government at the basic wage and it was settled policy in the early twentieth century for the state governments to expand their works in winter, which was the slack period for private employment. These measures were not however sufficient to take up all the unemployed, and in the 1920s unemployment rose sharply. Australia now had a new model for coping with unemployment. Britain had adopted unemployment insurance and health insurance in 1911 and there was a growing interest in comprehensive social security insurance in Australia. Leader writers, intellectuals and political leaders espoused it. Insurance had a particular appeal to conservatives worried about the sapping of self-reliance if people received benefits to which they had made no contribution. The federal government authorised detailed examinations of social insurance and made two attempts to introduce insurance schemes, in the 1920s and the 1930s. Its particular interest, Rob Watts argues, was in reversing the 'mistake' of funding the Commonwealth old age pension out of consolidated revenue. A comprehensive social insurance scheme would establish contributions for pensions as well as other benefits and reduce the drain on the Treasury. In its 1928 proposals the government decided not to include a scheme of unemployment insurance. For this omission it had the sanction of its *Royal Commission on National Insurance*. Under the British system of unemployment insurance, employers, employees and government contributed equal shares to the insurance fund. The Commission had examined employer and union representatives around the country and found that most were opposed to a contributory scheme and generally to any scheme of unemployment insurance. The Commission summarised the views it had encountered:

> The giving of food or sustenance is not advocated as it is stated that there is no other solution worth considering than that of providing work for the unemployed in order that they may retain their self-respect and independence. There should be no payment without work in return, as the genuine unemployed wants work and not charity. Further, that it is undesirable to hand out charity to men willing to work when so much national work of a reproductive nature is required to be done in Australia. It is contended that every person in the community should have the right to work, and that if a man is willing and able to work, and work is not forthcoming, then the government should provide full sustenance for him and his family while he is unemployed. Full sustenance is said to be the basic wage … It is suggested that this financial responsibility would force the government to provide work for the unemployed.

'There is no other solution worth considering than that of providing work': this was Australia's defiance of Britain and all those European countries which had adopted unemployment insurance. The Commission recommended that state governments should develop and refine their existing practice of expanding public works to give the unemployed work.

There was a remarkable tendency towards convergence in the views of those employer and union representatives whom the Commission examined. There were differences in emphasis and different reasons for holding the same opinion but in substance their approach to dealing with unemployment was similar. The unions stressed the right to work, but employers supported the policy of providing public works which was how the 'right' was to be exercised. It was employers rather than unionists who pointed to how much scope there was for public works and were more nationalistic in claiming that unemployment insurance was inappropriate for a young country where there was so much still to be done. Both groups feared the consequences of supplying a money dole. The employers were afraid that it would lead to a weakening of work discipline, though they conceded, as the unionists insisted, that most men wanted work rather than handouts. The unionists were afraid that if a dole were provided there would be less incentive for governments to provide work. Hence the demand that if there was a dole it should be equivalent to the basic wage so that governments would want to get work in return, which employers insisted should always be done when benefits were granted. Employers and unionists were completely at one in the desire not to pay contributions to an unemployed insurance fund, the employers arguing that it was a further tax on industry which would lead to less employment opportunities, the unions because workers on the basic wage were barely surviving as it was.

The attitude of the Labor Party and the unions made the introduction of any contributory insurance scheme difficult if not impossible. The Labor Party line was that if there were to be money payments to the unemployed they should be paid for out of consolidated revenue and the extra funds needed should come from taxing the rich. Despite this, a few union witnesses before the Commission were prepared to consider contributory schemes. They were pounced on by the Labor appointees among the Commissioners and asked whether they would not prefer all the funds to come from consolidated revenue, to which it seemed churlish not to agree. Where he could, Senator Grant (ALP, New South Wales) encouraged witnesses to say that unemployment would never be completely solved until the Labor platform was fully implemented and society was entirely remade. The unemployment insurance schemes in Germany and Britain had been implemented before the workers' party was a major force in the state and in part in an attempt to prevent it from becoming so. A contributory scheme which required a wide measure of support to succeed would be difficult to launch against opposition from the party which was the alternative government. If it were launched, the unions had a weapon to thwart it. They made it quite clear to the Commission that if compulsory contributions were levied they would seek an increase in the basic wage to cover their costs. Employers would then pay both their share and that of the workers.

To read the evidence and report of the Royal Commission on unemployment insurance is to become aware how inappropriate, for this matter at least, is the standard question being asked about our welfare history: why after such promising beginnings at the turn of the century did Australia lag behind the rest of the developed world? Australia did not 'lag behind': it was holding out for something much better than the rest of the world had settled for. It wanted regular work for all at a living wage – an ideal generally supported and the aim, though far from realised, of its official policy – and its workers insisted that if there were to be a dole they should not have to pay for it.

The Depression of the 1930s, as everywhere else, took the problem of coping with the unemployed into a new dimension. It removed one relic of Australia's founding years – the benevolent asylums and societies, still the major source of outdoor relief in some states, could not cope with the massive numbers and were superseded. The state governments themselves all provided food to the unemployed. But to have thousands of men and their families existing on these handouts was repugnant to the unemployed themselves and to the community at large. All states except South Australia introduced special taxes on those still in work to pay for the food doles and to provide relief work for the unemployed. The relief work was rationed: a man was allotted so many days work a week according to the number of his dependants. The wages were below award level, but were designed so that men earned considerably more than the value of their food entitlement. By

1934 in New South Wales, 75 per cent of those in receipt of relief were working for it. Western Australia did best – by 1935, 95 per cent of those on relief were at work. That other relic of the founding years – the practice of finding work for the unemployed – still survived.

The distinctiveness of this response to the Depression has not been generally realised. In Britain in the 1920s when unemployment was already high there was some relief work rationed according to need, but it catered for only a tiny proportion of the unemployed and was abandoned in 1931. In the United States massive sums were spent by the federal government to provide relief work in the 1930s. At first the work was arranged by local bodies on the rationing system, but from 1935 the federal government itself controlled the program and the rationing system was dropped. It was condemned as inefficient since work could not be properly organised with men constantly coming and going and as failing to provide what the men could regard as a proper job. Under the federal scheme all work was on a full-time basis. This was clearly better for those who obtained it, but many missed out. At best one-half of the unemployed were on relief work; the usual figure was between one-quarter and a third. In Australia there was a stronger determination to get everyone in work whatever the imperfections of the work offered.

The federal government made a concerted attempt to introduce a national insurance scheme in 1938. Two British experts were brought out to design it. The expert on unemployment insurance drew up a scheme based on the British system of contributions from employer, employee and government. He criticised the system of relief works and judging the matter with the values of an accountant explained that jobs were more expensive for governments to provide than doles, something which Australians well knew since they had paid special taxes rather than see men left without work. He attempted to shame Australians with their backwardness:

> Relief works had been adopted in many countries from time to time as a temporary method of relieving unemployment, but the method that is being most universally adopted as a permanent means of relieving unemployment is that of unemployment insurance.

He was at pains to point out that unemployment insurance only provided relief to the unemployed; it did not cure unemployment. The method he condemned as temporary and ad hoc, which Australians had been following for a hundred years, was much more a cure since it gave the unemployed not 'relief' but a job. The federal government accepted his scheme, but wanted the states to pay two-thirds of the government contribution. The premiers refused and the scheme lapsed.

During the war the Labor government introduced the unemployment benefit along with other new social welfare measures. They were to be paid for out of consolidated revenue, but the scope of the income tax was widened so that for the first time workers had to pay it. They were to contribute to their welfare benefits. The government well knew that the unemployment benefit was not a cure for unemployment and it committed itself to a Keynesian policy of managing the economy so that serious unemployment would not occur. It is only in recent times that it has become possible to assess the full consequences of these policies. What happens when the management of the economy falters? The workers were right to fear that once there was a dole there would be less incentive for governments to provide work. Ministers now govern without having to encounter deputations from the unemployed demanding work. After its colonial defiance, Australia has rejoined the old world.

*

Mechanics institutes began in Britain in the 1820s. Their aim was to instruct mechanics – that is, skilled men – in the rules and principles of their own trades and in science generally. There were to be lectures, classes, and the provision of scientific reading matter. The institutes spread rapidly, but very quickly their social composition and purposes changed. They ceased to be exclusively institutes for working men and were usually composed of the highest sections of the working class and the lower sections of the middle class. Their lectures, if they continued to be given, were on literary and historical topics or matters of current interest. Dramatic and musical recitals were held. The running of a library became a central function of the institutes but the books were general rather than scientific literature and increasingly works of fiction.

Institutes were established in Australia from the 1830s. In Victoria and Western Australia they were called mechanics institutes; in New South Wales and Queensland the alternative British name of school of arts was used (by 'arts' had been meant mechanical arts); in South Australia they were called simply institutes. A similar change occurred in their purpose and a much more marked change in their social composition. The migrants who came to Australia from the 1830s to the 1850s were overwhelmingly from those groups for which the British institutes catered – the upper sections of the working class and the lower middle class. In Britain they comprised a part of the population; in Australia very near the whole. In Australia, particularly in the suburbs and country towns, the institutes became community centres used by people from a wide range of occupations. They were not established by one group for the use of another as the first Australian institutes had been on the British model; the men who established them wanted to use their services themselves. They provided a place for meetings, lectures, debates by the 'model parliament' societies, entertainment, and dances; they ran a library; they frequently had a billiard room. Throughout the nineteenth century the number of institutes continued to increase and there were mechanics institutes and schools of arts where there might be no more than a handful of mechanics. But providing for them in particular had long ceased to be thought of as their function, though the original names were not abandoned. By 1900 there were about 1000 institutes, a greater number than ever existed in Britain. The vital function they played in Australian society was recognised by governments which gave financial aid for the building and the running of a library.

In the 1930s the institutes still ran Australia's public libraries apart from the one central library maintained by state governments in each of the capitals. In 1934 Ralph Munn, director of the Carnegie Library of Pittsburg, was invited to Australia to survey its libraries and suggest improvements. He was appalled at the institute libraries. Most were run by amateurs; only in a few large institutes was there full-time paid staff; in the medium size there might be a librarian cum billiard marker cum janitor. The books were overwhelmingly light, ephemeral novels. What non-fiction there was was usually hopelessly outdated. 'It is

pathetic,' he wrote, 'to observe the pride and complacency with which
local committees exhibit wretched little institutes which have long
since become cemeteries of old and forgotten books.' Munn was an
advocate of rate-supported free municipal libraries run by professionals. These would be better libraries and reach more people than the
institutes which still required a subscription from their library users.
He was puzzled why Australia, which had 'led the world towards
government ownership of public service and socialised activity', should
lag so far behind the rest of the English-speaking world in the provision of free libraries.

In Britain municipal councils were empowered by the 1850 Public
Libraries Act to set up free libraries. As councils opened libraries, the
mechanics institutes libraries were either absorbed or superseded. The
number of mechanics institutes reached their peak in the 1860s and
then declined. In Australia there was no need to follow the example of
the Public Libraries Act for the institutes provided a comprehensive
service. As Munn reported, on the evidence of the books they still held,
the libraries were much better in the nineteenth century than they
were by the 1930s, and as he had to concede they were able to function
in places too small to support a professionally run rate-supported
service. Despite their rapid growth, the mechanics institutes in Britain
never covered the whole country, and there would have been many
people reluctant to use a library housed in a building called a mechanics institute.

From the 1930s dates the campaign to establish free municipal
libraries in Australia. The leading campaigners were the Australian
Council for Educational Research, funded by the Carnegie Foundation,
and the professional librarians. The report by the American library
expert on Australian backwardness was one of their most powerful
weapons. The new municipal libraries are undoubtedly better than what
they replaced, but I imagine their chief business is still in ephemeral
fiction. Not all is gain, however. The professional librarians have a
quaint belief that children should read only wholesome fiction. So they
banned from their shelves Enid Blyton and Biggles and whatever the
modern equivalents are. I borrowed scarcely anything else from our
library, though I always had to look hard to find them for there was

neither catalogue, nor book numbering, nor alphabetical order at the Clarence Park Institute.

*

Friendly societies underwent a transformation similar to that of the mechanics institutes when they were transferred to Australia. Friendly societies were mutual benefit associations which flourished in England from the late eighteenth century. The societies which came to Australia were the affiliated orders such as Manchester Unity and Foresters which had a central organisation co-ordinating the activities and pooling the resources of numerous local lodges. These provided the most comprehensive benefit packages – in return for a weekly contribution members were eligible to receive free health care, sick pay, and a decent funeral. The cost of these services meant that the poorer sections of the working class were excluded from membership. The membership, as with the mechanics institutes, came generally from the higher section of the working class and the lower section of the middle class.

In Australia the friendly societies had a much wider membership. My information on their membership and much else besides comes from Nancy Renfree's excellent study of the societies in Victoria. Men who had done well and no longer had the financial need for the benefits remained subscribers and continued to associate at the weekly lodge meetings with those who had not been so fortunate. Employer and employee within the lodge called each other brother. Skilled working men were the largest occupational group in the lodges, but membership extended as it did not in England to include significant numbers of labourers. Information on the occupation of lodge members was gathered in official returns. The religion of members was not officially recorded but in her detailed study of Castlemaine, Renfree established that Protestants and Catholics were members of the same lodge. In the suburbs and larger country towns a very high proportion of the adult males were members of lodges – in the early 1870s in Collingwood 53 per cent, Williamstown 62 per cent, Maldon 45 per cent, Creswick 51 per cent and Castlemaine 63 per cent. It was entirely fitting that the leading nationalist institution in the late nineteenth century should have been a friendly society – the Australian Natives Association, which has been wrongly characterised as 'middle-class'; its membership ranged from professional men to labourers.

The doctors came to regard the friendly societies with hostility. The societies contracted with the doctors to provide a service to their members for which they were paid so much per member per year. The societies reserved the right to carpet the doctors for poor performance and to reduce their payment as punishment. The strength of the societies meant that doctors had fewer patients paying the full fee for a consultation and they were forced into relationships which they increasingly saw as incompatible with their social and professional standing. They were particularly incensed that men who could well afford to pay their fees came to them as lodge patients. At the intercolonial Medical Congress in 1887 it was noted:

> In Australia the most prominent feature is the extent of the club practice ... To the newcomer the extent to which the lodge system is carried is astonishing. He is amazed to find well-to-do and opulent men – Members of Parliament, lawyers, Government officials – not only ordinary members of a lodge, but expecting, and demanding, treatment as lodge patients. This should not be, and could only have arisen from a misconception of the origins of Friendly Societies.

The origins of the societies were working class, and while they remained chiefly that in England doctors were prepared to make special arrangements for servicing their members; as community organisations in the new world they were threatening.

Once the doctors' professional organisation became more powerful they were better able to reduce the friendly societies to their proper role. The Australian division of the BMA insisted that contracts with friendly societies were unacceptable unless the societies excluded from their benefit schemes those whose incomes exceeded a certain amount. The societies did their best to stave off these demands, but they could do little finally against the doctors' power simply to boycott them. In 1909 the New South Wales societies implemented an income limit on membership. After a long dispute in Victoria during which over 400 lodge doctors refused to renew their contracts the societies conceded in 1918.

But for the doctors greater dangers loomed in the new century. They had to fight off the plans of the state to introduce national health insurance schemes which, if they were to follow the British model of 1911, would give them the same relationship with the state as they had with the friendly society lodges. They would have a panel of patients and be paid so much per head. In fighting the government's insurance schemes in 1938 the doctors were joined by the friendly societies which feared a further downgrading of their own role. The opposition of these two bodies helped kill that proposal, but the doctors knew they could not forever forestall plans to make health care more accessible. From the 1930s they encouraged and themselves founded new insurance organisations which gave contributors a cash payment to offset the costs of doctors' services. This kept doctors from being subject to the insurance body and allowed them to charge fees to all-comers. Doctors insisted that this should be the model for any national scheme of health insurance. The Menzies government introduced a scheme of this type in 1953 by making federal health benefits available to those who insured with organisations which made cash payments. In 1950 the BMA had announced that all contracts with the friendly society lodges would cease. The friendly societies survived by becoming insuring bodies of the new sort. They now have more members than they ever did, but not members who meet together in brotherhood and sit in judgment on doctors.

The association of men of very different economic circumstances in the lodges was paralleled by the attendance of children from across the community at the new state schools. In the first decade of their operation in Victoria there was a great shift of children into state-supported education, the newcomers being made up of both poorer children (since fees were no longer charged and attendance was compulsory) and the well-to-do (since the teaching was superior to that of many small private schools). After the introduction of the 1872 Education Act the state school in South Yarra was swamped by 'young ladies'. At St Kilda, 'the children of doctors, the children of clergymen, the children of professional men and the children of everyday labourers … sit side by side'. The elite generally continued to regard such schools as unsuitable for their children, but what a tiny elite it was! After ten years operation the state schools had 82 per cent of all school enrolments. If those attending Catholic schools are set aside as a religious rather than a status minority, the proportion was 92 per cent. The new schools were modelled on the Board Schools set up in England in 1870. These were provided by town councils to educate working-class children not reached by the National Society and the British and Foreign Society whose schools continued to receive government support. Varying from locality to locality there were status differences as between these schools which all catered for the working class and lower middle class. A London artisan would keep his children away from the Board school so that they might mix in better company at a National school. And beyond were the gulfs which separated all these schools from the grammar schools and public schools. In Australia, by contrast, setting the Catholics aside, what would have been known as Board Schools in England took virtually all children at the primary level.

The transformation of the mechanics institutes and friendly societies can be understood chiefly in the social composition of the migrating population – the institutions of a section of the population became those of the whole as migrants distributed themselves across the occupational structure in the new land. But this does not wholly explain why these institutions lost their sectional character. In Britain they were identified in the social order according to those who belonged to them. In the new world the colonists, anxious for the best sanction of all for their activities, gave them a new dimension by identifying them as British and using them to establish those civilising activities which made the colonies seem more like home. The social bearing of these institutions became even more indeterminate because in the new society there was not in the same configuration the social groups in which they originated and by which they were originally defined. They were ready for new purposes and a new membership. It is thus that we can understand why men who had no experience of these institutions in the mother country or had positively shunned them were ready to join them; why they continued to hold a membership diverging in economic circumstances; and why few saw the incongruity of maintaining such names as mechanics institutes.

*

It is this second process which we should bear in mind when attempting to understand the colonial career of the last of the British working-class institutions to come to Australia – the labour party. Whatever the local circumstances precipitating its foundation, it was undoubtedly a borrowed institution, something which those historians who seek to explain its origins and success by reference to class configuration in Australia sometimes overlook. The trade unions, the Trades and Labour Councils and their parliamentary committees were replicas of British models. Many of the movement's members and most of its leaders had come to Australia in the migration of working men in the 1870s and 1880s. The great development of new unions in Britain and the increased interest in parliamentary representation in the late 1880s were spurs to similar developments here. In 1886 the British Trade Union Congress established a Labour Electoral Association which was soon describing itself as the National Labour Party. Its aim was to increase working-class political influence though not necessarily by running its own candidates. Their first attempt to elect an independent Labour man occurred in 1888 when Keir Hardie ran for Mid-Lanark in a by-election which attracted national interest. Support for independent political action was strongest in the industrial north. The Scottish Labour Party was formed in 1888; the Bradford Labour Union in 1891; and at Bradford in 1893 the Independent Labour Party, which was constituted chiefly from associations in the north and Scotland, was established. When the Australian labour parties were launched in the early nineties they immediately achieved much more than had been secured in Britain, but their leaders had the encouragement and sanction of British practice. The legitimacy of what they were attempting in the labour interest was generally accepted and so they brought to this agricultural and pastoral country with its commercial cities a class institution of an advanced industrial economy.

The rapid expansion in electoral support for the Labor Party, especially in the early years of the twentieth century, was phenomenal. In Britain the Labour Party was and was seen to be a party of the working class, a group quite rigidly separated geographically, in status and style of life from the rest of the population. In Australia the party could not have this identity. The workers who formed it were members of mechanics institutes and friendly societies; they sent their children to the state schools – institutions which in England had a distinct lower-class character but in Australia were patronised by wide sections of the population. In these circumstances so long as Labor had suitable policies there was less to inhibit those outside the ranks of the unions and manual workers from supporting the party. Adelaide and its suburbs, the small farmers, the Tasmanian apple-growers were all won over to Labor. Labour in Britain was the party of the working class; in Australia the party of those who worked and on this basis could be persuasively presented as both a 'class' and a 'national' party.

But the Labor Party in this society without a large industrial working class became a different party from the British one. In 1918 when the British party adopted its socialist objective it had only fifty-seven seats in the House of Commons. It gradually consolidated its support in the working class and sought support outside with a socialist program, which it went some way to implementing when it first obtained office in its own right in 1945. When the Australian party adopted its socialist objective in 1921, it had already ruled in the Commonwealth and in five of the states, and what Labor governments did and did not do had been settled.

*

Hartz has difficulty in deciding on the essential nature of Australian colonial society: was it collectivist, proletarian, or radical? The impulse behind the determination not to have a poor law can scarcely be identified as collectivist or proletarian. 'Radical' may be closer, but in a specific sense which Hartz does not envisage – opposition to burdensome taxation which was an important part of the radical program in the early nineteenth century. Those in Australia who wanted to increase opportunity by removing the threat of taxation were nevertheless in their refusal to set up a poor law committing themselves, however indirectly, to the view that Australia would not have Britain's social problems. When unemployment did occur, the unemployed were thus well placed to get their demands met. The *Argus* said of Governor Hotham's provision of roadworks for the unemployed in 1855 that it would 'greatly relieve the public mind, and we shall no longer be oppressed by the supposition that poverty and misery find lurking places here almost as numerous as those of the old world'. It is in the provision of work for the unemployed that we can trace the origins of the Australian living wage which was a distinctive character-istic of this fragment. In his attempt to characterise the ideologies of the fragments Hartz sometimes attaches them to certain key European figures. When among other stabs he fixes on Cobbett for the Austra-lian ideology he may have chosen well. Cobbett was neither proletarian nor collectivist, but he was radical. He wanted to reduce the taxation of the old order which oppressed small property holders and producers and yet he insisted that labourers must live in decent comfort.

Hartz wrote of a proletarian or collectivist ideology being national-ised in Australia. I have outlined instead how British working-class institutions were nationalised in this country. The mechanics institutes and the friendly societies were of course far from being collectivist in spirit. Their aim was to help their members to self-improvement in a moral and cultural sense and to better their economic circumstances. Hartz's account of Australia is seriously flawed because he followed the old Whig view of Australia's history which posits a weak middle class, and a large, confident working class and he derived from this the view that Australian democracy was 'dedicated much less to the capitalist dream than to mateship'. Australians did want a career open to talent and the desire for economic independence was strong. But the member-ship of the mechanics institutes and the friendly societies suggests some limitations on this which may not have their equivalent in that liberal capitalist society par excellence – the United States. Those who had done well were willing to associate with respectable working men whose worth and respectability were not impugned because they had failed to make fortunes. The mutual seeking of self-improvement is not collectivism, but nor is it unalloyed individualism. The respectable working man was part of a culture which spread a long way beyond his ranks. It is in these terms that I would explain the widespread accept-ance of the Labor Party.

Hartz, by contrast, ascribes the easy victory of the Labor Party to a pre-existing collective ethos. One of the difficulties with his thesis is to know when the fragment 'breaks away'. He implies that this had happened before the formation of the Labor Party, but if this were so he has the difficulty of explaining why an inward-looking fragment should be borrowing a British institution. One of the reasons for the absence of a strong labour or socialist party in the United States is that by the time these movements emerged in Europe the United States was a self-confident society, absolutely sure of its superiority to Europe and ready to condemn labour organisations and socialism as alien and un-American. The social structure of Australia in the late nineteenth century was much closer to that of the United States than of Britain, and indeed Australia may have been a more open society, but the continuing eagerness to follow British models brought to it with a large measure of acceptance what was regarded as alien in America.

It is difficult for even a friendly critic of Hartz to date the 'departure' of the Australian fragment and impossible to see the multifarious activities which are following or departing from British models as moving in unison. When Australia borrowed the new unions and the Labor Party, other matters were already settled in ways which were no longer British – mechanics institutes as the chief providers of libraries, for instance. In some places Hartz dates the departure of the fragment when the society is composed chiefly of the native-born who do not know Europe and for whom the fragment is naturally the whole world. That would put Australia's departure about 1900. But its separate life would then be very short-lived for, as this paper has detailed, in the twentieth century the intelligentsia and the professionals were in Hartzian terms taking Australia back to the old world. They successfully attacked the institutions of the migrant population of the nineteenth century – mechanics institutes libraries, public works for the unemployed, lodges for health insurance. The attackers were the people most open to outside influence and whose professional standing was most threatened by the 'amateurism' of the migrant institutions.

I do not want to suggest that *The Founding of New Societies* or some refinement of it should be our sole guide. There are other ways that dependence must be explored. But Hartz is worth a second look and the issue he dealt with we must continue to confront.

1984

Egalitarianism

'Egalitarianism – see under myths': so runs the index entry in a standard sociological text on Australian society, and it illustrates a stock way of handling this vexed question. One can understand the despair behind this approach – why won't the populace who believes this is an egalitarian society read the books on social stratification and class formation? To this there may be an obvious answer. While historians are also interested in the development of myth, for them egalitarianism has a more substantial existence. The desire for equality in social, political and economic realms has been a major force in our history, with results that are quite palpable.

One of the difficulties of the term is the variety both of the equalities which have been sought and the standards by which they have been measured. This applies even to historians or sociologists studying egalitarianism in Australia, who have not always made their own positions clear enough or taken care to separate them from those of the people they are studying. Some egalitarians, for example, seek equality of opportunity: they regard unequal outcomes in wealth and social prestige as acceptable so long as all have an equal chance of obtaining them. To egalitarians of another sort such outcomes are unacceptable: they wish to see equal material outcomes, or at least no gross differences in material rewards between various occupations. There have been egalitarians of these two sorts both in our history and among the observers of our society. Those who deride the view that Australia is an egalitarian society point to the undoubted existence of class structures and status hierarchies. On the other hand, Australians who claim their society is egalitarian may believe that opportunity is open to all or be pleased that people of different status address each other as equals and that everyone has the vote. This introduces two other kinds of equality: that of manners, and that of political rights. The failure to distinguish between various forms of egalitarianism has not only produced confusion; it has precluded discussion of the relationship between them, now and in the past. I don't intend to offer here anything like a full account of egalitarianism in our history. The paper gives some impressions derived from my study of nineteenth-century New South Wales society, and it bears mainly on equality of opportunity, of political rights, and of manners. Much of the paper is concerned with some of the inequalities that developed when equality of opportunity was the ideal.

*

Egalitarianism, in the sense of opportunity for all regardless of birth, has rightly been considered as something which the great bulk of the free migrants of the mid-nineteenth century wanted to see enshrined in the new country. Any attempt to recreate here a closed system of privilege was fiercely resisted. Nominated members of Legislative Councils were anathema to a generation brought up on the battles against Old Corruption. Wentworth's attempt in 1853 to found a colonial aristocracy for his constitution was laughed out of court. The terms on which squatters held their land were seen as an attempt to restrict land ownership to a few hands, and (worse) to re-establish a feudal order of lords and serfs. The squatters were relentlessly pursued and politically crushed. The land, the prime resource of colonial society, was thrown open to all.

There is a widespread view, to which serious historians have given support, that the migrants were also egalitarian in another sense: having escaped an old-world society, they are said to have been opposed to the creation here of a society of deference, ranks and titles. On this view, the history of the egalitarianism of manners would begin at this point. On the face of it, there are grounds for doubting this. The old society which denied migrants their opportunities would also have ingrained in them its own signs of success. In so far as the motive for migration is the desire for social advancement, a society of migrants will not forget the old marks of social pre-eminence.

Political democracy was not part of the old world, and its establishment in New South Wales in the 1850s might be thought to signal an acceptance of the intrinsic worth of every man which would also have affected manners. Clearly, democracy does imply the social worth of every man, or it may be justified in such terms, but this was not the bearing it had in New South Wales at its foundation. The introduction of political democracy was not accompanied by the establishment of a democratic ideology. There were many reasons for this, not the least of them being that the word 'democracy' itself was still suspect. It had not altogether lost its associations with direct popular rule and republicanism. The Liberals could not afford to be seen as un-British in their constitutional plans, for the British constitution was still widely revered. When Wentworth had declared that he wanted a British and not a Yankee constitution, the Liberals accepted this, and argued that their plan for two elected houses was a better embodiment of the principles of the British constitution than his own, given the colony's different social composition. In this they were fortunate to have the authority of leading British statesmen, who declared that there was no longer any necessity for colonial constitutions to be closely modelled on the British. The time was past when a departure from a nominated upper house in a colonial constitution was taken as threatening to the House of Lords at home. There was also in the 1850s respectable British precedents for widening the franchise. Chartism, which had been a handicap to the cause of colonial democracy, was finally defeated in 1848. Middle-class reform groups then reappeared with more limited programs, and the cause had been taken up in the House of Commons by no less a figure than Lord John Russell, the hero of the first Reform Bill, who had now renounced his earlier view that that measure was final. These movements in British opinion were relied on heavily by the Liberals and were crucial to their success. Such a strategy precluded the emergence of a democratic ideology that would have implied too thorough a denunciation of British society, from which the colonial constitution still had to be able to derive its authority and to which colonial society still gave its loyalty. There is a striking contrast between the fierceness with which the privileges of nominated Legislative Councillors and pastoral lessees were attacked and the gingerly approach to manhood suffrage. Indeed, the very form in which the franchise was extended indicates the limited commitment to democracy: the old property qualifications for the vote were retained and the manhood qualification was merely added to them.

The introduction of political democracy can best be seen as a measure adopted by those who were close to success in order to strengthen their hands for the final battle against the squatters. The supporters of manhood suffrage were warned that they would eventually become victims of the forces they were prepared to unleash. These warnings were ignored; some say because there was less reason in Australia to fear the multitude. Perhaps so; but the impatience and recklessness of the aspiring migrant must also be considered. He had no care or respect for society until he had attained what he considered his proper place. This was the migrant's dilemma: would he in his destructive phase be so successful that there would be no basis finally upon which to claim the distinction he craved?

What would be the basis for distinction in a colonial society was a central concern of a very perceptive lecture given in Melbourne by Archibald Michie in 1859. Michie was a Liberal, a supporter of manhood suffrage and a defender of the Eureka rebels. He gave his lecture the rather cumbersome but pertinent title, 'Colonists: Socially and in their Relations with the Mother Country'. It begins by welcoming those aspects of colonial society which distinguish it from England: here everyone – gentle and simple, educated or ignorant – works for his living. There is no disdain for manual labour, and no pathetic attempts by the genteel poor to keep up appearances. 'The revolution set in when gentlemen began to dress sheep for the scab. The revolution surely is complete when a French marquis is driving a dray in Collingwood and the son of an English peer is in the police, and ex-fellows of colleges are in the deep sinkings of Ballarat.' But these changes in fortunes and in old certainties have not established – and, Michie insists, never can establish – entire social equality. Like-minded people will want to associate with each other; and what is seen and criticised as exclusiveness is frequently no more than that. Furthermore, men will continue to want to be distinguished from their fellows by titles and other marks of honour. In democratic America men grasp at any title they can lay claim to and are constantly be-captaining each other. This is a natural human vanity – and a beneficial one; for would it not be 'disastrous for society – nay, could society even exist? – if we were in the mass utterly indifferent to the good or ill opinions of our fellow citizens'. For Michie, the colonists were merely Britons overseas, and they should be eligible for all the titles available to the inhabitants of the United Kingdom – a surprising view for a colonial Liberal to voice while the battle against privilege still raged. Michie went so far as to put in a good word for Wentworth's peerage scheme. A peerage should perhaps only be conferred in rare cases, but the principle for which Wentworth contended was correct: a colonist held a degraded rank as a British citizen if he were deprived of the opportunity of gaining British honours.

The *Sydney Morning Herald* was delighted by Michie's lecture. Fighting a losing battle against the New South Wales Liberals, it was pleased to take up and strengthen Michie's views. The affected contempt for titles of honour, it claimed, was hypocrisy: 'Social distinction is everywhere desired, and nowhere more than in democratic countries, where the passion for rising in the world is stimulated by the possibility of it.' Was the *Herald*'s view of its enemies correct? Were the distinctions of the old society still sought in the new democracy?

*

The social distinction most readily available to the aspiring colonist was that of becoming a gentleman. Gentlemen had a distinctive dress – frock-coat, top hat, kid gloves – and received public recognition from other gentlemen. Policemen were instructed to salute them. In letters addressed to them and in any formal listing of names they were given the title 'Esquire'. Working people addressed them as 'Sir'.

The history of the gentleman in Australia has suffered much from the aristocratic bent of its historians. Paul de Serville in his study of Port Phillip gentlemen is much concerned with gentle birth and good family. Geoffrey Bolton associates the colonial gentleman with the ownership of broad acres. By traditional English standards, these are the correct criteria to adopt; but in the colonies, gentlemen did not have to meet them. In the 1850s in New South Wales the men claiming to be gentlemen and recognised as such were squatters, landowners, merchants, bankers, professional men, chief clerks and those of independent means. This rather lax conception is reflected in Burke's *Colonial Gentry* published in the 1890s – a work that both Bolton and de Serville find puzzling. De Serville takes it to task for belying its title:

> The genealogies are exiguous, often covering no more than three generations although attempts are made at times to graft new branches onto old trees. The heraldic aspects are even less impressive. An English critic pointed out that at least a third of the entrants are technically not gentlemen, lacking coats of arms ... Nor could the 563 odd entrants be said to compose a gentry in the accepted sense of the term, since many were not landed, much less members of historical or ancient families of the untitled nobilities.

Bolton is a little more prepared to see standards relaxed but was it not, he asks, 'generous to include W. O. Hodgkinson, Micawber-like journalist and mining speculator who happened to be Minister for Mines in Queensland in 1891 and had neither wealth, permanent position, nor ancestry beyond a father who was a Mr Hodgkinson of Birmingham?' No, it was not generous. He was certainly a gentleman – as was Mr Micawber of course, once he was in Australia and had become a sheepfarmer.

The widening of the ranks of the gentleman in the colony was made possible because in England there was a long-standing ambiguity about the term, pressure for widening of the ranks, and uncertainty about where the line of exclusion fell. Gentlemen were of good family and held land, but they also had to possess the gentlemanly virtues – they were scrupulously honest and considerate. A man who lacked these virtues could be described as 'no real gentleman' even though he had land and an ancient lineage. But if this were so, could the practice of the gentlemanly virtues entitle one to the status of gentleman even without land and lineage? It was at this point that those without the traditional claims could exert pressure. Not that gentlemen had ever formed a closed order; old families had married new wealth, and after one or two generations, new wealth was old enough. Undoubtedly, it was now much easier, in the nineteenth century, to become a gentleman, or to seem to become one; but the uncertainty about the term was still only at the edges of a group that could be recognised clearly enough by the old criteria.

In Australia the balance changed. The core of true gentlemen was small and not self-sustaining; the claimants at the edges numerous. There were enough true gentlemen to retain the rank's traditional prestige, but too few, owning too few resources, for the traditional criteria to maintain a commanding influence. Everyone in the colonies – including those with the best claims to be gentlemen – was closely involved in money-making. This was traditionally forbidden the English gentleman, who could invest his fortune to advantage but was essentially a man of leisure, not preoccupied with money matters. If trade in sheep or cattle, or speculation in squatting runs, was allowable, on what grounds could merchants be excluded from the gentlemanly ranks? Both the Australian Club in Sydney and the Melbourne Club – the institutions of the gentlemanly elite – had merchants among their founding members. No doubt these were men who came closest to the gentlemanly ideal in character and education, but their acceptance into the Clubs meant that the traditional prejudice against trade could not be used to deny gentlemanly status to other merchants. All merchants became gentlemen, even if they were not all accepted into the Clubs. The rule against trade took on a new form in Australia: it was used to draw the line below merchants and so to exclude shopkeepers. Wholesale trade was allowable to a gentleman; retail trade was not.

The groups which became gentlemen in Australia were making (or were soon to make) claims to that status in England, but there, these claims could be resisted or made to look doubtful. In Australia, they could not, with the paradoxical result that there was ultimately less uncertainty about who was a gentleman in Australia than in England. In Australia, the criteria of good family (which was particularly limiting) and land ownership disappeared; 'gentleman' became the status of anyone holding a certain position in the occupational hierarchy or possessing independent means. Membership of a traditional English rank thus became available to the successful migrant of whatever background.

But one uncertainty remained. The new-made colonial gentlemen knew they were doubtful gentlemen by traditional English standards, which were overlooked in the colonies but not forgotten. The colonial gentlemen set about to meet them as best they could. By old-world standards many of these attempts were pathetic. Paul de Serville laughed at family trees that went back only three generations; what would he think of vague references to 'good yeoman stock'? Or of the ex-convict pastoralist claiming that his ancestors must have been people of some consequence because of the quality of their tombstones in the village churchyard? The gentlemen in Australian cities – merchants, bankers, company directors, professional men – frequently sought a country 'estate': ten acres, sometimes more, sometimes less, beyond the city proper where they built their mansions and villas. They worked in the city but lived in what might just be called country. The grand town house did not flourish in Australian cities, because town wealth immediately claimed gentlemanly status and tended to move out of town. In Adelaide, a country life for city gentlemen was most happily accomplished: the Adelaide Hunt Club met at the gentlemen's mansions and followed the trail over their estates and the neighbouring farms, all within sight of the city itself.

The widening of the ranks of gentlemen in the colonies was a fairly rapid but traumatic process. Gentlemen who had, or thought they had, good traditional claims to gentlemanly status regarded themselves as superior to the would-be gentlemen; but would-be gentlemen with the summit of their ambition in sight were not disposed to accept a subordinate place. They subjected any claims to superior status to remorseless analysis: How had so-and-so made his money? What was the real reason for his coming to the colony? Who were his wife's people? Such was the staple of day-to-day gossip, and often of public feuding. Men with new wealth, doubtfully acquired, could sometimes claim superior origins to those with old. Being an old family carried some status in New South Wales, but the old families were particularly vulnerable because some of the founders were of doubtful origin and all had made their money in ungentlemanly ways. Challengers could not meet the traditional criteria, but they used them to denigrate occupiers. Just because the new men could not be excluded, the contentions for place and precedence were fearsome. In small societies, where so many were parvenus and the traditional standards were being set aside, there could be no agreed basis for the ranking of gentleman. The result was the bitter personal feuding and the litigiousness we find in early Sydney and Melbourne – and in other colonial societies where status became problematic.

In England, a gentleman needed no title to have an unequivocal claim to his status. In the colony, as the traditional tests were being set aside, titles, official recognition and official position became more significant. If you could occupy an official position traditionally held by an English gentleman, then your claim to be a gentleman was more secure or precedence could be claimed over other gentlemen. In England, some men who had no other claims became gentlemen by this route – most notably, military officers. But though all officers were accepted as gentlemen, they were always eyed narrowly: there were regiments and regiments, and officers could well be rootless men, adventurers and jilters. As one officer was well pleased to find, no such suspicion attached to officers in New South Wales. A captain or a lieutenant – the title itself – was something solid and certain when other old-world claims were doubtful and contentious. In this uncertainty begins the amazing career of the Australian doctor whose title meant little in England but worked wonders here.

To be received at Government House became an important acknowledgment of gentlemanly status. Government House was not a court at the apex of society. Having begun as a place where all the colony's officers and gentlemen gathered, all who became gentlemen expected to be received there. At levees, they all could go. A levee at St James's was a gathering of the kingdom's elite, who in the 1850s and '60s still wore court dress to the Palace; at Government House in Sydney, it was a gathering of the colony's gentlemen, who wore gentlemen's evening dress. Governors differed in policy about whom they invited to dinners and balls, but because invitations to Government House held such significance, the tendency was to liberality. Certainly, invitations were not left unquestioningly to the governor's discretion. Lady Denison, whose husband was successively governor of Van Diemen's Land and New South Wales in the 1850s, records the difficulties they had with invitations. After invitations had gone out for a ball, every day brought a number of protest letters to the A.D.C. asking whether his Excellency had heard anything prejudicial to the writer's character or whether it was considered their situation disqualified them from the honour of an invitation. Some, more indignant, wrote direct to the governor. So vital to status was official recognition that the clerks in the Ordnance Office threatened to write home to the Board of Ordnance to complain at the indignity of being overlooked.

The House of Commons was a gathering of gentlemen, and those few members who might not have been true gentlemen enjoyed the title. Before responsible government in New South Wales, the Legislative Council was similarly composed overwhelmingly of those whose gentlemanly status was already secure. After responsible government and with the introduction of manhood suffrage, men of lower status entered the parliament: small traders and dealers, shopkeepers, publicans and country newspaper proprietors. These men and all their colleagues took the title of gentlemen. The securing of this status was one of the attractions of becoming an MP. A good many members who voted for manhood suffrage were still getting used to the feel of a top hat.

*

In England the Justice of the Peace was the epitome of the country gentleman, serving his monarch and dispensing justice to his inferiors. In New South Wales the Justices, as in England, constituted the Courts of Petty Sessions and took a large part in local administration. But the position became valued for its social prestige. In England the title of J.P. could add some lustre to a gentleman's name; in New South Wales it was the best endorsement of gentlemanly status and local pre-eminence. A place in the Commission of the Peace was therefore much coveted, and colonial success stories did not end merely with riches, but with the hero on the magisterial bench. This, for example, was the clearest way that Dickens could signal Mr Micawber's success; indeed, the position was especially valued by colonists just because its message was so clear not just to local eyes but to relatives and friends at home. Every aspiring emigrant was conscious of the audience he had left behind.

With responsible government the right of appointing Justices of the Peace passed from the governor to the ministry of the day, and the seal of gentlemanly status became one of the spoils of popular politics. Places in the Commission of Peace were used to secure support in the House and to reward constituents – just as with roads and bridges, but with the advantage to government that they cost nothing. The first premier, Donaldson, a Conservative, asked all members to submit suggestions for additions to the magistracy. This resulted in 177 new appointments. The Liberals who quickly supplanted the Conservatives were more prodigal. In his five years of office to 1863, Cowper, the Liberal premier, made some 800 new appointments. At one time he reported he had 200 applications on his desk. There was no attempt at a careful scrutiny of these candidates. When there were complaints that new magistrates could not write or make themselves understood, Cowper blandly replied that all appointments were recommended by someone. He was a master of the patronage business. He always spoke as if magistrates were appointed in order to better supply the bench of the local courts. Certainly, there were regular complaints that court business had to be postponed because magistrates did not appear. But since a position in the magistracy was sought chiefly for its social prestige, and not because men wanted to spend one day every week on the bench, appointing more magistrates did not necessarily improve attendance at the courts. The 'need' for more magistrates was thus never ending.

In the country, the new Liberal appointments to the bench included storekeepers and other town business-people. These men were local leaders of the Liberal cause, but even by colonial standards had doubtful claims to be gentlemen. The existing country magistrates, chiefly landed men, were now being forced to accept them as equals. Cowper boasted that in making his appointments he broke with the usual practice of asking local magistrates whether new appointments were acceptable to them. In many cases they clearly were not, and

Cowper provoked the old order into a counter-revolution. Magistrates declared that they would not sit with the new men and at Goulburn and Mudgee magistrates resigned en masse. They focused their objections on one particular appointment, declaring that the new man was unfit by social position and antecedents for the bench and was transparently being rewarded for political services. The townspeople of Goulburn and Mudgee enthusiastically supported the new appointments, and were angry that the local gentry should attempt to keep in their hands an honour which the Liberal government in Sydney was opening to them. In the colony at large, the grounds of objection taken by the resigning magistrates – social position and antecedents – were widely condemned. But the old magistrates won these battles, though not the war. It was true, as the Goulburn magistrates alleged, that the new appointment there, the editor of the local paper, had been dismissed in his youth from the Public Service for offering to bribe his supervisor. The government could not ignore this objection, and it was for this reason, and not because he had once run a pub on the Yass road, that his commission was withdrawn. At Mudgee the new appointment, a storekeeper, had once briefly served as a police constable under the supervision of the magisterial bench of which he had now been made a member. This was the particular circumstance used by the old magistrates to support their general case against appointments of this sort. The government ignored their protest, and the newcomer would have remained on the bench had he not over-played his hand. In answering the objections made to him, he proclaimed his own gentility – his father was an Irish gentleman of 'independent but not very large means', and many near relatives were peers of the realm – and attacked the antecedents of the local magistrates at their weakest point. Mr R. W. Blackman was now a landholder, but his parents had kept a public house at Mudgee. The storekeeper magistrate declared they had been suspected of sly-grogging and that the mother of the J.P., still living, was a drunk. When threatened with legal action for libel, he publicly apologised and lost his place on the bench.

'Social position', which the protesting country magistrates made a test for the bench, was rejected by the Liberals. Cowper said the tests were character and intelligence. A Select Committee that had examined the question in 1858 had opted for character and education but a requirement for formal education the premier thought too restrictive. Among what survived of the Conservatives in the Legislative Assembly, there was sympathy for the resigning magistrates, but given the constraints of popular politics they could not talk of 'social position' with impunity. James Martin, the Conservative leader in the House, and the *Sydney Morning Herald* accepted the tests of character and education, and criticised many of Cowper's appointments for failing to meet them. Under the protection of parliamentary privilege, Martin could detail his objections to new appointments. He declared that Chapman, a Sydney paper-hanger, was unfitted for the bench, but although the social slur in this reference to occupation was clear enough, Martin insisted that his objection concerned the paper-hanger's fitness and not his social position: the education a paper-hanger might receive suited him for mechanical pursuits, but not for dispensing justice. But such a test was no more acceptable than social position. Chapman's virtues were self-evident. As one of his many parliamentary defenders said, he was upright, honest and had raised himself by his own industry. And what could be said against a country-town worthy, also queried by Martin, who was as well-known as the town itself 'for he has grown with its growth and strengthened with its strength'? Education, as Cowper said, was too narrow a test. Instead, stress was laid on the virtues of shrewdness, knowledge of the world and sound common sense. A too close attention to the character and abilities actually needed to perform duties on the bench could not be allowed. Something other than a career open to talent was being contended for: a title had to be open to self-made wealth.

'Character and intelligence' rather than social position served their turn in opening the ranks of the magistracy, but they had their dangers. Strictly applied, they meant that anyone – no matter what his wealth, class or status – could be a magistrate. The ambiguity in the position of the magistrate – was he a man of a certain social rank or a man with certain abilities and qualities of character? – was similar to that surrounding a gentleman. If the virtues a gentleman should possess were made the sole defining characteristics of gentlemanly status, then gentlemen would cease to occupy a pre-eminent place in the social and economic hierarchy. Cowper's government had to face this implication of their policy when it was revealed that they had made a working man, a lowly employee at a sheep station, into a magistrate. The government was seriously embarrassed by this. No record could be found of who had made the recommendation. The government's final defence was that the appointment had been a mistake. Some Liberal supporters suggested that their enemies had smuggled the name in to discredit the government. A few bold Liberals made a show of defending a working-class appointment to preserve the integrity of the 'character and intelligence' principle. But working men were by general consent not eligible for the honour. A limit had finally been reached.

James Martin became premier in 1863, and his government undertook a revision of the magisterial lists. Its declared aims were to exclude those unfit by education, means or character; all members but one of a family in the same neighbourhood; people in active business (this would exclude shopkeepers) unless no-one else was available; and those who rarely or never attended the bench. There were by now 1250 Justices of the Peace, and Martin reduced these to 628. It was generally conceded that a culling of the lists was necessary if only to exclude the dead and the departed, but a purge of these dimensions shook the social foundations. After the first howls of rage came demonstrations that the government had not been true to its own principles, and claims that it had been as much influenced by political allegiance as its predecessors. The gross inconsistencies, which even a cursory examination of the list reveals, suggest that this must have been so. The furore over the exclusions was such that Martin had to reinstate twenty-six of the excluded. His tampering with the Commission was partly responsible for his defeat in Parliament as soon as the House reassembled and at the election which followed. Cowper returned to power and ninety-eight more of the purged were reinstated within twelve months.

*

How far could the democratising of social distinction proceed? The distinctions became more defensible as access to them was widened, but would the new men so lower the tone that respect would vanish?

My impression is that in the 1860s and 1870s the positions of gentle-man, certainly, and of magistrate, more doubtfully, retained their prestige. With parliamentarians the case was different. There was a rapid collapse in respect for them. This was not solely a response to the widening of the social positions from which parliamentarians came, extreme though that was. A criminal record excluded a man from the magistracy but not from a seat in the House. What sealed the parlia-mentarians' fate was that in their deliberations they outraged the gentlemanly ideal. The House was frequently in uproar; insults and imputations were freely hurled; there was none of the restraint and good manners which should characterise the gentleman. The accounts of colonial history which describe this as the age of the bourgeoisie are a poor guide to the government and politics of the period. First, because the parliamentary benches were not filled by the solid bour-geois. As Chris Connolly concludes it is truer to say of the new Assem-blies, as one Conservative did at the time, that they were made up in large part by 'publicans – expiree convicts – journeyman mechanics – Wesleyan lay preachers'. The great merchants who had helped the Liberal movement early soon deserted to the Conservative side. Connolly described the Assembly as 'middling class'. Secondly, the Assembly in its deliberations did not display the sobriety which one associates with the bourgeoisie. They failed as gentlemen, which was what they claimed to be; they could not even meet the tests of decency and respectability. But to the dismay of the respectable, the larrikin members were regularly returned by their constituencies. If the 'Age of the Bourgeoisie' is a poor guide to the politics of this period, the 'hegemony of the mercantile bourgeoisie' is worse. The wide popular franchise gave parliament a distinctly unrespectable odour.

Just as the respect for parliament and public life was falling, new honours became open to leading public men. An honour from the queen was immune from the dangers which might lower the value of colonial distinctions. It came from the fount of honour herself, and it associated its local recipients with the venerable orders of the mother country. The award of imperial honours remained a prerogative of the Colonial Office. It received recommendations from governors but even these were not always acted on. Governors were lobbied by ministers, individual aspirants and their friends. In the 1860s the Australian colonies were the most clamorous for honours of all the self-governing colonies, and received the most. Since I haven't examined the situation in other colonies, I cannot be sure of the reasons for this, but I suspect that imperial honours were sought more avidly in the Australian colonies because political power had passed from the hands of the social elite. Before responsible government, a place in the Legislative Council marked a man as one of the elite. With manhood suffrage and the coming of the 'middling class' to the Assembly, a place in the House, even a leading place in the House, no longer had this cachet, especially as there was a clear tendency for old wealth to shun and despise the parliament – to which in any case it had difficulty in gaining access. But what did old wealth matter, if the new political leaders could answer its taunts with royal honours?

During the 1860s the Colonial Office deliberated on how it could accommodate the growing demand for honours, chiefly from Australia. There were too few vacancies in the Order of the Bath. If the existing orders were expanded to take in the Australians, would they lose status in English eyes? If a special order were established for the colonies would Australians be prepared to accept it? Finally in 1868 the Order of St Michael and St George, which had been inherited by Britain with the Ionian Islands and which had been used to reward services in the Mediterranean, was expanded into a general colonial order. It had the advantage of a grand name and a lineage. It was to reward services for the colonies as well as in them. The first appointments to the new order included the distinguished Colonial Secretaries Lord Derby, Lord John Russell and Earl Grey. With these baits, the order was successfully launched and gratefully received in Australia.

The New South Wales Liberals took a prominent part in pressing for honours. The cabinet, meeting as the Executive Council, passed resolutions recommending particular people for honours, to the dismay of the Colonial Office which was not prepared to allow colonies to be self-governing on this issue. A continuing concern of the Liberal government was to secure an honour for its premier, Cowper. His Conservative predecessors had been honoured, even though their hold on office had been so brief; and the Liberals saw no incongruity in seeking a similar mark of royal favour for the man who had introduced manhood suffrage and swamped the Upper House.

I trust that I have said enough to show that liberal democrats, the victors of the battles against old world privilege, wished still to retain social distinctions which were marked by titles, special modes of address and of dress. Against this must be set the many features of late colonial society which shadow forth a different world, closer to our own, with less deference and more egalitarian manners. There was the independence of working men, arising from high wages and labour shortage; the disrespect of the Irish for English pretension; the 'egalitarianism tempered by the checks of respectability' that characterised the wide membership of friendly societies and mutual improvement groups; the wide support for common schooling in the new state schools. There is some evidence – I wish I had more – that the only acceptable terms for social mixing were those of equality, with the result, as de Tocqueville noted in America, that cross-class socialising declined. Yet for all these signs, commentators insisted on the Britishness of the colonial social order, especially in New South Wales, even while noting some aspects of life that we now take as constituent parts of our egalitarianism. Trollope referred to the maintenance of the British mode of thinking on 'social position', a view not disturbed by close observation of those archetypal egalitarians, the nomad pastoral workers whose attitude to their superiors he described as 'civil'. Froude, who visited Australia in 1886, detected no reluctance to respect men of high rank, and declared, 'There is room in Australia for all orders and degrees of men', though admittedly he did not move very far from the Government Houses and the people he met there. Twopeny observed more widely. He records the independence of servants, and the prickliness of tradesman if they thought they were going to be patronised, and yet he writes confidently of the gentlemanly order and of polite society, and takes a favourable view of the future of the Australian aristocracy after four generations. Australia's fascination for overseas observers was its newness and its democracy, and yet their message is that neither characteristic had had a transforming effect on social relations. Trollope specifically drew the comparison with the United States where:

all institutions of the country tend to the creation of a level, to that which men call equality, – which cannot be obtained, because men's natural gifts are dissimilar, but to which a nearer approach is made in America than has ever been effected in Europe. In Australia, no doubt and especially in Victoria, there is a leaning in the same direction; but it is still so slightly in advance of that which prevails among ourselves as to justify an observer in saying that the colonies are rather a repetition of England than an imitation of America.

*

Colonial society wore a double aspect. It was a new society and by its own standards an egalitarian one, in that opportunity was open to all regardless of old-world tests of rank and birth. But so long as success dressed itself in traditional garb, colonial society could also look, or be made to look, like the old world reincarnated. This was its vulnerability. From the 1880s, a new radicalism and socialism reached the colony from the mother culture. A democratic society committed to equality of opportunity and the absence of old-world distinctions – like the United States – might have been largely impervious to these forces. New South Wales with only a half-hearted commitment to democracy, and nurturing old-world distinctions, was not. Herein lies one answer to the question which Geoffrey Bolton has asked: why did Australia, with a social structure like the United States, acquire British class institutions? It was from this time also that the egalitarianisms with which we are familiar were firmly established. I will briefly refer to three of the new egalitarian forces: the Labor Party, the *Bulletin*, and the literature of Lawson and Paterson.

Those who want to highlight the tameness of the early Labor Party draw attention to the number of items in its first programs concerned with democratic reform: the abolition of plural voting, which the retention of the old property qualifications had allowed; the relaxation of resident qualifications to give votes to nomadic workers; the reform of the Upper House; the introduction of the referendum. Those who want to explain Labor's success should note the great advantage it acquired by being the first party in a democracy to be thoroughly committed to democratic principles. It had everything to gain by democracy becoming more complete; and its moral claim to represent the people was greatly enhanced by advocating principles that could not readily be denied. The party could use the principle of political equality to assert the worth of the working man and to claim attention for his needs. But the working men the party sent in to parliament were always suspected of being likely to betray the cause; and for this reason, if no other, they did not put on the garb of gentlemen. Unlike some earlier members of low status, they were noted for their sobriety and attention to their duties. Previously men had used parliament to advance their own status; the effect of Labor in parliament was to dignify the working class.

The final catch-all point of Labor's first platform read: 'Any measure that will secure the wage-earner a fair and equitable return for his or her labour'. 'Fair and equitable': here begins the egalitarianism which Hancock traced in the pages of his *Australia*. The success of the Labor Party with that formulation derived in part from its ability to make it a democratic cause. The egalitarianism of equality of opportunity had, as we have seen, made little claim on political democracy; democracy was first fully exploited by an egalitarianism of distributive justice.

The *Bulletin* of J. F. Archibald exercised an immense influence, and yet it did not persuade Australians to renounce imperial titles or break the ties with Britain, two causes for which it campaigned relentlessly. What it conveyed more persuasively was a style: cheeky, irreverent, opposed to all humbug and pretence, delighting to find the hypocrite in the advocate of any cause it did not support. These attitudes are rightly taken to be widespread in Australia, and they form one of the cornerstones of the egalitarianism of manners. So integral are they to the Australian ethos that it is tempting to think that they must have been well entrenched long before the first *Bulletin* rolled off the press in 1880. Archibald himself did not think so. The natural tendency of Australians as British colonists was to toadyism and flunkeyism. He deplored the fact that while Australia was rightly expected to adopt ways and means best suited to itself for its 'commerce and money-grubbing', it slavishly followed England in 'politics, social relationships, and religion'.

Our understanding of Archibald has been greatly enhanced by Sylvia Lawson's biography, *The Archibald Paradox*, which presents him as a cosmopolitan nationalist. Archibald wanted Australia to sever its connection with the rottenness of aristocratic England, yet it was the English republican and radical movement which inspired and encouraged his republicanism. In the mid-'80s Archibald visited England, and sent back articles to the *Bulletin* on the caste, monopoly, and privilege that disfigured the society which Australians called 'home'. In London, he had his vision of what the future held: the Liberals as a reform party were finished; it was the party of idleness, privilege and great wealth, of that 'gilded bauble' the crown and the Whig nobles with broad acres stolen from the people. A social revolution was imminent. The Labor Leagues were rallying and had plans to send working men into the Commons. Soon there would be over 200 of them and they would wear cheap tweed suits or, better still, affront that perfumed Assembly with a grimy Crimean shirt. These men would speak for the toiling masses, the millions who lived in one room. Australians should follow this lead. The two representatives of labour in the New South Wales Assembly were a disgrace: they had put on top hats and frock-coats, which are as 'offensive … marks of what the world calls social superiority as are stars and garters and Windsor uniforms'.

Archibald knew something of both sides of the coming revolution in the metropolis, and he used the standards of both in the *Bulletin* to show how pathetically provincial New South Wales was. He told the 'aspiring vulgarians' who scrambled after honours and Government House invitations what the old world thought of them. A travelling Lord, after being feted by these people in Australia, returns to his London club and says, 'A very good kind of people, you know; awfully vulgar and coarse, but anxious to please.' But what made Australia's hankering after old-world titles and distinctions even more pathetic was that the old world itself had seen through them. The social revolution would sweep them away. Australians, to universal laughter, would be running after the 'gewgaws of titles' while the rest of the world was discarding them. Archibald, the man from the provinces, who knew himself the disdain for the colonial, and feared the world's laughter for his country, saw the way to make the province into a metropolis.

Australia could seize its chance and become the leading democracy of the new order. Without entrenched interests and ancient wrongs, it could quickly sweep away monopoly, caste and privilege. Then the rest of the world, still struggling with these evils, would turn to Australia for inspiration and instruction. To prepare Australia for this role, everything sacred had to be profaned. What we take to be typically Australian attitudes in Archibald's *Bulletin* were the responses of a cosmopolitan intellectual to a provincial culture.

The *Bulletin* made its impact through cartoons as much as text. One of its standard cartoon figures became the fat man, the bloated capitalist, dressed in top hat and frock-coat. During the coal-mines' strike of 1888, Capital as a portly gentleman first appeared in a tug-of-war with a working man. The working man says: 'Hello! Who's the joker in the white gaiters and shiny beaver? I've never seen him down in a mine.' The gentleman's garb signifies fastidiousness and remoteness from the realities of toil. Many wearing this dress in Australia were self-made men who had indeed known hard toil, but that is not how they dressed themselves to appear. They wore the clothes of an English gentleman for whom it was a point of honour not to work and never to have worked. But although this dress gave a false message about background, as indeed many of its wearers wished, it was a very good guide to Labor's enemies. The cartoonists of the *Bulletin*, and later in the Labor press did not have to dress Capital up for ridicule; they found it already dressed fit to kill. There could be no doubt as to who would win in the image stakes between the soft hat and the bell-topper, and between sleeves rolled up and frock-coat. Gentleman's dress was now held up as a badge of shame. This was the cartoonists' contribution to an egalitarianism of manners.

The irony is that English gentlemen in the 1880s were abandoning the frock-coat and the top hat for ordinary street wear. Australian gentlemen were reluctant to follow this shift in fashion. Governors and their staffs, fresh from home, tried in vain to woo them from it by wearing tweeds and bowler hats, a style much less domineering than the old and more suitable to the climate. Men's fashion, writes one of its historians, tends to harden into a uniform, unlike women's which is always changing. Australian gentlemen might have clung to their uniform because it had assumed a greater significance in defining the gentle-manly order since the old-world tests did not apply. It was this uniform that many had struggled for the right to wear. However, from the 1890s tweeds and lounge-suits did become more common. Is it too fanciful to suggest that the cartoonists had succeeded where the Governors had failed? But the cartoonists were not happy with the change. Up until World War I they still dressed Capital in top hat and frock-coat even though the real capitalist was becoming inconspicuous.

The nationalist writers of the '80s and '90s, nurtured by the *Bulletin*, must be understood as operating in the same radical milieu as Archibald. This is a point insisted on by Graeme Davison and Richard White in recent times. Both have argued that Russel Ward's treatment of the writers in *The Australian Legend* is inadequate because he is too prone to regard the literature as a conduit, carrying the values and attitudes of the nomad bush workers to a wider audience, and because he underplays the creative power of the writers themselves. Graeme Davison insists that instead of studying the bush men as they were, a perplexing matter in itself, 'we do better to begin, as we would any other exercise in the history of ideas, with the collective experience and ideas of the poets and story-writers themselves'. I accept all that Davison and White say in this regard. The creative writers were chiefly urban men, influenced by the social and political reform movements of their day; they reacted to an urban environment with an idealised version of country life, giving an Australian celebration of the common man which was then a vogue in European society generally. But none of this excuses us from looking at the literature itself, and considering what constraints and opportunities faced the writers whose scene was pastoral Australia. The writers who were 'inventing Australia' did not work on *tabula rasa*.

Taboos were broken in pastoral life which were upheld everywhere else in Australia. Gentlemen worked with their hands; they worked alongside their men; and in pioneering days at least wore the same clothes as their men. An age-old inequality disappeared as employees took to horses and met their masters eye to eye. Pastoral properties were not managed from homestead offices. Whoever was in control had to ride as well as the stockmen and boundary riders he employed, to move around the property, to assist on occasion in the real work as well as supervise it. A pioneer squatter might eventually leave the work to a manager, and keep more to his homestead or retire to the city; some proprietors were absentees who had never left the city; but always there were gentlemen squatters directly involved in the dirty work of the pastoral industry. The term 'bushman' was first applied to those who possessed the bush skills, whether they were owners or workers.

The literature of Paterson and Lawson is described by Russel Ward as portraying the bush workers as egalitarian collectivists combining to outdo the wealthy squatters. Had the bush workers really been depicted in this way, the literature could not, in a capitalist society, have gained the acceptance and influence Ward claims for it. Certainly, when unions are mentioned – they are by no means a common theme – they are treated favourably, and good bush men support them. But squatters are not portrayed unsympathetically. They are respected as pioneers, and judged on an individual basis. The mateship between workers is generally personal and limited in scope; a man is loyal to his mate or mates, which is not quite the same as loyalty to the working class. The social dichotomies are not chiefly between employers and employees, but between bush and city, and between Australians and the English. The dominant impression of the bush workers is of their unassertive self-confidence. They are completely at home in their environment, suffering no enduring indignities on account of their status as employees. They become romantic figures in a way no peasant or yeoman farmer could, because of the roving nature of their work. In most industries so to dignify and celebrate the life and skills of the worker would imply some devaluation of the owner and employer – as parasites, exploiters or simply effete. The cult of the peasant and manual worker in Europe had this subversive edge. But in the pastoral industry, as the literature takes no pains to hide and as everyone knew, the employing class possessed bush skills as well and had furthermore the aura of hard-working pioneers. Thus the unique character of the pastoral industry, where employers and employees at the extremes of the status hierarchy toiled in the same enterprise, allowed for a most potent yet unthreatening message to be conveyed about the worth of working-class figures. The literature is democratic in its implications, and not socialist; the status order is subverted, but not the economic. The more noble and romantic the bushman became, the more he confounded the socialist account of the plight of the working man under capitalism. The literature could thus be accepted into the schools and the homes of the middle class. Its acceptance has grown with time, and becoming as it were the Holy Writ of the Australian nation, it must be rated as one of the most powerful forces sustaining the view that Jack is as good as his master, a view that sustains in turn the egalitarianism of manners. Jacks have often enough thought themselves as good as their masters, even if only silently; what has been rare is for their masters to agree with them. We have to find in Australia the reasons why, to use Craig McGregor's words, the wealthy 'feel under some pressure to be accepted by ordinary working Australians rather than the other way round'.

The egalitarianism of manners is generally acknowledged to be one egalitarianism that does really exist in modern Australia. To give an adequate account of its history would require a much closer attention to the details of social life than I have been able to give. My impression is that it made its greatest advances, not in the 1850s, but in the 1880s and 1890s. Certainly, it was then that it first had firm ideological support, in the general sense that the worth of working people was being proclaimed and the pretensions of others were being derided, and issued in specific injunctions. Lawson's verse is well known:

> They tramp in mateship side by side –
>> The Protestant and Roman,
> They call no biped lord or sir,
>> And touch their hat to no man.

These lines would have had no point if these marks of deference had disappeared thirty or more years earlier.

The egalitarianism of manners is regarded as a trifling thing by those who want to see complete equality of opportunity or equality in the distribution of material goods. I don't think it should be under-valued. Despite the growth of the social sciences, most people still spend little time filling out questionnaires on status systems. They do spend a lot of time meeting other people. If those encounters do not induce the heartache and corroding anger that can be the other side of deference, then egalitarians of all sorts should rejoice.

1986

The Pioneer Legend

Schools have been the most influential purveyors of the pioneer legend and in literature for children it occurs in its purest form. The first item in the Fifth Grade *Victorian School Reader*, in use for two generations or more earlier this century, was the poem 'Pioneers' by Frank Hudson:

We are the old world people,
Ours were the hearts to dare;
But our youth is spent, and our backs are bent,
    And the snow is on our hair ...

We wrought with a will unceasing.
We moulded, and fashioned, and planned,
And we fought with the black, and we blazed the track,
    That ye might inherit the land ...

Take now the fruit of our labour,
    Nourish and guard it with care,
For our youth is spent, and our backs are bent,
    And the snow is on our hair.

This legend is very different from the radical, collectivist legend of the bush worker discussed by Russel Ward in *The Australian Legend*. It celebrates courage, enterprise, hard work and perseverance; it usually applies to the people who first settled the land, whether as pastoralists or farmers, and not to those they employed, though these were never specifically excluded. It is a nationalist legend which deals in a heroic way with the central experience of European settlement in Australia: the taming of the new environment to man's use. The qualities with which it invests the pioneers – courage, enterprise and so on – perhaps do not strain too much at the truth, though it assumes wrongly that owners always did their own pioneering. Its legendary aspect lies more clearly in the claim that these people were not working merely for themselves or their families, but for us – 'That ye might inherit the land'. The pioneer story can also be described as legendary because of what it leaves out: there is usually no mention of the social, legal or economic determinants of land settlement. The pioneers are depicted in a world limited by the boundaries of their properties, subduing the land and battling the elements. Their enemies are drought, flood, fire, sometimes Aborigines; never low prices, middle men, lack of capital, or other pioneers.

The pioneer legend can scarcely help being conservative in its political implications. It encourages reverence for the past; it celebrates individual rather than collective or state enterprise; and it provides a classless view of society since all social and economic differences are obliterated by the generous application of the 'pioneer' label. In claiming that the pioneers were working for us, it puts on later generations a special obligation not to tamper with the world which the pioneers made. One of the first of the epic pioneer poems was written in 1898 by Robert Caldwell, a conservative politician in South Australia. It concluded with an attack on land reformers and socialists for wanting to deprive the pioneers of their rightful heritage. During the 1890 Maritime Strike the *Argus* declared 'this country should remain what the pioneers intended it to be – a land free for every man who is willing to work, no matter whether he belongs to a union or not'. The travelling lecturer of the Victorian Employers Federation used the same theme to keep the country safe from socialism and it has remained a minor strand in conservative rhetoric since.

Though the pioneer legend is very different from the other legend, in its origins it is quite closely linked to it: it began at the same time – in the 1880s and 1890s – and was celebrated by the same people. It owes much to Paterson and Lawson.

*

The term 'pioneer' came into common use in Victoria and South Australia sooner than in New South Wales. It was applied to those immigrants who had come to the colonies in their early years and so was not limited to those who had settled and worked the land. The pioneers were much honoured at the jubilee of South Australia in 1886 and during the Melbourne Centennial Exhibition of 1888. New South Wales could not look back with similar confidence to its origins or so readily identify its 'pioneers'. In Victoria the members of the Australian Natives Association, looking towards the future of the coming Australian race, showed only a formal respect for the pioneers – many of whom resented the arrogance of the native-born – and were seeking genuinely national symbols and causes. The honouring of early colonists as pioneers reflected the growth of colonial and local patriotisms; they clearly could not serve as heroes for the new nation.

'Pioneers' acquired its present primary meaning – that is, those who first settled and worked the land – in the 1890s. The older meaning survived, and still survives, but it now took second place. The shifting of meaning is nicely illustrated in the special Old Colonist number of the Melbourne *Tatler* in 1898. Under the heading 'The Pioneers of Victoria' appeared biographies of many early colonists, including bishops, officials, merchants, professional men, as well as settlers on the land. These were pioneers according to the earlier meaning of the word. But the cover illustration depicted a settler pushing his way through the bush and carried two lines from a woeful poem, 'The Pioneers', which appeared in full inside: 'Can you not follow them forth/Through the black treacherous bush'. This was the new meaning of the term, but it was not well-deserved by many of the worthies featured inside who had moved straight from the ship to Melbourne and had never pioneered in the bush. The pioneers as settlers on the land were a much more anonymous group than pioneers as early colonists, who always had an establishment, who's-who air about them. They were not identified with a particular colony and were much more closely connected with the land itself. The pioneers as immigrants had been first identified and honoured by the old colonists themselves. Pioneers as settlers and national heroes were the creation of poets and writers. It is to their work we now turn.

Ken Inglis in *The Australian Colonists* has outlined the largely unsuccessful search for national heroes in the years prior to 1870. We can see the difficulties facing a nationalist writer of this period in the work of Henry Kendall, the native-born poet who, like his friend Harpur, knew that poets can make a nation, and saw that as one of his tasks, but who never found the words or the audience to succeed. At the last, however, he touched on the pioneer theme which was left to others to develop. Kendall's views of what a proper hero should be were heavily influenced by the classical tradition of Greece and Rome. Heroes had to be statesmen or soldiers, preferably those who died for their country. For statesmen Kendall offered Governor Phillip, Wentworth, Blang, Lang and other politicians of the 1840s and '50s. This civic theme was extended by the celebration of those who built the Australian cities; this rather than the settlement of the land was the great triumph of colonisation, and one that could be described in classical terms. Melbourne is 'Like a dream of Athens, or of Rome'; Sydney is 'this Troy'. Australia had no great warriors, but the explorers in their bravery and in their deaths were acceptable substitutes. Kendall frequently celebrates Cook, Leichardt, Burke and Wills. In a later poem 'Blue Mountain Pioneers' (1880) he moves away from the more heroic big-name explorers and celebrates the work of Blaxland, Lawson and Wentworth in crossing the Blue Mountains in 1813. This was a short expedition and it didn't end in death, but it could be linked much more closely than other expeditions to the settlement of the land.

> Behind them were the conquered hills – they faced
> The vast green West, with glad, strange beauty graced;
> And every tone of every cave and tree
> Was a voice of splendid prophecy.

What that conquest foretold was the settlement of the western lands, but Kendall was tied so closely to the notion of the heroic as public and civic, that he never celebrated the coming of the settlers themselves. For him 'pioneers' was reserved for the explorers.

This poem was published posthumously in collected editions of Kendall's work in 1886 and 1890. There Paterson must have read it for it forms the basis of the historical section in his poem 'Song of the Future' which is the classic statement of the pioneer legend, frequently reproduced in anthologies and school magazines. This poem is much more ambitious than his usual ballad or bush-yarn work. It calls for a new response to landscape and nature in Australia, and to the history of European man in the continent. Paterson begins by criticising Adam Lindsay Gordon, Marcus Clarke and others who had written in gloomy terms about the Australian scene, and he rejects the stock claims that Australian birds were songless and its flowers scentless. On Australian history he acknowledges that there has been no 'hot blood spilt' – a commonly held prerequisite for worthwhile history – but Australians do have something to celebrate: 'honest toil and valiant life'. This introduces the historical section of the poem. The treatment of the crossing of the Blue Mountains is more extensive than Kendall's and it is told as a great saga of the people, rather than as a celebration of individual heroes. The names of the explorers, significantly, are not mentioned and the poem is more concerned with the achievements of those who came after them.

> The mountains saw them marching by:
> They faced the all-consuming drought,
> They would not rest in settled land:
> But, taking each his life in land,
> Their faces ever westward bent
> Beyond the farthest settlement,
> Responding to the challenge cry
> Of 'better country farther out'.

Paterson measures the extent of this achievement by dealing with a sceptic who declares 'it was not much' since the resistance to expansion was slight and – the stock objection – not much blood was split.

> It was not much! but we who knew
> The strange capricious land they trod –
> At times a stricken, parching sod,
> At times with raging floods beset –

Through which they found their lonely way,
Are quite content that you should say
It was not much, while we can feel
That nothing in the ages old,
In song or story written yet
On Grecian urn or Roman arch,
Though it should ring with clash of steel
Could braver histories unfold
Than this bush story, yet untold –
The story of their westward march.

This poem, more than any other single piece, did bring about that new perception of Australia's past which Paterson sought. He still had to defend his heroes against those of Greece and Rome, but soon the heroism of the pioneers was accepted without question and the reference to the classical tradition ceased.

Lawson was more consistently preoccupied with Australia's past than Paterson. In a contribution to the *Republican* in 1888 he called for much more Australian history to be taught in schools. As a nationalist, he wanted to give his country a past to be proud of. In the early stories and poems Lawson follows the orthodox line of dating Australia's greatness from the gold rushes, and so he accords heroic status to the diggers. These were the men 'who gave our country birth'. He rates their achievements higher than those of the explorers, the ranking heroes of the time: 'Talk about the heroic struggles of early explorers in a hostile country; but for dogged determination and courage in the face of poverty, illness, and distance, commend me to the old-time digger – the truest soldier Hope ever had!' For the settlers on the land and particularly the selectors, Lawson in his early years had scant respect. He criticises the selectors for their slovenliness, dirt and ignorance, and depicts settling on the land not as an heroic endeavour, but as a madness. But this attitude changed with time. His early emphasis on the wretchedness of the selector's life had had a political purpose, since he wanted to discredit those who saw small holdings as the cure for Australia's social ills. He never abandons the view that the life of small settlers could be wretched and narrow, but he becomes more willing to celebrate their powers of endurance and the co-operations between them, and, in the Joe Wilson series, the satisfactions and pleasures which their small successes gave them, though here Mrs Spicer, watering them geraniums, is still present as counterpoint being worn literally to death. In his verse, where he always wrote at a higher level of generality and usually with disastrous results, he came to see the settling of the land as the central theme of the nation's history, which could comprehend much more than the coming of the diggers. 'How the land was won' (1899) is a complete statement of this theme, and is the counterpart to Paterson's 'Song of the Future'. The settlers are described firstly as immigrants leaving the old world, and the poem tells of the variety of hardships and deprivations which they experienced in Australia. These two verses give the flavour of the whole, perhaps too favourable a view, since six verses of hardship become a little tedious, though the quality of the verse is better than Lawson's average:

> With God, or a dog, to watch, they slept
>> By the camp-fires' ghastly glow,
> Where the scrubs were dark as the blacks that crept
>> With 'nulla' and spear held low;
> Death was hidden amongst the trees,
>> And bare on the glaring sand
> They fought and perished by twos and threes –
>> And that's how they won the land!
>
> They toiled and they fought through the shame of it –
>> Through wilderness, flood, and drought;
> They worked, in the struggles of early days,
>> Their sons' salvation out.
> The white girl-wife in the hut alone,
>> The men on the boundless run,
> The miseries suffered, unvoiced, unknown –
>> And that's how the land was won.

In the early twentieth century scores of pioneer poems by many hands rang the changes on these hardships. Two important aspects of the legend are embodied in 'How the land was won': in the first verse (not quoted here) we are told that the land was won 'for us'; secondly, there is no differentiation of the settlers – they are all simply 'they'. This conflation is the more noticeable in Lawson since elsewhere he gives such particular detail about social conflict on the land. Nor can the co-operation among the settlers – in the stories he describes young men putting in crops for sick men and widows, and women caring for bereaved neighbours – find a mention here, since the pioneer legend prefers to see hardships overcome, if at all, by further individual effort. It is a sign of the attractiveness of the pioneer legend to nationalists that Lawson was ready to abandon so much to produce his simple compelling saga. Of course the Lawson of 1899 had abandoned much of his early radicalism, and in his disillusionment the struggle on the land took on an elemental, purifying quality, but changing personal views will not wholly explain 'How the land was won'. The pioneer legend is a literary mode or a type of history which shapes material in its own way. Writing on a different assignment in the same year he composed 'How the land was won', Lawson highlighted the gossip and bitchiness of country towns and hinted broadly that incest was frequently practised in the isolated selectors' huts. That would never do for the pioneers.

In Lawson's prose there is little explicit glorification of the pioneers, but here Lawson made his most powerful contribution to the pioneer legend with his description of bush women. 'The Drover's Wife' occupies an important place in the pioneer canon. There is a sense in which all his bush women are heroines because, as he insists time and again, the bush is no place for women. When her husband had money the drover's wife was taken to the city by train – in a sleeping compartment – and put up at the best hotel. For Lawson, women deserve the attention and comfort which this signifies, and which bush life denied them. While she waits for the snake, the drover's wife reads the *Young Ladies Journal*, but Lawson does not use the hard life of a country woman to deride the artificiality of the woman's journal world; rather, he accepts that as legitimate, and so emphasises the sacrifices of the women who are obliged to live a different life, and in many cases do the work of men. The theme of women as pioneers was taken up by G. Essex Evans, a Queensland poet of the '90s, in his 'Women of the West'.

This, together with his other pioneer piece 'The Nation Builders', have frequently been reprinted in the children's literature and anthologies.

The work of Paterson and Lawson is described by Ward as the chief vehicle for spreading a democratic, collectivist, national mystique. How was it that these writers also celebrated the pioneers which meant frequently the squatters, who had been, and were still, the enemy of democrats and radicals? In *The Australian Tradition*, A. A. Phillips has noted how sympathetic writers of the '90s were in their description of individual squatters, despite the squatters being the class enemy. Phillips offers a number of explanations for this. He wonders first whether 'the triumph of human sympathy over social prejudice' reflected the breadth of feeling one would expect in any good writer. Scarcely so, he concludes, since in other areas, notably the description of Englishmen, the writers reveal severe limitations and create caricatures. The writers knew some squatters personally and this no doubt helped them to write individualised, sympathetic portraits. But more importantly, according to Phillips, the squatter was a bushman too, and had shared with his men 'the pride and expansiveness' that came with the escape from 'fetid slums and the tight little hedgerow squares' of the old world, into the vast spaces of the new continent where the strength of individual character as a man determined success or failure. He concludes that the democratic tradition embodied in the literature reaches deep back into the pastoral age. But we must remember that what squatters had felt, or others had felt about them, may well be different from their depiction in imaginative literature. The tradition of the pastoral age did not flow automatically onto the pages of Lawson and Paterson. The writers were making a tradition as well as reflecting one – how much they created and how much they reported has been one of the matters debated in the argument over *The Australian Legend*. We can extend Phillips's analysis and come closer to understanding these writers' attitude to the squatter–pioneer if we examine what influenced their view of the pastoral age.

Both men were disturbed and angry at the new harshness and poverty which drought, depression and strikes brought to the colonies in the 1880s and 1890s. They were cast into a world they did not like, and like many others before and since in this predicament they began to exaggerate the virtues of the world they had lost. Lawson's poem 'Freedom on the Wallaby' is well known. It was written in Brisbane in 1891 to support the shearers' strike and its last verse contains the much-quoted threat of violence: 'If blood should stain the wattle'. Less well-known is the previous verse:

> Our parents toiled to make a home,
> > Hard grubbin' 'twas an' clearin',
> They wasn't troubled much with lords
> > When they were pioneerin'.
> But now that we have made the land
> > A garden full of promise,
> Old Greed must crook his dirty hand
> > And come ter take it from us.

Those who know Lawson's usual description of the Australian country – unyielding, desolate, drought-ridden – will scarcely credit that he could describe it as a garden; domestic, fruitful, a symbol of paradise. Lawson's explanation for the lowering of wages and the assault on the unions is that Greed has invaded this garden. It was a theme he used many times. Sometimes Greed had invaded the countryside from the cities, on other occasions it was an unwelcome import from the old world into the new. In the poems the particular forms which Greed assumed were not always defined. The stories identified the process more explicitly. In the countryside it meant the increasing ownership of pastoral properties by banks and companies, and the replacement of resident proprietors by managers. Before this process began were the good times, and squatters of that time, or who have survived from it, are described as squatters of the 'old school'. In describing Black, the squatter who employed Joe Wilson, Lawson outlines their virtues: 'He was a good sort, was Black the squatter; a squatter of the old school, who'd shared the early hardships with his men, and couldn't see why he should not shake hands and have a smoke and a yarn over old times with any of his old station hands that happened to come along.' A. A. Phillips errs when he says Black is Lawson's only portrait in any detail of a squatter. There were several other good squatters – Baldy Thompson, Job Falconer, Jimmy's boss – and their goodness is carefully explained: they are resident proprietors of long standing, not managers for absentees. Job Falconer, for instance, was 'Boss of the Talbragar sheep station up country in New South Wales in the early Eighties – when there were still runs in the Dingo-Scrubs out of the hands of the banks, and yet squatters who lived on their stations'. Lawson's one detailed portrait of a bad squatter is that of Wall, the man who, until it was almost too late, refused to send his employees to fight the fire on Ross's farm. Until this last-minute repentance Wall was a hard man who had done all he could to make the selector Ross's life impossible. But he had not always been so: 'Men remembered Wall as a great boss and a good fellow, but that was in the days before rabbits and banks, and syndicates and "pastoralists", or pastoral companies instead of good squatters.' The pattern is clear: it is not only that managers for absentees are mean: all resident proprietors of the old days were good.

In Paterson's work there was much less overt social commentary than in Lawson's, but briefly around 1890 Paterson was a committed reformer, and in his poem 'On Kiley's Run' published in December 1890, he gives a clear picture of the world which Greed had disrupted and the new world it was making. The poem describes the 'good old station life' on Kiley's run. The squatter was resident, swagmen were welcome, there was plenty of good fellowship and horseracing with neighbouring stations, and relations between squatter and his men were excellent.

> The station-hands were friends, I wot,
>   On Kiley's Run,
> A reckless, merry-hearted lot –
> All splendid riders, and they knew
> The boss was kindness through and through.
> Old Kiley always stood their friend,
> And so they served him to the end
>   On Kiley's Run.

But droughts and losses forced the squatter into the hands of the bank, which finally took possession of the stock and sold the station. The new owner is an English absentee; a half-paid overseer runs the place, shearers' wages and all other expenses are cut, swagmen and drovers receive short-shrift – and the name of the run has been changed to Chandos Park Estate. Paterson felt this transformation very keenly, for at the end of the poem he adds, for him, a rare call to arms:

> I cannot guess what fate will bring
> > To Kiley's Run –
> For chances come and changes ring –
> I scarcely think 'twill always be
> Locked up to suit an absentee;
> And if he lets it out in farms
> His tenants soon will carry arms
> > On Kiley's Run.

'The Song of the Future', Paterson's classic pioneer piece, in its last section contains a similar lament for the old bush life and urges that the land be thrown open to all to reduce poverty and unemployment.

Men live by myth and golden ages have frequently been created. What is odd about this one is that it was placed in the very recent past. The democrats and land reformers of the 1850s had denounced the squatters as monopolists and tyrants: they were the lords who would make everyone else serfs if they could. In their defence the squatters had actually attempted, fruitlessly, to attach to themselves the name of 'pioneers' and so justify their claim to retain their lands. Thirty years after their political defeat, they were accorded that title, among others by the poets of democracy. How could they overlook the denunciations made so recently? A large part of the answer is simply that Lawson and Paterson, like most other people in the 1890s, knew very little of the struggles of the 1850s. John Robertson had given his name to the Selection Acts and had achieved legendary status, but he was not seen as part of a wider movement. The Australian born certainly did not learn of the land reform movement in school. Those who had survived from that era, like Robertson himself and Parkes, did not talk freely of their early struggles, chiefly because, one supposes, the bitter social and economic divisions of those years and the whiff of republicanism which hung over the reform movement were no longer apt for their present political purposes.

The Sydney *Bulletin* was republican, a constant derider of British aristocrats and Australians who fawned on them, and it had no qualms about disturbing the liberal consensus over which Parkes and Robertson had presided, but it too did little to inform its readers – among whom were Paterson and Lawson – of the democratic movement of the 1850s or to celebrate its triumphs. The *Bulletin* ran a very crude line on New South Wales history: it insisted that very little had changed in the colony since the convict days. The British had created an abomination in the convict system, and since its influence was still potent, New South Wales could never establish a truly democratic society until the British connection was severed. It wrongly attributed the flogging of criminals and other evils to the survival of the spirit of earlier times. Victoria, by contrast, had managed something of a fresh start with its gold rushes and the Eureka rebellion, whose anniversary the *Bulletin* wanted to celebrate as Australia's national day. Such a view of the past could not allow that there had been genuine and far-reaching reforms in New South Wales in the 1850s and 1860s. The history which the *Bulletin* promoted was Price Warung's *Tales of the Convict System*. This was the stick to beat the British with. The triumphs of Robertson over the landowners and squatters would not have suited its purpose.

We are now in a position to understand better why Paterson and Lawson were among the founders of the pioneer legend. Their work is suffused with a generalised nostalgia – "Twas a better land to live in, in the days o' long ago' – but they also created a highly specific past which was free from the social evils of the present. Before Greed invaded the land there were humane employers and decent class relations in Australia. Having made that past, and as they made it, they elevated the early settlers into pioneers. That they could create this past so freely gives new meaning to the dictum that Australia had no history. For Paterson and Lawson, the 1840s and 1850s when the squatters were the popular political enemy might never have existed. No democratic tradition had survived from these years.

In broad terms, the creation of the pioneer legend can be explained by the growth of nationalism in the 1880s and the 1890s and the need to find new national heroes and symbols. Paterson and Lawson were attracted to the pioneers as nationalists, but also as radicals. They used the past to condemn the present. However, the pioneer legend quickly shed its radical overtones. Paterson's classic statement 'Song of the Future' is very simply rendered innocuous in anthologies and school readers by the omission of the last section which urges that the land be thrown open to all. In any case, the golden age of pioneering was, in some respects, rather uncertain in its political implications. Paterson's claim, though false, that there had been a time when land was freely available to all did relate clearly to the current radical demand for land taxes and breaking up of large estates. But the depiction of the old station life of hard work and mutuality between boss and men can serve the conservative cause, for clearly there were no unions or industrial arbitration or parliamentary limitations on hours worked on Kiley's Run. Reform movements which aim to purify and simplify government can appeal with some chance of success to golden ages; once radicalism is associated with state regulation and ownership, as it was in Australia from the 1890s, the ideal society needs to be placed in the future rather than the past. In finding a glorious past for Australia, Paterson and Lawson ultimately did more to help the conservative cause than their own. Once there is a valued past, the future is more confined. 'She is not yet' Brunton Stephens had written of the Australian nation in 1877. Because we are nationalists as they made us, we still enjoy the celebrations of Lawson and Paterson and we forget that as well as being an affirmation, their work marked also a retreat: the nation was no longer yet to be, it had arrived, and, more amazing still, its best days were already passed.

*

In 1904 Frederick McCubbin painted 'The Pioneers', a massive work in three panels which is the classic embodiment in art of the pioneer legend. The first panel shows a settler and his wife on their first arrival at their selection in the forest; the second shows the selection established; and in the third, the 'triumphal stanza' as the *Age* described it, 'A country youth, with reverent fingers, clears away the undergrowth from the rough wooden cross marking the last resting place of the gallant couple. In the distance the spires and bridges of a glorious young city and the stooks of a rich harvest field tell of the joys that another generation is reaping from the toil of the once lusty pioneers now gone to dust.' The painting was, and is, enormously popular, and the *Age* successfully urged that it be purchased for the National Gallery. It described the work as a 'poem of democracy'.

The conservative implications of the legend have already been noted; in what sense is the legend, nevertheless, a democratic one? In the first place it accords historic status to the ordinary man – frequently the pioneers were squatters, but small settlers were also honoured with the title. The pioneer legend transformed the low status selector of the nineteenth century into a nation builder. The legend also proclaims that success is open to all since all may possess the requisite qualities of diligence, courage and perseverance. Secondly, the legend provides a simple, unofficial, popular history of the nation. When it was formed the standard histories were still organised by the terms of office of the various governors, to parallel the British histories which dealt with monarchs, the dates of their accession and death, and the chief events of their reign. Governors made some sense as organising principles for the period before responsible government, but in some works their comings and goings continued to be crucial events even after responsible government. In contrast to history as high politics and administration, the pioneer legend offered social (and economic) history and declared that the people had made the nation. The 'people' in the pioneer legend have always included women. Feminists may object that too often they are seen merely as helpmeets for men, but their complaint that women have been omitted altogether from Australian history is not true of the popular history fostered by the pioneer legend. There are Pioneer-Women gardens and memorials in Melbourne, Adelaide and Perth. In the celebration of state and national anniversaries, pioneer women have been honoured in special ceremonies and commemorative histories. The pioneer legend is a people's legend, in this sense it is democratic; its conservatism is not the conservatism of deference, but of communal pride in what the people have achieved.

Of democracy in the sense of a system of government, the legend has nothing to say, since it implies that politics were unnecessary or irrelevant to the work of pioneering. It is a further instance, then, of the Australian tendency to isolate politics from the heroic or the good. Paterson claimed his pioneers as worthy of Greece and Rome, but in fact he had abandoned the classical tradition which found its heroes in those who served the state. Kendall, true to that tradition, thought that an Australian democracy would want democratic statesmen for its heroes, but he was wrong, and he worked in vain on Deniehy and Lang.

The pioneer legend had a significant influence on the writing of formal history. It solved the problem which formal historians could never overcome satisfactorily: the embarrassment of the convict origins of the nation. The pioneer legend, by proclaiming the settlement of the land as the chief theme in Australia's history, found it easy not to mention the convicts at all. If you begin Australia's history with Governor Phillip it is very difficult to avoid the convicts, though some histories for children managed it. The first formal history to reflect the influence of the pioneer legend was James Collier's *The Pastoral Age in Australasia* (1911). This dated Australia's freedom from the opening of the pastoral lands west of the mountains and rejected the traditional view that the gold rushes marked the divide from the convict origins. Collier described the old society to the east of the mountains as static, unfree, with the settlers relying on governments for land, labour, stock, and markets. The new pastoral society was dynamic, independent, a wild free life that 'lifted the community to a higher plain, and started it on a new career'. He conceded that convicts were still employed but in a 'radically different' way, which was never explained. Stephen Roberts in *The Pastoral Age in Australia* (1935) celebrated the pastoral expansion in a similar way and from Collier borrowed the image of the protoplasm of the nation, long lying dormant, and in the magic year 1835 showing at last what form it was going to take. The theme is present too at the opening of Hancock's *Australia*: 'Wool made Australia a solvent nation, and, in the end, a free one.' The concentration on the pastoral expansion meant that Sydney's merchants and trades went unexamined. So it was only recently that historians rediscovered the importance of the whale industry and the Pacific trade, which had been known to the older historians like Rusden (1883) and Jose (1899) whose approach was strictly chronological and who wrote uninfluenced by the pioneer legend. The pioneer legend, having first excluded convicts, eventually enabled them to be rehabilitated and given a place in the nation's history. Convicts could be regarded as pioneers. In this role Mary Gilmore depicts them in 'Old Botany Bay':

> I was the conscript
> > Sent to hell
> To make in the desert
> > The living well;
>
> I split the rock;
> > I felled the tree:
> The nation was –
> > Because of me.

By the early twentieth century a new meaning of 'pioneer' had come into common use. It was now also applied to people who were at present at work on the land, and particularly on new farms or at the edge of settlement. This extension of meaning occurred at a time of heightened concern for racial strength and purity and a new awareness of the vulnerability of the nation. Cities were now seen as dangers to national and racial health, and further development of the land was considered on all sides as essential for the nation's survival. The pioneer's struggle with the elements and the nation's struggle to survive in a more hostile world became fused. 'The people in the bush were fighting the battle of Australia every day and every year', said George Reid in 1909 at the foundation of the Bush Nursing Association which was formed to bring medical help to remote country areas. 'From a national point of view,' the Association declared, 'the lives of pioneers and their children are of the utmost value to the State.' G. Essex Evans, one of the important makers of the legend, caught these new concerns in 'The Man Upon The Land'.

The City calls, its streets are gay,
　　Its pleasures well supplied,
So of its life-blood every day
　　It robs the countryside.

How shall we make Australia great
　　And strong when danger calls
If half the people of the State
　　Are crammed in city walls ...?

The concluding lines of the poem are its refrain:

And the men that made the Nation are
　　The men upon the land.

The change of tense here illustrates nicely how the men upon the land gained in glory from the heroic status of their predecessors. Well before the Country Party was formed, its ideology had been made – by no means solely by country people – and the pioneer legend gave it added force.

After the landing at Gallipoli, Australians acquired a legend more powerful than either those of the bush men or the pioneers. In *The Australian Legend* Russel Ward has outlined the way in which the legend of the digger embodied aspects of the bush men's legend. A similar process occurred with the pioneer legend. *The Anzac Memorial*, published in 1917, carried a poem by Dorothy McCrae, 'The First Brigade', reproduced subsequently in the Victorian *School Paper* with the subtitle 'The Pioneers of Australia':

They cleared the earth, and felled the trees,
And built the towns and colonies;
Then, to their land, their sons they gave,
And reared them hardy, pure, and brave.

They made Australia's past: to them
We owe the present diadem;

For, in their sons, they fight again,
And ANZAC proved their hero strain.

The first celebration of Anzac Day in 1916 posed a problem for the compilers of the Victorian school calendar. Since 1911, 19 April had been set aside as Discovery Day. This was the anniversary of Cook's sighting of the Australian coast and was devoted to the celebration of explorers and pioneers. Since it fell so close to Anzac Day, it was suspended in 1916, but on Anzac Day teachers were encouraged to link diggers, explorers and pioneers together: 'The lessons and addresses on Anzac Day will, no doubt, include matter appropriate to Discovery Day, such as reference to the discovery, settlement, and development of Australia.' The connection between 'settlement and development' and the Anzac spirit took substantial form after the war in the soldier settlement schemes. Diggers were to become pioneers.

The subsequent history of 'pioneer' and the legend cannot be fully traced here. The legend still survives, though its foundations are not as firm as they were in the early twentieth century. It has suffered inevitably from the waning of faith in progress and the virtues of European civilisation. No-one now writes of the pioneers as Paterson did, though his pioneer verse and others' is still collected in anthologies. Historians have for a long time escaped the romanticism of Roberts' *Squatting Age* and have emphasised the clash between squatters' interests and those of the rest of the community. Paterson's golden age has received no help from them. The legend, which was made by creative writers, was eventually attacked by them. Brian Penton in *Landtakers* (1934) overturned the view that the squatter's life was exhilarating and free. His theme was the coarsening and hardening of a well-bred English emigrant as he coped with life in a 'gaolyard' and then on the frontier, with 'the grind and ugliness and shame of Australia'. Xavier Herbert's *Capricornia* (1938) is still the most devastating anti-pioneer piece in our literature. It confronts the legend explicitly. Herbert's Northern Territory society is brutal, chaotic, hypocritical and drunken. The book is an indictment of the white settlers of the Territory for the destruction which they brought to Aboriginal society and for their continuing exploitation of Aborigines and half-castes. 'The Coming of the Dingoes' is how Herbert describes the arrival of the white man in the Territory. Herbert was, in fact, the first to write black history in this country. Pioneers were the enemy to the original inhabitants of the land, and as sympathy with Aborigines grows and the brutalities of the frontier continue to be highlighted, the pioneers' reputation will suffer more. The growing concern with the environment will damage the pioneers still further as their ruthless exploitation of the land comes under closer scrutiny. And yet, sympathetic accounts of pioneering men and women continue to be written, among the most notable are Margaret Kiddle's *Men of Yesterday*, Patrick White's *Tree of Man*, and Judith Wright's *Generations of Men*. While not endorsing the crudities of the pioneer legend, these works nevertheless depict the pioneers as a creative, ordering force, whose work gives their lives a certain nobility and completeness. *The Tree of Man* describes in its first pages the arrival of Stan Parker at his uncleared land in a forest, a similar scene to that McCubbin depicted in the first panel of 'The Pioneers':

> Then the man took an axe and struck at the side of a hairy tree, more to hear the sound than for any other reason. And the sound was cold and loud. The man struck at the tree, and struck, till several white chips had fallen. He looked at the scar in the side of the tree. The silence was immense. It was the first time anything like this had happened in that part of the bush ...
>
> The man made a lean-to with bags and a few saplings. He built a fire. He sighed at last, because the lighting of his small fire had kindled in him the first warmth of content. Of being somewhere. That particular part of the bush had been made his by the entwining fire. It licked at and swallowed the loneliness.

We may come at last to see Stan Parker merely as a destroyer of the natural environment or as a labourer transforming himself into a small property holder, but so long as our spirit stirs in other ways at this scene the pioneer legend will not be without its force.

Popular history is still very much pioneer history, embodied in new forms now in the reconstructed pioneer villages and settlements which have proliferated throughout the country in recent years. What is conveyed by these is in some ways rather different from the classic pioneer statements in literature. The concentration is much less on the struggle on the land, partly because the encounter with the elements, which was central to the drama, cannot be reproduced. But the buildings and their fittings strike the visitor with a sense of the pioneers' achievement, in making their homes or farms or businesses where nothing was before, and with a sense of the pioneers' hardships in contrast to his own life. We noted earlier how the legend confines pioneers to their land and ignores their wider society. The pioneer villages carry this tendency to its ultimate by leaving out people altogether. We are shown empty buildings, disembodied achievement, and are told nothing of the social and economic factors which determined who had the chance to achieve what. Buildings cannot speak readily of social conflict; these pioneer villages are powerful contributors to the consensus view of Australia's past.

Early immigrants generally, as distinct from the first settlers on the land, are still honoured as pioneers. In New South Wales there is a Pioneers' Club, formed in 1910, and in South Australia a Pioneers' Association, formed in 1935, to keep their memory alive. These organisations define categories of membership by year of arrival of ancestor, construct genealogies and exercise a declining influence on the edge of the old state establishments. The pioneer–immigrants continued to be associated more with state than national loyalty. They were also honoured more frequently by those who wished to stress the British identity of Australia, and who saw its history as the winning of new areas for the empire. The British heritage these pioneers brought with them was as important as their accomplishments here. Pioneers as settlers on the land were more purely nationalistic heroes. At some times in the twentieth century – particularly in South Australia with its clear and clean foundation – pioneers as first immigrants may have had greater standing than pioneers as settlers on the land, but there is no doubt now of the latter's primacy. The two groups of pioneers are, of course, not totally distinct. The pioneer poem at the beginning of the Fifth Grade *Victorian Reader*, quoted above, is concerned chiefly with the struggle on the land, but the pioneers are identified clearly as British immigrants – 'We are the old world people' – and this is part of their virtue – 'Ours were the hearts to dare'. The pioneer legend has served local, Australian and imperial patriotisms.

The survival of the word 'pioneer' itself means much. The word originally applied to those in an army who went as pioneers before the main body to prepare the way by clearing roads and making bridges and so on. It was then extended to the initiator of any new enterprise or new undertaking who 'showed the way' for those who came after. In this sense it could well be used as Kendall used it in 'Blue Mountain Pioneers' for the explorers. In the new world, first in North America and then in Australia, the meaning was again extended to refer to first settlers on the land. But to whom or in what were the first settlers showing the way? Their aim was to occupy the land for their own use and to keep others out. The metaphor of showing or preparing the way was now being stretched further to make them pioneers in a very general sense; they showed the way to the generations or the nation which came after them, and benefited from their labours. In this way the word itself obscures the private interests which they had in acquiring the land and depicts it as a service, as something for which we should be grateful, thus embodying a central concept of the legend. Let any who doubt the significance of the word consider what would have to change before we consistently referred to the first settlers as, say, landtakers, which was Penton's term.

This paper shares Russel Ward's assumption about the significance of a nation's legends, or its dreaming: 'The dreams of nations, as of individuals, are important, because they not only reflect, as in a distorting mirror, the real world, but may sometimes react upon and influence it.' That the legend which Ward describes exists is unquestionable; he is misleading, however, when he implies that this was the only national legend. Ward claimed with very little analysis that Lawson and Paterson embodied the legend which he had described; what they in fact embodied was a great deal more complex and varied. We have already noted their favourable view of the squatters, which A. A. Phillips identified. Ward takes too little account of this in his attempt to stress the radical collectivist aspect of the legend. Phillips is closer to the literature in writing of 'The Democratic Theme'. The anti-police aspect of the legend is not well reflected in Lawson, who nearly always makes his policemen good cops, sympathetic to the poor and outcast, and who wrote a poem celebrating the bravery of a police trooper. And both writers fostered the development of the pioneer legend.

Some of Ward's critics, over-reacting perhaps to his less guarded claims for the legend's influence, have attempted to deny its existence or force by citing social behaviour which runs counter to the legend. This is, of course, very easy to do, but when faced with this criticism Ward can retreat to very safe ground and declare that he was merely tracing the origins of the national legend which is not fully founded in fact, nor vastly influential. Those who feel that Australia has not been made according to the legend would be better advised to establish the other legends, stereotypes and symbols Australians have made or adopted. The pioneer legend is one such. It is a national rural myth, democratic in its social bearing, conservative in its political implications.

1978

Federation: Destiny and Identity

Australians know little and care less about the origins of their nation. Historians have commonly encouraged them in this response by depicting federation as a business deal or a compact hammered out by hard-headed politicians looking after their own colonies. They find little here to inspire later generations.

This is a strange outcome because the people who devoted themselves to the creation of the federation regarded it as a holy or noble or sacred cause which would carry the people to a higher form of life.

Federation would supplant the mutual suspicion and hostility between the colonies with brotherhood, a widening of human sympathy which was the hallmark of moral progress. The petty and provincial concerns of colonial politics – the struggle over roads and bridges, the endless deputations to ministers begging favours – would be replaced by a politics that dealt with a national life and the fate of a whole people.

Federation itself – the means by which Australia was to become a nation – wore a progressive air. It represented so clearly a stage in social evolution from simple to complex forms. It was by federation that men envisioned that the British empire, the Anglo-Saxon race, the English-speaking peoples and finally the world, would be united. Tennyson, the poet laureate, sang of 'the parliament of man, the Federation of the world'.

In looking for the motives for Australian federation, historians usually are far too instrumental in their thinking. The Commonwealth government was given power over various subjects and the puzzle of

why federation occurred is reduced to ranking these in order of importance. Was federation chiefly to secure a customs union, or a united
immigration policy, or a national defence? To federalists none of these
things was sacred; the whole forty-two powers given to the Commonwealth did not together make federation sacred. It was the making of
the nation, apart from anything it might do, which was sacred.

Because federation was a sacred cause, poetry was considered the
most appropriate medium to express its rationale and purposes. It was
poetry's role to deal with what was noble, profound, and elevating.
There are innumerable federation poems by hundreds of different
hands. The nation was born in a festival of poetry. Historians have
noticed the poems, but haven't quite known what to do with them.
Most of them are valueless as poetry. One leading scholar who produced a bibliography of federation sources decided that it would be
kinder to his readers to leave it all out. He thus removed from consideration the best guide to the ideas and ideals which inspired the movement. You are not to be spared, but I will be very selective in my
quotations.

The poets considered that God or destiny intended Australia to be a
nation. The evidence for this was in the first place physical. They forgot
Tasmania (which was inconsiderate since it was always keen about
federation) and saw the nation-to-be as a single geographical unit, a
whole continent with only natural boundaries. This was a special bene-
diction. Other nations had man-made frontiers; Australia's were the sea.
A common word for the sea in this role was 'girdle' and in its verbal
form 'girdled' or 'girdling' or 'girt'. 'Advance Australia Fair', written by
Peter McCormick in 1878 and now the national anthem, uses 'girt' and
assumes the implications of the sea boundary do not have to be spelled
out, recording merely 'our home is girt by sea'.

The social uniformity within the continent also marked out
Australia for nationhood. The people were of one blood or stock or
race; they spoke the same language; they shared a glorious heritage
(Britain's), the most celebrated part of which was political freedom
which had been extended in Australia to all men so that the country
was the freest on earth.

The best federation poem, written very early (1877), does not argue that Australia should be one, but assumes it and deals instead with the ideal becoming real. It is the most powerful expression of the idea that union was Australia's destiny. The author was James Brunton Stephens, a headmaster at a Brisbane state school.

His federation poem was called 'The Dominion of Australia: A Forecast':

> She is not yet; but he whose ear
> Thrills to that finer atmosphere
> Where footfalls of appointed things,
>   Reverberant of days to be,
> Are heard in forecast echoings
>   Like wave-beats from a viewless sea,
> Hears in the voiceful tremors of the sky
> Auroral heralds whispering, 'She is nigh'.

The middle part of the poem develops an elaborate comparison between the silent force carrying Australia to its destiny and the underground rivers which some experts assumed must run under the parched lands of the outback and which one day might be released to make the desert bloom:

> So flows beneath our good and ill
> A viewless stream of Common Will,
> A gathering force, a present might,
>   That from its silent depths of gloom
> At Wisdom's voice shall leap to light
>   And hide our barren feuds in bloom,
> Till, all our sundering lines with love o'ergrown,
> Our bounds shall be the girdling seas alone.

When Parkes opened his campaign for federation in his famous speech at Tenterfield, he quoted from this poem. He did well to quote from Stephens' poetry rather than his own. At the time he launched his campaign he was revising the proofs of his next book of poems, *Fragmentary Thoughts*. In the preface he said with his usual mock humility that he would be happy to be judged no great poet, but lest anyone dare to make that judgment he reproduced a letter from his friend Lord Tennyson which praised his efforts, how guardedly Parkes probably did not notice. In Brisbane a few days before his Tenterfield speech, he had refused to disclose his federal plans to the *Courier*'s reporter but had been very willing to discuss poetry. He passed the proofs of his poems to the journalist for his opinion. He declared Stephens to be the best poet in Australia, a compliment Stephens returned in his review of *Fragmentary Thoughts* which contrived to be favourable without pronouncing definitely on the quality of the poems.

In his new collection Parkes rehearsed a standard theme in 'The Flag':

> God girdled our majestic isle
>> With seas far-reaching east and west,
> That man might live beneath this smile
>> In peace and freedom ever blest.

He was a much better phrase-maker in his speeches.

As federation became a firm proposal, it met opposition as well as the old indifference. The poets identified the forces which frustrated it as selfishness, greed, and faction, by which they meant a sinister political combination. Men were damaging the union already created by God. The symbols of this divisiveness were the customs houses on the colonial borders, which were hated not as a commercial inconvenience, but as a moral outrage. So to reveal the Australian nation, men had to repent and return to God. In a Christian culture this was a powerful theme. It was best expressed by William Gay in his sonnet 'Federation' written in the early 1890s:

> From all division let our land be free,
>> For God has made her one: complete she lies
>> Within the unbroken circle of the skies,
> And round her indivisible the sea
> Breaks on her single shore; while only we,
>> Her foster children, bound with sacred ties

Of one dear blood, one storied enterprise,
Are negligent of her integrity. –
Her seamless garment, at great Mammon's nod,
    With hands unfilial we have basely rent,
    With petty variance our souls are spent,
And ancient kinship under foot is trod:
    O let us rise, united, penitent,
And be one people, – mighty, serving God!

Deakin quoted Gay's sonnet to conclude his great speech that launched the 'Yes' case in Victoria in 1898.

According to the poets, the prospects for the new nation were unrivalled. Australia had no ancient feuds, no privileged caste, no bar to anyone making money from its abundant resources; a land of freedom and opportunity. Always imagined as female, Australia was young, pure, virginal. The themes are present in 'Advance Australia Fair', though again rather minimally. Australians are young and free; the land is rich in opportunities – golden soil – which are open to those ready to work: wealth for toil.

There was a constant insistence that no blood had been spilt in this land. This is a puzzle to us who are now so conscious of the violence done to the Aborigines. In part the claim could be made because the slaughter was simply being forgotten, though the forgetfulness was more complete in the early twentieth century than in the nineteenth. It was possible to know well enough what had happened on the frontier and still see Australia as pure. In *Fragmentary Thoughts* Parkes wrote of the Australian flag: 'It bears no stain of blood and tears./ Its glory is its purity.' In the same volume is a poem that gives a chilling account of the murder of an Aboriginal boy by settlers on the Hawkesbury in 1794. He was tied hand and foot, dragged through a fire until his back was horribly burnt, and then thrown into the river and shot:

Loud talk ye of savages
    As they were beasts of prey! –
But men of English birth have done
    More savage things than they

The two thoughts remain unconnected. It was easy not to make the connection when Aborigines were not seen as part of the future nation since they were dying out and in any case unworthy of its citizenship. Furthermore, when they spoke of no blood spilt, the poets had in mind the European experience of warfare ravaging the land and being constantly renewed.

The best poem on Australia as a new world free from all the ills of the old was written by John Farrell. He was a brewer turned journalist and poet. In the late 1880s he was editor of and chief contributor to a radical Sydney newspaper which supported land nationalisation along the lines of Henry George's single tax:

> We have no records of a by-gone shame,
>> No red-writ histories of woe to weep:
>> God set our land in summer seas asleep
> Till His fair morning for her waking came.
> He hid her where the rage of Old World wars
>> Might never break upon her virgin rest:
>> He sent His softest winds to fan her breast,
> And canopied her night with low-hung stars.
> He wrought her perfect, in a happy clime,
>> And held her worthiest, and bade her wait
>> Serene on her lone couch inviolate
> The heightened manhood of a later time.

The sexual theme was never more explicit. The men worthy to take Australia, the 'manful pioneers', only leave Europe when freedom has dawned there:

> They found a gracious amplitude of soil,
>> Unsown with memories, like poison weeds,
>> Of far-forefathers wrongs and vengeful deeds,
> Where was no crown, save that of earnest toil.
> They reared a sunnier England, where the pain
>> Of bitter yesterdays might not arise:
>> They said – 'The past is past, and all its cries,

Of time-long hatred are beyond the main …
And, with fair peace's white, pure flag unfurled,
    Our children shall, upon this new-won shore –
    Warned by all sorrows that have gone before –
Build up the glory of a grand New World.

The new Commonwealth did not seem designed to build up a grand new world since it was to have limited powers. In the 1890s Australia was gaining a reputation for progressive social and economic legislation, but this was and would remain chiefly the responsibility of the states. Only at the last minute was the Commonwealth given power over old-age pensions and interstate industrial disputes.

It was in the name of the federation that the delegates most clearly expressed their sense that Australia represented a new dispensation. The name 'Commonwealth' was suggested by Parkes at the 1891 convention and was taken up enthusiastically by Deakin who lobbied the delegates on its behalf. After being narrowly adopted by the convention's constitutional committee, it won general acceptance in the convention and outside it because it embodied an Australian view of the nature of government. The state existed not to aggrandise an elite or to embark on conquest, but to serve the common weal, the common good. It was this view of government which was to make the Commonwealth much larger than its formal powers implied.

The entry which won the New South Wales government prize for a poem celebrating the inauguration of the Commonwealth deals with its name. These are its best lines; the poet was George Essex Evans:

Free-born of Nations, Virgin white,
    Not won by blood nor ringed with steel,
Thy throne is on a loftier height,
    Deep-rooted in the Commonweal!

On 1 January 1901, and for the days before and after, the newspapers gave over a large part of their space to poetry. There was Evans' prize-winning poem; a new poem by Brunton Stephens whose 1877 work was now very well known; and the words of the anthem sung at the inauguration which had been written by John Farrell who had celebrated Australia as a grand new world.

These poets are now almost entirely forgotten. The poets of the turn of the century who are remembered, honoured and read are Banjo Paterson and Henry Lawson. They have helped to define the Australian nation. They were newcomers in the 1890s. The critics, while acknowledging the appeal of their work, regarded it as light, ephemeral verse. Paterson's poems had sold in the thousands, but would anyone keep the book on their shelves? He lacked the nobility, the profundity, and moral elevation thought proper to poetry. Brunton Stephens was generous about Paterson's achievement, but could not believe that poems about racecourses and backblocks life would endure. He regarded William Gay as the true, new poet of the 1890s. Evans conceded that Paterson was a master of the bush ballad, but thought Stephens would always be acknowledged as the founder of the national literature. Of course, no-one in the 1890s ever imagined that a whole nation could come to treasure a Paterson poem about a Snowy River horseman and a Paterson song about a sheep-stealing swagman.

Historians examining what part nationalism played in the creation of federation find it hard to imagine the founding fathers reciting 'The Man from Snowy River' and assume that nationalism's role was small. They overlook the whole school of nationalist poetry which flourished from the 1870s, whose leading practitioners were in a double sense the established poets of their time. Their reputation stood high and they were encouraged and supported by leading colonial politicians who became founding fathers of the Commonwealth. When Griffith took to translating Dante he sent his efforts to Brunton Stephens and Essex Evans for their professional criticism. The flier advertising Gay's book of sonnets carried endorsements from Parkes, Barton, and Deakin. When Gay produced a book of essays on federation he attracted contributions from Deakin, Inglis Clark, and Griffith.

The nationalism of these poets was a civic nationalism, concerned with the state and the principles and values it should protect and advance; its symbol was female, a young virginal goddess in the classical tradition. The nationalism that grew from Paterson's verse was social and masculine, concerned to honour men of the outback and their values. It was the civic nationalism, now lost to sight, which inspired the federation movement. It was dignified, earnest, Protestant, not raffish, Irish-Catholic or working-class.

I don't think I can talk safely for much longer about the idealism that underlay the movement to federation. You hard-headed realistic Australians will want to know what was the true driving force of the movement. It can't be poetry.

Australian historians who doubt the force of national feeling in federation have looked to economics to reveal the selfish motive behind it. They overlook the motive that is quintessentially selfish and integral to nationalism, the desire for identity and status. As the Italian patriot Mazzini declared: '... without a country you have no name, no identity, no voice, no rights, no membership in the brotherhood of nations.'

The federalist who was most revealing about this was Samuel Griffith, the chief draftsman of the Constitution. Griffith came to Australia as a boy of eight. His father was a Congregational minister who gave his bright son a good education, hoping he would follow him into the ministry. But Griffith would not be bound by his parents' narrow puritanism. His ambition was to become pre-eminent in the law, rich, and famous. There was no open rupture with his parents; the young man kept his exploits with women and drink secret and outwardly conformed. He took to drinking when he was at university in Sydney; at home in Brisbane during vacations he went with his parents to teetotal meetings. From the start there was something unruffled in his progress. Until his father died he attended the Congregational Church and then he switched to the Anglican. Religion did not mean much to him. He invested far more in the masonic lodge, whose codes he studied as assiduously as the law and where his advancement was equally rapid.

He was a man of principle, a legal philosopher in politics who could not rouse a crowd, but could argue a case from first principles. He pursued his personal ambition in politics with the same rectitude, as if he were taking only what was his due. As premier he directed the government's legal business to himself and brought his political career to an end in 1893 by getting himself appointed Chief Justice, but only after Parliament had increased the salary.

He liked the trappings as well as the substance of success. At twenty-one he designed the coat of arms that he hoped would be his; at forty-one he secured it when he was made a Knight of the Order of St Michael and St George. One of the jobs of Queensland's Agent-General in London was to lobby the Colonial Office for honours for Premier Griffith. After gaining his knighthood, Griffith wanted to be promoted to Knight of the Grand Cross. Once he was Chief Justice, he set his sights on being in addition Lieutenant-Governor. On formal occasions he delighted in wearing all his badges and ribbons. He was always well dressed; a tall, spare, dignified figure.

On great occasions, when Griffith was called on to detail the advantages of federation, he spoke, quite uncharacteristically, in a personal and heartfelt way. He said, 'I am tired of being treated as a colonial.' Even when the English were being considerate, he continued, they could not hide their disparagement of the colonist. In the eyes of the world, Australians were nothing but children while they remained as colonies. As a nation, they would meet the rest of the world as equals and the status of every Australian would be raised.

As premier of Queensland, Griffith was well aware of the difficulties involved in inter-colonial co-operation and the advantages union would bring. He was a conscientious administrator. Yet at the deepest level, he wanted federation not so that public affairs might be handled differently, but so that he might be someone different. His assiduous application and lobbying for honours could not prevail against one barrier: there would have to be an Australian nation before Samuel Griffith ceased to be a colonial.

Griffith wanted to constitute an independent Australian nation which would remain in the empire, but without being subordinate to Britain; the only link to Britain would be the crown. Britain would be an equal and an ally and all the people of the empire would share a common citizenship. This was the arrangement not formally achieved until the passage of the Statute of Westminster in 1931. Legally, Griffith could not produce that outcome in 1901, but he had it in mind as he drew up the Constitution. When Australia became independent, the Constitution did not have to be changed.

Griffith took great satisfaction from the fact that immediately the

Commonwealth was established the colonies were to be reconstituted as its states. So the word *colony*, the badge of inferiority, would no longer be used by Australians talking of themselves, nor, Griffith hoped, by other people, particularly the English, in talking about Australia and its people. In England *colonial* meant second-rate or at least suspect.

Australians laboured under a double handicap because *Australian colonist* also suggested 'convict', or the descendant of convicts, or the associate of convicts and their descendants. The Australian rule was not to talk about the convicts – unless to insult New South Wales in inter-colonial feuding – but Australians knew that the world had not forgotten. They were very anxious to find and parade signs that the stock had not degenerated despite this taint. Victories over England at cricket were very comforting.

Australians were annoyed and sometimes angry at British disdain, but they could not easily reject or ignore Britain. Most of them admired Britain and its civilisation and wanted British interest and approval. By the late nineteenth century there was more British interest in the colonies than thirty or forty years before when the colonies were widely viewed as an encumbrance, but old attitudes persisted. Simple ignorance abounded. People in Britain did not know the names of the various colonies or their location. Letters arrived with bizarre addresses: 'Melbourne, near Sydney, Victoria'. Visitors to England were asked where they learnt to speak English.

In the 1880s the leading colonial politicians, among them Samuel Griffith, were brought into a new relationship with British ministers and officials as they sought to influence the empire's defence and foreign policies. The men who were accustomed to govern their own societies were cast into the role of lobbyists and petitioners at the metropolis. Frequently they found it a frustrating and humiliating experience. They felt themselves very much the colonials. 'We are children,' said Griffith, 'dependent on a superior people.' They thought the British did not care enough for them. If their submissions were rejected, their first response was to assume it was because they and the people they represented were mere colonists.

The leading politicians gave as one of the advantages of federation that the colonies would speak with one voice and more notice would be taken of them as a nation. Britain would no longer ignore them. Australians would benefit from this increased stature and strength, but so in a very particular way would they as their representatives and spokesmen. They would cease to be colonial politicians. They might be Australian statesmen. It was notable that the founding fathers, having declared that they must limit Commonwealth power and keep the states strong, immediately transferred to the Commonwealth on its inauguration.

The man who hoped to lead the new nation as prime minister was Henry Parkes, an intention clearly indicated by the frequency with which he disclaimed it. He was the best-known politician in Australia and the only Australian politician well known in Britain, but he still knew the hurt of being colonial. It was part of his success as a politician that he could fuse his own pursuit of a greater glory with the emancipation of a whole people. In the series of speeches with which he launched his campaign for federation he promised to remove humiliation and slight and bring dignity and pride:

> Instead of a confusion of names and geographical divisions, which so perplexes many people at a distance, we shall be Australians, and a people with 7000 miles of coast, more than 2,000,000 square miles of land, with 4,000,000 of population, and shall present ourselves to the world as 'Australia'.
>
> We shall at once rise to a higher level; we shall occupy a larger place in the contemplation of mankind, the sympathies of every part of the world will go out to us, and figuratively, they will hold out the right hand of fellowship. We can not doubt that the chord awakened by such a movement will be responded to in the noble old country where our forefathers' graves are still. All England has awakened with sympathy to this movement through its press.
>
> We shall have a higher stature before the world. We shall have a grander name.

These are the desires that make nations.

The committed federalist leaders – Parkes, Deakin, Griffith, Barton, Inglis Clark and others – were pursuing a sacred ideal of nationhood. They can be thought of as both selfish and pure. Selfish, in that the chief force driving them was the new identity and greater stature they would enjoy – either as colonists or natives – from Australia's nationhood. Pure, in that the benefit they sought did not depend on the particular form federation took. In a sense any federation would do. They knew of course that interests had to be conciliated and other ideals not outraged; they shared some of these themselves. But they were not mere managers or lobbyists; underneath all the negotiation and campaigning there was an emotional drive. Those who only considered economic and provincial interests when they contemplated federation understood this quality in the federalists. They called them federation-at-any-price men, enthusiasts, or sentimentalists.

It might be objected that these enthusiasts were only a minority. Sometimes the test for the role of national feeling in federation has been how widespread it was. So relatively low turnouts for the choosing of convention delegates and at the referendums have been used to indicate that national feeling played a small part in federation. But the role of national feeling is not to be measured by taking the pulse of the community at large. Nationalism has always possessed one section of the population first – whether poets or intellectuals or a new middle class or local officials of an empire. They become passionate for the nation while the mass of the people remain attached to their chiefs, villages, or provinces and can see no benefit in creating a new government. Nationalism in its creative phase is a minority movement.

The practical people, the hard-headed men, saw no need for federation. If the colonies needed to take more joint action, let them co-operate more closely. If the border customs houses were a nuisance, let a customs union be formed. It was the nationalists who wanted a nation and it is to them we owe our federation.

2001

Labor and Conscription

There are very few critics of the American alliance as hard-headed as David Martin. He insists that the alliance can only be abandoned if we are ready to take the necessary measures to provide for our own defence. His book *Armed Neutrality for Australia* sets out his plans. To establish the circumstances in which armed neutrality can work and the defence systems which it requires he examines five countries which follow this policy – Switzerland, Sweden, Finland, Austria and Ireland. Of these, he discovers that four conscript young men in peace-time. That policy, he immediately recognises, could not be adopted in Australia: 'universal conscription in peace-time would divide Australia'. He quickly moves on to examine other methods which could raise the numbers of our army.

This hiccup in David Martin's advocacy is highly significant. The natural constituency for a proposal to break with the United States – broadly those people on the left – are attached to traditions, particularly anti-conscription, which make them opponents of the measures that we would need to adopt, or at least consider, if ANZUS were to be abandoned. Here the past weighs very heavily on the present and constrains the future. Those like myself who have some sympathy with David Martin's position have good reason to re-examine the history of defence and conscription in this country. Why, in particular, have all the movements which are labelled 'Australian', 'independent', and 'nationalist' not produced a tradition or a constituency for David Martin to build on?

*

In the early twentieth century Australian politicians increasingly began to doubt whether the British Navy, the front line of their defence, could protect them. To meet growing threats in Europe from Germany, Britain concentrated its fleet in the North Sea and was hence less able to match the growing power of Japan in the Pacific. Britain considered this threat was contained by its 1902 treaty with Japan, but this piece of paper was not accepted by the colonists as granting them protection from the power which had the capacity to overturn the White Australia Policy by main force. Australian governments, on a bipartisan basis, took two measures to counter the Japanese threat. First, they introduced compulsory military training for boys and young men so that if Britain did lose control of the sea and Australia was invaded the men conscripted into the militia would give a good account of themselves. Second, an Australian Navy was built.

Compulsory military training was at odds both with British liberal tradition and Labor's anti-militarism. Its adoption indicates the strength of the new nation's fears and of its desire to be as self-reliant as possible. Billy Hughes of the Labor Party did most to shake thinking about military compulsion out of its usual grooves. In a democracy, he argued, universal training on a part-time basis prevented the emergence of a military caste and of militarism. The soldier was the citizen in arms. Citizenship was the concept which legitimated the new obligation and the organisation which trainees joined was known as the Citizen Military Forces (the name of the militia until recent times).

The creation of the Australian Navy was long delayed because the Admiralty, wedded ever more firmly to the blue-water school, opposed this development. It argued that nothing Australia could do in the way of coastal defence – for an ocean-going fleet was beyond its resources – could affect the outcome of a naval engagement between Great Britain and another first-class power and on that would depend Australia's fate. If Australia was concerned at the erosion of British naval supremacy, it could do no better than increase its subventions for the maintenance of British ships. New Zealand was prepared to entrust its security to Britain and in 1909 offered to pay for the full cost of a Dreadnought battleship which was to be presented to the Admiralty with no strings attached. This won them the admiration of Churchill:

'No greater insight into political and strategical points has ever been shown by a community hitherto unversed in military matters.'

The Australians did not want to follow this course because their nationalist aspirations would not allow them to continue to purchase their naval defence from someone else. And yet they accepted the broad tenets of the blue-water school which meant that they had to wrestle with the conundrum that the nationalist course appeared to diminish rather than enhance their security. They marked out a niche for an Australian navy by arguing that though the decisive battle might be fought far from Australia, local destroyers and submarines could protect Australian shipping and if the decisive battle went the wrong way they could take toll of an invading fleet. The Admiralty succumbed to Australian pressure in 1907 and reluctantly agreed to colonial navies for coastal defence and then in 1909 it changed tack and encouraged the construction by the colonies of ocean-going vessels. A strong Pacific fleet would be constituted from Canadian, New Zealand, Australian and British vessels. The Admiralty's ploy was to make the dominions take full responsibility for the Pacific so it could concentrate its own efforts in the Atlantic. The promise of British vessels, which would not be withdrawn from the Pacific, was the bait. Australia bit and built its ocean-going vessels and then in 1913 Britain announced that because it was so hard-pressed by Germany it could not make its contribution to the Pacific fleet. The Australian government was still reeling from this betrayal when war broke out. Labor under Andrew Fisher won the election which was in process when war was declared. In 1915 Fisher retired and Billy Hughes, Labor's great advocate of conscription, became prime minister.

Before the war Australia had devoted much attention to building up its own defences. It was not unmindful of its obligations to empire for it knew that by its own efforts it could not defend itself against a first-class power, but its working motto had been Australia first, the empire second. The disaster scenario which took shape in these years had the empire unable to help Australia. Britain would be pre-occupied in some European conflict, Japan would descend on Australia, and Australia would have to hold out by its own efforts until help came. If Britain were unable to bring the help, then the United States seemed the only prospective saviour. Of course World War I unfolded very differently for Australia. The Anglo–Japanese alliance held and there was little direct threat to Australia. Australia's task was to reinforce Britain in Europe. To demand that Australia devote all its resources to this task was to overturn the common understanding of Australia's best course in defence and wore the appearance of resiling from Australia's national aspirations. Australia was being asked to assume towards the empire the posture of New Zealand. The Labor Party had been the firmest against adopting that position. For them it would have been the greatest wrench to assent to Hughes' claim that since Britain faced annihilation the boundaries between local and imperial defence no longer made sense and that if Australia were prepared to conscript for local defence it must do the same to save the empire and itself in France.

To discover why the bulk of the Labor Party would not agree to conscription for overseas service we shall not dwell long on the arguments they advanced during the conscription referendums. We have some understanding of how No cases are run: raise every bogey until you find ones that bite. Towards the end of the 1916 campaign the *Bulletin* wrote, 'Heaven may know what fresh reasons for voting No would have been manufactured if there had been another week … In one district a yarn was told that compulsory service was being urged so that everybody might be compelled to live at Canberra.' The bogey that conscription would endanger White Australia by denuding the country emerged late and bit hard, but had played little part in the development of Labor's anti-conscription stand.

The men who insisted that no conscription must be Labor policy were the industrialists, a group who had only recently identified and organised themselves. They were trade unionists disgusted at the moderation of Labor politicians and the failure of Labor governments to institute a new social order. They planned to take control of the party by instituting the system of card votes at conferences (which would strengthen the union influence as against the branches) and by excluding Labor politicians from any position within the party organisation. Their case against conscription was a class one: conscription was advocated by capitalists who were making great profits out of the war while the workers died; the capitalists' purpose was to break down all the workers' hard-won gains for once conscription was instituted any worker who protested would be shipped off to the front.

It was clear to contemporaries, and their assessment has been endorsed by historians, that conscription was as much the occasion of the Labor split as the cause of it. Industrialists were openly urging that the issue be used to purge the party of those elements which were frustrating its purpose. This is not to impugn the genuineness of the opposition to conscription. The Labor Party had supported the war and the great majority were still in favour of it, but nothing could be more at odds with what the labour movement had been instituted to achieve than the sending of men to slaughter in a clash of imperial powers in Europe. Opposition to conscription expressed the dismay at what the war had become and Labor's complicity in it. It was put to the party that it should be either for Australia's participation in the war or against it; and if for, it could have no objection in principle to conscription since it accepted it for local defence. The party's feelings about the war were too mixed for it to obey this logic.

The conscription issue was not settled at Labor Party conferences. When it was put to the people at referendum the anti-conscriptionists had to behave exactly as the despised Labor politicians did in front of the electors – they soft pedalled the class language. It might win votes at Labor conferences to claim that workers were the special victims of war, but not in the electorate at large where most families in all classes were touched by bereavement or lived in dread of it. As the class argument against conscription receded from prominence, it was replaced by the radical libertarian claim that the state had no right to compel a man to fight. This was elaborated and elevated to a sacred principle by H. E. Boote, the editor of the *Worker*, which was the key propaganda organ for the No case. Conscription was an outrage to the sanctity of the soul: 'The man who is forced to fight is as vilely outraged as the woman who is forced to fondle.' At the beginning of the second referendum campaign Boote declared:

There are a thousand arguments against conscription, and *The Worker* intends to use them every one. But the most powerful, the most far-reaching, and most comprehensive of them is formulated in these four simple words –

HUMAN LIFE IS SACRED

The move from class to liberty in the anti-conscription case can be followed in Claude Marquet's cartoons in the *Worker*. When conscription was being debated within the party the protagonists in the cartoons were fat capitalists and heroic workers; when the debate was before the whole electorate Australia is the potential victim, a noble, classical figure, and its oppressor is a jack-booted militarist or William Morris Hughes.

The defence of individual liberty was a new position for the Labor Party to adopt. It had made its way by opposing liberties – the liberty of property owners and employers – and by instituting new compulsions – to vote as caucus directs, to join a trade union. Conscriptionists within the Labor Party and outside it chided the anti-conscriptionists with gross inconsistency: how could they insist on compulsory unionism and be opposed to conscription for military service – in both cases non-joiners should not be allowed to let others make sacrifices for a benefit which came to all. In pressing home the contradiction *The Socialist Case for Conscription* declared: 'In presence of real danger these fire eaters of the Trades Hall become men of peace, preaching scabdom with a kind of religious zeal.' For use in the campaign Hughes collected statements from European socialists and trade unionists in favour of conscription. Ben Tillet wrote 'trade unionists are coercionists, and in a strike, absolute conscriptionists, but God help anybody who is a "conscientious objector"'. Leaflets for the Yes campaign urged workers not to scab on their mates in the trenches and not to scab on civilisation. On the whole, Australian historians have not seen a similarity in the military and trade union cases for they indulgently record the rough treatment and kidnapping of scabs and wax indignant at an unenlisted man being sent a white feather.

The most considered response of the *Worker* to the charge of inconsistency was this: 'Compulsion would be democratic in its concepts, incidence and results only if the property and privileges it protects and preserves were equally shared.' That is, only a socialist society can legitimately conscript men to fight. But generally the anti-conscriptionists did not bother to explain why compulsion was acceptable to build trade union strength but not for the defence of the country. They had little need to. Instead of having to contest the hegemony of liberal thought, Labor was now its beneficiary. Until very recently anti-conscription had been a central part of the British liberal tradition. Anti-conscriptionists depicted their battle for freedom as the latest in a long line of struggles against tyranny. Here is Curtin in the No leaflet 'Fight as Free Men':

> The seeds of Liberty which were sown in the blood-stained soil of Eureka has created an Australian environment which is responsible for the bold, courageous, and self-sacrificing characteristics which have made our sons admired by all the world. If you would preserve these freedom-loving aspirations, which is the very soul-force of true patriotism, then fight to the last gasp against the introduction of conscription into your country, because conscription is the very foundation and cornerstone of the servile state.

For the time being, at least, history had ceased to be the history of class struggle.

The libertarian case against conscription assumed that it would force unwilling men to fight. The pro-conscriptionists generally took the same view by describing those who had not enlisted as shirkers and cowards. Some men caught by conscription would have been unwilling, but far from all. Men were willing to fight but were reluctant to make the sacrifice while others equally or more eligible held back. Or they were restrained by family obligation and pressure which they did not feel able to defy. Conscription would have freed these people to serve willingly. Universal conscription induces consent because it guarantees equality of service. This aspect of the case was put clearly by two men, the young H. V. Evatt and William Watt, former premier of Victoria, both progressive liberals who wanted to reconcile conscription and liberty. 'Laissez-faire is dead,' wrote Evatt, 'and we are gradually giving up the idea that we can be in or out of the social order as we please.' If the people want conscription to be imposed by government, which is not a power external to themselves, then conscription would be 'a service of perfect freedom'. The people at the referendums indicated that they did not want the government to conscript, but we now know, thanks to the cliometric efforts of Glenn Withers, the contribution to the outcome of military-age males. They tended, slightly, to favour Yes. If they alone had voted – which the anti-conscriptionists said was what justice required – then possibly conscription would have been carried.

Those who elevated anti-conscription into an absolute principle, never to be broken whatever the circumstances, denied that they were depriving the state of the capacity to defend itself. A democratic state like Australia would never have difficulty in finding sufficient volunteers. During the referendum campaigns the anti-conscriptionists threw back at Hughes the statement he made early in the war that if men had to be conscripted to fight the country was not worth fighting for. The number of volunteers certainly fell away sharply in mid-1916. The anti-conscriptionists said that this was the result of the growing demands for the introduction of conscription. If that divisive issue had never been raised there would have been no slackening in the supply of volunteers. The matter is impossible to test. Given the nature of the war, *prima facie* one would expect that the volunteer rate would decline.

Conscription was proposed in Australia not to effect a full mobilisation, but to maintain the five divisions already in the field. Without conscription and with some nursing, the five divisions did remain intact, though if the war had lasted into 1919 the five would have had to have been reduced to four. This enabled the anti-conscriptionists to declare that they had been right all along: the voluntary system did not fail Australia and it never would. It is difficult to envisage it succeeding if a full-scale mobilisation was required. This is not simply because people vary in their willingness to contribute to joint efforts which benefit all, but because of the need to allocate people between military and civilian tasks. Since Australia's economy was not reshaped for war production in World War I, the appeal of conscription as an efficient allocator of resources was not strongly put. When it was used it usually related to the advantage of keeping married men at home and sending only single. In World War II when Australia did fully mobilise, conscription was used from the outset and a much higher proportion of men was recruited into the armed services than in World War I. Britain in World War I is the best test case for the view that there will be no stint in volunteering when the nation is in danger. War was near at hand and English towns had been shelled and bombed, and yet when conscription was adopted in 1916 only about half the eligible men had enlisted. This was the same proportion as in Australia when Hughes proposed to increase the rate with conscription.

The core of the Yes case was that the nation was in danger and since the voluntary system had failed conscription was the only alternative. The danger arose because the defeat of the empire would leave Australia without its protector. Hughes declared that if Britain lost the war, Australia would become a German possession. The outlying colony, sparsely populated and rich in resources, would feel the victor's vengeance more than Britain itself. This may have exaggerated the danger to Australia, but since it is now so common to assume that Australia faced no danger in World War I, it is worth quoting the sober assessments of two distinguished military and diplomatic historians on the likely result of a German victory.

W. J. Hudson wrote:

Had the German empire triumphed in Europe in 1914–18, Australia certainly would have been subjected to economic dictation, possibly to military dictation, conceivably to reallocation.

John Robertson writes:

The terms of a peace treaty might have geared Australia's economy to the needs of German industry and controlled other aspects of national policy, such as defence and immigration. Germany would certainly have resumed possession of its scattered island empire in the western and south-western Pacific and would probably have acquired Australian New Guinea as well, localities of great strategic importance to Australia. Germany would have had one of the most powerful navies in the world, and Australia's security and development would have been at its mercy. If challenged by Japan, the way would have been opened for eventual accommodation between Germany and Japan at Australia's expense.

The opponents of conscription did not query the war's significance for Australia; rather they said that Australia had already made a sufficient contribution and if every last man were conscripted it would not affect the outcome of a war in which millions of men were engaged. Answering the claim that Australia had done enough presented difficulties to the pro-conscriptionists. The instinctive response was to say that Australia could never do too much when the empire was imperilled, but this clashed with the promise that married men would never be called up and the reassurance that the country would not be denuded. It was easier for the pro-conscriptionists to explode the notion that small numbers could make no difference – the soldiers ferried out of Paris in taxis saved France in September 1914 and a handful of cooks had stemmed the breach at Ypres, and with 50,000 more Australians at the crucial moment Constantinople would have been taken.

Hughes came to believe that the calculating responses of the anti-conscriptionists to the empire's call hid a secret wish that Britain might be defeated. Sadly for him their public utterances on the outcome of the war could not be faulted for they declared that Britain was certain to win and, as one writer added, it was disloyal to suggest anything else! In support of this, they could cite the numerical superiority of the Allies, the unrelenting optimism of the censored press and the morale-boosting addresses of Allied leaders.

Was this just a debating point and the Prime Minister correct? Behind the public proclamations of the invincibility of the empire, were the anti-conscriptionists privately indifferent to its fate? I do not think so. The conservative *Argus*, fiercely pro-conscription, chided the Prime Minister for denouncing his opponents as enemies of the empire. Most of them, said the *Argus*, wanted a British victory and knew its importance for Australia; their weakness was that they believed Britain would always be ready to help Australia without Australia having to make any extraordinary effort to assist it. It does seem to me likely that those most suspicious of the British empire had most difficulty in imagining its defeat. For them Britain stood in the path of national achievement; their task was to distance themselves from this overwhelming presence. Such a cast of mind, preoccupied with the colonial relationship and its restrictions, is not likely to consider Britain as one of a number of powers and the one to be preferred as overlord no matter what the difficulties. That outlook could more readily envisage the defeat of the overlord.

The presentation of the case for conscription aroused the worst forebodings in those whose nationalism drew most strongly on anti-British feelings. Hughes usually used the language of *realpolitik*, but he sometimes and others regularly spoke of duty, gratitude and a filial relationship, all the talk that stifled a national spirit. In Britain this was matched by new declarations for imperial federation whose protago-nists assumed that dominion enthusiasm for the war indicated a new interest in closer union. In these circumstances to accept that Britain was in desperate danger appeared like an invitation to give up the nationalist enterprise. To preserve the nation Britain had to be thought of as invulnerable.

Hughes committed himself to conscription after returning from an extended visit to Britain where he had urged a more vigorous pros-ecution of the war and had been fêted in all the haunts of the estab-lishment. On this basis developed the Labor myth that the Australian nationalist and workers' friend had been corrupted in the metropolis. In return for a dukedom Hughes promised the British to introduce conscription to Australia. Actually, the closer Hughes got to the British the more he was convinced that they would neglect Australia's interest unless extraordinary pressure was put on them. During this trip he insisted on his right to speak as Australia's representative at the Allied Economic Conference in Paris and he outwitted the British bureaucracy, which was denying Australia shipping space, by buying a fleet of transports and creating a national shipping line. But once Hughes declared for conscription, in Labor eyes, he could be neither socialist nor nationalist and must be traitor to both class and nation. Hughes in turn thought of the anti-conscriptionists as traitors for not supporting to the utmost the one power which could protect Australia.

Such were the tensions imposed on a society whose great power ally was also the power against which its nationalism was asserted. The American alliance has been much less complicated and easier to maintain.

Most of the anti-British nationalists did not seriously contemplate full independence from Britain. Had they done so, they might have been, as Hughes alleged, secretly indifferent to its fate. The limitations of anti-British feeling have recently been described very well. John Rickard writes of 'Labor's historical lack of enthusiasm for the imperial connexion, expressed more in gestures than any argued alternative.' Beverley Kingston writes: 'There were plenty who did not like Britain, but they did not envisage a world in which Britain was not a powerful presence, nor British values the standard of behaviour.' Lovers fear the destruction of their beloved; haters may plot the destruction of their enemy; grumblers do not imagine a world without their grievance. Within colonial nationalism defiance degenerates rapidly to grumble because colonists do not wish to break their allegiance but renegotiate it.

The high profile anti-conscriptionist who gave the impression of not caring whether the empire won or lost was Archbishop Mannix. He was cool, detached, passionless, a witty and devastating critic who treated the war as some passing show in which other people made fools of themselves:

> Of course the imperialists will pour out their wrath upon anyone who talks of finance, while, as they say, the Empire is in danger. Next moment, they will tell us there is no danger, because England is never stronger than when she has her 'back to the wall'.

His detachment was infuriating. He gave as much offence by what he failed to say as by what he did – he did not denounce German atrocities, he did not commend the Allied cause, he did not encourage recruiting. He affected not to understand why his use of the slogan 'Australia first, the Empire second' gave offence. Of course this had been perfectly acceptable before the war, but once the empire was in real danger, to give priority to Australia looked like desertion of the empire.

Mannix did not content himself with issuing statements against conscription. He kept up a running battle with Hughes and the *Argus*, endorsed the Labor line on a wide range of issues and ended the war speaking the language of socialism. What he thought he was doing remains a puzzle. Certainly on the war and conscription he was not representing the views of Catholic people. They did not believe that the war was an 'ordinary sordid trade war' or that it was a disgrace to put on the king's uniform. They enlisted in the same proportion as other denominations until the end of the war. Nor did they show any strong tendency to vote No at the referendums. Irish Catholics adored Mannix, as Patrick O'Farrell explains, because he was a rebel, an Irishman who spoke up for his own and would not be suppressed.

Mannix gave great offence by urging that Ireland push the issue of self-government during the war when Britain was in difficulties because after the war Britain would be sure to revert to its double-dealing ways. This statement, nevertheless, assumed the empire would survive the war. Like other anti-conscriptionists, Mannix answered Hughes' claim that Australia was in danger of becoming a German possession by saying that Germany was not going to win the war. So did Mannix's detachment rest on an unexamined assumption of British invincibility? It seems so, because during the great German advance early in 1918 a new element entered his speeches: 'The Empire was never in greater danger. It badly required all the help that could be given.' With others who had said Australia had done enough and extra Australians would make no difference, he spoke of what needed to be done to boost recruiting numbers. It took German shells falling on Paris for these people to see that the wrong side might win.

For Hughes himself it is doubtful whether his greatest concern was that Britain would lose or that it would win without Australia playing a sufficient part. He had gone to Britain chiefly because he was concerned about the intentions of Japan, Britain's valuable ally in the Pacific. Already the Australian government, under pressure from Britain, had agreed that the German islands north of the equator, which had been part of German New Guinea, should pass to the Japanese. In London Hughes became fully aware of all the demands Japan was making on Britain as the price of its continuing support.

The Japanese ambassador personally presented to Hughes the Australian section of the shopping list: a commercial treaty and some relaxation of the immigration law. Hughes was prepared to consider trade relations, but the mere raising of the question of Japanese traders being admitted to Australia as residents convinced him that the Japanese had designs on the continent. 'By the time he returned to Australia,' writes L. F. Fitzhardinge, 'his latent fear of Japan had become an urgent apprehension amounting almost to an obsession.' He was now determined that Australia should play such a part in the war that at the peace it could successfully withstand Japanese demands and any British support for them. This rationale for supporting conscription was put to members of parliament in a meeting held behind closed doors. It could not be aired publicly for to bring discredit on an ally was an offence under the government's own War Precautions Act. During the campaign Hughes declared that if only he could share all he knew opposition to conscription would vanish. The anti-conscriptionists broke the confidence of the closed meeting and, defying the censorship, used Hughes' alarm about Japan's intentions to argue that every man must be kept in Australia to defend White Australia against imminent attack. To which Hughes replied, that if Britain were defeated Australia could not stand alone against the Asian masses: 'I bid you go and fight for White Australia in France.'

In his own appeals to the electors Hughes insisted that Australia must at least contribute as many men proportionately as Britain. The set of his mind was revealed very clearly on one occasion when he said this obligation would be the same even if Australia were much smaller and able to contribute much less in absolute terms. It was Hughes rather than his opponents who calculated most finely what Australia's contribution to the empire had to be. He did not carry the case further and talk of the need to go to the peace conference with a strong hand. Other pro-conscriptionists made the point on his behalf. A prime minister calling the nation to great effort and sacrifice can scarcely admit that men must fight and die not to win a war, but to give him a better bargaining position at its termination. During World War II the Curtin government kept Australian troops fighting in the islands for no strategic purpose so that Australia would be in a better position at the peace – a motive Curtin was prepared to acknowledge in the semi-public forum of a Labor Conference. Even though Hughes was rebuffed over conscription he went to Versailles in a strong position. Australian soldiers had played a conspicuous part in the final defeat of the enemy and overall more Australians had died in the war than Americans. On this basis Hughes laid claim to German New Guinea and defeated the Japanese proposal to have a declaration of racial equality inserted in the preamble to the League of Nations Charter.

At its first meeting after the Armistice the Council of the Melbourne Trades Hall, which had been the headquarters of the anti-conscription campaign, resolved to honour the Australian people who had voted No. The commemorative plaque with the numbers of No and Yes voters at the two referendums still adorns the wall inside the Trades Hall entrance. The Labor Party treasured those two moments when it carried the people with it. The victory had been won against the capitalist press, the Protestant churches, all the people who mattered, and the party's own leaders; it had been won despite the censorship and police harassment; it had been won by the efforts of ordinary men and women who had organised meetings, marches and the distribution of literature; it seemed to presage a time when the world would be transformed from below. Such a victory became more precious as Labor had few others to celebrate. Its fortunes had declined ever since it had declared against conscription and expelled its leaders. At the general election held between the two referendums Hughes and the other Labor renegades now in league with the Liberals had routed the Labor Party on a win-the-war platform. In the next twenty-five years Labor would hold office at national level only once and for a mere twenty-six months. In the wilderness Labor's attachment to anti-conscription strengthened with time and became its bond with the people and the test of true heartedness. It had become much more than a policy relating to defence.

Labor's boast was that in defeating conscription it had saved Australia from militarism. If militarism is taken to mean the subordination of civilian life to military ends, Labor's efforts were unnecessary because there is no reason to suppose that conscription for full-time service would have been continued in the peace. If militarism is taken in a weaker sense to mean the imbuing of civilian life with a martial spirit, then Labor's efforts were counter-productive. In the absence of conscription, the recruiting drum had to be beaten until the end of the war with the appeals to enlist becoming more shrill, pervasive and intrusive. Since military service had been disassociated from citizenship, the men who had volunteered to fight regarded themselves as an elite with a special claim to guide the nation and receive its homage. By opposing conscription the Labor Party gave the RSL its unique status.

The case which Labor had developed against conscription during the war made it illegitimate in all circumstances and for any purpose. When conscription is opposed for a war considered unjust, much of the case against conscription can rest on the unjustness of the war, as it did in regard to Vietnam. Since the anti-conscriptionists in 1916 and 1917 did not question the justness of the war, they had to plumb the depths and ascend the heights to find reasons against conscription. They had thus undermined Labor's policy for local defence which was compulsory training and conscription into the militia in time of war. The most fervent anti-conscriptionists wished to resolve the contradiction thus created in the simplest way – compulsion of any sort must be removed from the Defence Act. At the 1918 conference they were successfully resisted by those who argued that the party must have a credible local defence policy. Scullin, the future prime minister, declared that he had not been opposed to conscription overseas on the basis that human life was sacred (Boote's famous formulation), and that if Australia was under threat from a 'certain power' he would cheerfully conscript the manhood of Australia. At the 1919 conference the resistance crumbled as socialism, internationalism and anti-imperialism reached their zenith and the Labor Party became consistently and completely opposed to compulsion in military affairs. It was a government led by Scullin which abandoned compulsory training in 1929. Until 1940 Labor's policy for the army was to maintain a small permanent force which by law excluded infantry, to allow volunteers to train in the militia, to call on volunteers in time of war, and in no circumstances, not even on the invasion of the continent, to conscript men to fight.

As World War II progressed step by step these positions had to be abandoned. Finally Curtin as Labor Prime Minister proposed that conscription for overseas service would have to be introduced. He did so reluctantly; he was acting under great pressure from Douglas MacArthur, the American commander in the South-West Pacific, who was concerned at official and press criticisms in the United States of Australia's no-conscription policy. That was threatening his battle to get troops and supplies for his theatre.

Only with great difficulty did Curtin carry the policy for conscription in the South-West Pacific area through the Party conference and the Parliamentary Party. To placate the critics he had to abandon his intention of merging the militia and the AIF into one army and to lop large chunks off the South-West Pacific area. To the north the boundary for conscripts was to be the equator and so the Philippines, MacArthur's goal, was put beyond their reach. On the west the boundary was to be longitude 110°E which bisected Java and Borneo. Curtin's chief point in urging the change was that since the Japanese were bombing Darwin from Timor, the edge of the continent was not the boundary for the defence of Australia, but in making the change he agreed to boundaries strategically more absurd. This was a setback for the Party's strategic education but did not interfere with Curtin's purpose in proposing the change whose expected benefits were reaped while it was still only a proposal. On 19 November 1942 the *Christian Science Monitor* reported that Australia's credit had gone up sharply in Washington since the policy which had 'perplexed and disturbed' US officials was to be abandoned. In late January 1943 MacArthur rated the new policy a success even before it had received parliamentary approval. It had come just in time. He had heard that a personal assistant to the President had been about to propose that lend-lease assistance be withheld from Australia.

Curtin claimed that he was not seeking change so much as an interpretation of existing policy: the Party was agreed that the immediate defence of Australia was its priority rather than adventures in Europe but where was the boundary for the defence of Australia to be set? The purists would have none of this. The policy said unmistakably no conscription for service *overseas*. The Victorian branch of the Party, the most resolute against conscription in 1916–17 and again in 1942–43, resolved that there was no difference between the proposals of Hughes and Curtin. The anti-conscriptionists asked if the boundary were moved where would it finally come to rest. It could be said that Australia had vital interests in the Mediterranean and the Suez Canal and so a case could be made for sending conscripts there. The thin-end-of-the-wedge school was correct – it would be much more difficult to settle defence policy by thought rather than taboo.

Much of the case against conscription for overseas service as it had been developed in World War I told against conscription for any purpose. In World War II the Labor Party had accepted conscription for home defence (after a delay) and conscripts had already fought in New Guinea. The anti-conscriptionists of 1942 needed to find an argument why they should not fight in the islands adjacent or in Dutch New Guinea. Most of Curtin's opponents ignored this challenge and simply said what they had been saying for twenty-five years – that conscription was the policy of capitalists, that it denied the freedom of man's body and soul, that conscripts would be replaced by coloured labour, that it was morally offensive for those not eligible for conscription to propose it for others (now turned with particular savagery against Curtin himself), and that military conscription would lead to industrial conscription. This last point was harped on by Senator Cameron, Minister for Aircraft Production in the Curtin cabinet, which had already introduced industrial conscription and had disciplined striking coal-miners by threatening them with army service!

Of Curtin's opponents only Maurice Blackburn and Henry Boote, still editor of the *Worker* newspaper, focused clearly on the point at issue. Blackburn argued that there was a moral difference between compelling a man to fight at home and overseas. At home he was being asked to do what was instinctive – to protect his home and family – and so conscription was merely organisation. Overseas the issue was never so clear-cut and soldiers might be asked to kill not simply other soldiers, but civilians against whom they had no grievance. Conscripts for defence at home, only volunteers for offensive action overseas: this has its appeal, but would all countries agree to follow Australia and be islands and have two armies? It is amazing that someone seriously involved in shaping the defence policy of the nation should indulge in these speculations in 1942 when German conscripts were at Stalingrad,

Japanese conscripts in Timor, and American conscripts in New Guinea. But that the world should take its cue from Australia was part of the anti-conscriptionist faith. When it was put to anti-conscriptionists that they were being defended by US conscripts, Calwell replied that they had not asked the United States to send conscripts.

Boote acknowledged the difficulty of arguing against a small extension of the area in which conscripts should serve after so much military and civil compulsion had been accepted. He now saw that Labor had been in error to abandon voluntaryism, from which a democracy had no need to depart, and to accept this compulsion: 'Let it be admitted frankly and with contrite hearts ... Our patriotism got in the way of our reasoning faculties.'

Did patriotism have to be curbed to save anti-conscription? Opposition to conscription was carrying men who thought of themselves as patriots into strange paths as they grappled to hold on to a principle which they had been sure was universally valid. It carried Frank Brennan to indifference as to his country's fate. Why, he asked, should he break party tradition and support conscription?

> Is it that Australia is threatened? Surely that cannot justify ... a wrong done by one person to another.

It carried Henry Boote to urging the use of United States troops (in effect conscripts) while Australia's were kept at home:

> No-one has ever ventured to argue that Australian conscripted forces are essential to expel Japan from the Pacific. From every angle of consideration that is America's job. And America has nearly twenty times our man-power, and more than thirty times our resources.

It led Blackburn to prefer the Japanese Co-Prosperity Sphere to the American plan to roll it back from Australia:

> Our greatest danger comes from the fact that Australia is the base for American offensive operations against Japan. If it were not for the fact that Australia is the base from which America will strike at Japan,

Japan would be consolidating the empire it has acquired. It has to be ready to attack Australia because Australian men and materials may be sent out against it.

It might seem merely prurient to follow the case against Curtin's proposal into its ugly death throes, but these are not the views of a discredited minority because after the war Labor's traditional policy of no conscription for overseas service was automatically reinstated. Japan's demonstration that Labor had chosen the wrong boundary for Australia's defence was taken to be not conclusive. Blackburn is remembered in the Labor Party not as a pathetic figure who lost his bearings over conscription in the changed circumstances of World War II, but as a man who did well to stick to his principles till the end. He is a model for all those who believe that the world would have been transformed if Labor politicians had only been true to the Labor platform. His biographers contrast him with Curtin to the latter's disadvantage. Blackburn was the upholder of principle whereas Curtin was 'concerned only with Australia's safety'. *Only* with Australia's safety! These admirers are true to the purity and unworldliness of the no-conscription principle which must rank as one of the strongest and most damaging faiths held in this country.

1994

The Gallipoli Landing

The history of the colonial psyche is the struggle to manage the disdain of the metropolis. For Australians this was particularly difficult because of their convict origins. As was common in that era, they believed in blood and breeding even though those concepts called so firmly into question their own physical and moral capacity. When the Australian troops fought so magnificently in the tangle of hills and gullies at Gallipoli – and when all the world acknowledged it – there was an almost palpable settling of the national mind. Not everything was resolved of course, but the greatest uncertainty, that Australia would be tried and found wanting, that the worst suspicions of the metropolis would be confirmed, was now behind them. Australians said that they became a nation at Gallipoli and this was because the greatest obstacle to their feeling themselves to be such had suddenly been removed.

One of the recent 'advances' in scholarship is the questioning of Australian military prowess at Gallipoli. This occurred in stages. At first scholars, noting the enormous impact of the news of the Gallipoli fighting in Australia, began to examine the news carriers. These were firstly Ashmead-Bartlett, a British war correspondent, and then Charles Bean, the Australian correspondent, who both wrote of the landing in glowing terms. The assumption behind these studies was that the reporting was almost more significant than the fighting, for if the reporters had not been present (and they were not always so close to the fighting during the war) the event would not have had such an impact in Australia. Then the students of myth, language and text took up the issue. For them what actually happened is even less important. Reality is not events themselves but the talk about them. Whether Australians were good fighters or not became increasingly a matter of indifference; it may indeed be a matter on which knowledge cannot and should not be sought. But in military affairs above all reality will keep breaking in. Either this line of soldiers is advancing or that one is; or in the case of Anzac, the Australians are either digging in and holding on or they are being thrown into the sea.

Nothing better demonstrates the fatuousness of much of today's social science than that the study of the fighting capacity of Australian troops has become the province of literary critics, semioticians and linguists. They have produced a whole series of articles and a full length book, *Big-Noting: the Heroic Theme in Australian War Writing*, by Robin Gerster. One of the chief objects of their attention has been Bean's *Official History of Australia in the War of 1914–1918*. This makes large claims for the fighting capacity of Australian troops which are ascribed in the final analysis to the open, democratic nature of Australian society. Bean's work was notable for being uncensored, for its treatment of the hesitation, confusion and cowardice of troops as well as of their bravery, and its determination to depict operations from the perspective of the man in the front line rather than of the general at headquarters. It is a magnificent work, never fully acknowledged at the time of its publication, and resurrected recently through the efforts of Ken Inglis at the Australian National University who saw its virtues so clearly. Its honesty, subtlety and grandeur have been proof against the attempts of these modern critics to 'deconstruct' it.

Here are two examples of their work:

Bean's Digger is not merely laconic and relaxed; when roused he is also extremely dangerous … Here in terse blow-by-blow detail, he commemorates the courage of a junior officer at Villers-Bretonneux: 'Captain Sayers leapt among three of the enemy in a shell hole; he hit one of them on the head with the man's own steel helmet, strangled the second, and the third escaped.' Bean's strategy for the promotion of the Australian warrior depends upon the cumulative effect of such incidents. Sensibly, he tries to avoid big-noting of the overt kind,

> cunningly framing his heroic boasts in the form of the accolades of
> foreigners, whose words of praise often appear in footnotes to the
> main text. – Robin Gerster in *Big-Noting*

Cunningly? If foreign observers had been critical of Australian
troops, it would have been cunning of Bean, to say no more, to hide
their comments in footnotes. Their praise appears to me *prima facie*
good evidence that Australian troops were in fact outstanding and is
properly cited to support such claims. (The objection, one suspects,
is not to the misuse of this evidence, but to its existence.)

> Bean's *History* is also relatively frank about Australians running away
> during battles. At various points in the account of Gallipoli landing
> Bean described weary, half dazed and confused men running back
> from the enemy, or straggling in the gullies. Yet despite this frank-
> ness, Bean once again used value-laden language which defined the
> incidents as not too serious, not typical of the Australian soldier or
> the force generally, or at worst the inevitable consequence of strain.
> – Alistair Thomson in *Australian Historical Studies*

What should Bean have done? Made these incidents the centrepiece
of his account? – which would have been appropriate perhaps if the
Australians had been routed at the Anzac Cove landing. It happens
that, though under fire while defenceless in open rowing boats, though
having to wade ashore, though lacking the direction of officers, though
facing unknown and unexpected cliffs, though under constant fire, the
Australians did dislodge the Turks and establish a beach-head.

John Robertson, an old-fashioned military historian rather than a
textual critic, assesses this achievement in his recent book *Anzac and
Empire*. He makes comparisons with other landings. By World War II,
specialised landing craft had been developed, flat-bottomed to come
close to shore, steel-walled to protect the troops from enemy fire, and
delivering them almost dry-shod as the front wall swung down as a
ramp. Even the British reinforcements landing at Gallipoli in August
1915 were brought ashore in self-propelled steel-plated barges, a fore-
runner of later landing craft. In the Falklands War of 1982, British

troops landed unopposed in daylight on East Falkland Island. They had good maps and were put ashore in the right spot. Even so, the landing turned into a shambles with units mixed up. It took some time for the brigade to sort itself out before moving inland. The Australians at Anzac faced the difficulty of being mixed up in addition to all the others. One reason it deterred these soldiers so little was that they had so recently been inducted; fighting was for them a novelty, to fight without officers was nothing. Overall, concludes Robertson, the landing was 'an ordeal that has never been imposed on any other substantial body of Australian troops'.

Assessing the fighting capacities of troops is a routine business for military professionals, just as they assess weaponry and the lie of the land. They do not believe that troops are more or less the same or that there is no rational basis for comparing them. When the British Prime Minister was told by the military that they planned to use Australians at Gallipoli he asked, naturally enough, whether they were good enough for it. From several quarters he received advice that they looked very promising. Robertson is meticulous in reporting these professional assessments of the Australians and the many more that were made after the landing. A British staff officer who had seen the Australians storming their way up the hills, went ashore after the landing and reported: 'it seemed almost incredible that any troops could have done it ... How they got up fully armed and equipped over the rough, scrub clad hillsides one can hardly imagine.' By a score or more of these professional assessments, Robertson destroys the nonsense that it was only journalistic hype which made the Australians into good soldiers. But the attachment to text and word is the fashion and Robertson's book will probably make no impression on those whose pleasure it is to be agnostic about the fighting record of our soldiers. What would change them? If we lifted them from their books and told them that they had to fight a battle with the choice of commanding either an Australian or an Italian battalion? Or what if our country were in danger? Perhaps only then would they abandon their games and be prepared to accept that our soldiers have a deserved reputation for valour and resource.

1990

The Communist Threat

There is a profound ambiguity in the treatment of communism by left historians of Australia. In their writings on the Communist Party and old communists, they treat them respectfully, if not reverentially. However, when discussing the movements to counter or suppress the Communist Party they declare there was nothing there! – the party was tiny and without real influence; those who opposed it were alarmist, paranoid or kicking the communist can for electoral purposes. Why is it that they are allowed to take the communists seriously and the opponents of communist are derided for doing so? They warm to the communists for their thoroughgoing radicalism and yet are surprised that they provoked a savage response. What do they expect? Agreement? Silence?

At first this ambiguity appears to be absent from Andrew Moore's study of the Old Guard and its predecessors, the secret armies organised in New South Wales in the 1920s and 1930s to counter the communist menace (*The Secret Army and the Premier*). Dr Moore is a serious historian whose sleuthing has given us the first full and reliable account of these shadowy organisations. Although he has no sympathy at all for the Old Guard, he is concerned to understand the world as they saw it. He reports that they were men of integrity who genuinely feared a communist revolution. They discussed it in their private letters and not just to alarm the public. Dr Moore is also an orthodox Marxist for whom the possessors of wealth are automatically 'the ruling class'. Since the communists were planning to appropriate private wealth and end class rule, it was perfectly understandable that the leaders of

Sydney's business world should fight back with organisations like the Old Guard. The '20s and '30s were also, as he reports, a tempestuous time in New South Wales politics when to fear a breakdown in civil order was not altogether fanciful. Yet, despite all this, Dr Moore encourages the common view that the response to communism was exaggerated, an over-reaction touched by paranoia.

This may well have been so. For readers to judge how far it was so, they need to know something of the operation of communists in New South Wales in the 1920s and early 1930s. On this matter Dr Moore is mostly silent. He informs us of communism indirectly through the fears of its opponents, his procedure being to cite their attacks on communists and invite his readers to see them as absurd. It was absurd, no doubt, for anti-communists to denounce communists as 'unkempt, unwashed, unclean', a parallel to the left's depiction of capitalists as obscenely bloated figures in top hats. But was it absurd for anti-communists to claim that communists took their orders from Moscow, were cunning and unscrupulous, exercised great influence over the labour movement, and were planning a revolution? To answer that we should at least be told the following:

1. With encouragement from the Bolshevik Consul, a communist party was formed in Sydney in 1920. In 1922 it was officially recognised by the Comintern, based in Moscow, as the Communist Party of Australia (section of the Communist International).

2. The leader of the Communist Party was Jock Garden, who was secretary of the Trades and Labour Council, the chief executive, that is, of the peak council of the trade union movement. Nearly all the other members of the Council executive followed their leader and became communists. The Labour Council affiliated itself to the Red International of Labour Unions. In 1922 Garden visited Moscow where he met Lenin and announced that communists would come to power in Australia through controlling Labour Councils (as he did Sydney's) and through them the trade unions. In the annual report of the Labour Council in 1924 Garden proclaimed:

> Every day the Communist issue in politics becomes more and more the main issue. The shadow of Communism is over the

Labour movement. All efforts to banish Communism and the Communists are bound to fail. The good old times of playing at politics are gone. Revolution has stepped upon the stage.

3. In the early 1920s the commitment within the labour movement to socialism as an immediate goal was stronger than it has ever been before or since. The socialisation of production, distribution and exchange was adopted as the Labor Party's objective in 1921. Since communists shared the same goal, it was difficult for socialists within the Labor Party to regard them as the enemy, especially since they half feared that parliamentary action would not bring the millennium. There was hence a great deal of sympathy for the communists, which they were very ready to exploit. In 1923 the New South Wales Labor Party Conference, on the motion of Jock Garden, granted affiliation to the Communist Party. The following year this was revoked on a vote of 160 to 104, the size of the minority indicating that the issue was far from being settled.

4. From 1929, following a new policy directive from Moscow, the Communist Party ceased to work within the Labor Party and instead set up 'front' organisations, that is, bodies devoted to some particular cause with broad support which the communists would control by tight organisation and hiding their true purposes. The most success-ful of these 'fronts' were the Militant Minority Movement, which worked in the trade unions with the aim of creating a revolutionary situation through a general strike, and the Unemployed Workers' Movement, which claimed a membership of 68,000 in 1934.

5. The parliamentary leader of the Labor Party from 1923 was Jack Lang, who had little sympathy for socialism and was a fierce anti-communist, but nevertheless attracted the support of the left in the extra-parliamentary party by a seemingly determined attempt to abolish the Legislative Council. At first the left thought it had found a parliamentary leader who meant business. To secure his place he was voted parliamentary leader by the Conference and given extraordinary powers to control the party. Lang needed this extra-parliamentary support because his parliamentary colleagues, who normally elect the leader, were deeply dissatisfied with him. One of

the machine men working to keep Lang in office was Jock Garden, who had now left the Communist Party. During Lang's second premiership from 1930, which coincided with the onset of the Depression, he was increasingly reckless and demagogic, and the extra-parliamentary organisation became more insistent that socialism must be the immediate goal of the party. A minority of socialists within the party openly urged revolution and the dictatorship of the proletariat.

*

There were thus good grounds for the claims made about communists which Dr Moore invites his readers to pass over with a smile. The communists as yet had no deep penetration into the unions, but they clearly had some purchase there. To have captured the Trades and Labour Council was an outstanding and, for their opponents, a very disturbing success. Some unions, unhappy with this leadership, disaffiliated from the Council, but the big unions remained.

In the battle for the control of the Labor Party, particularly complex and vicious at this time, the communists and their sympathisers were significant players. The ultimate outcome, of course, could not be known. Nor could an outside observer know whether Lang was in charge of his party or whether he had become hostage to the increasingly militant socialists within it.

There was plenty of alarm within the Labor Party at the extent of communist influence. Here is the young Dr Evatt, campaigning as an independent Labor candidate for Balmain in 1927 after having his official pre-selection revoked by the communist-backed executive:

The great Australian labour movement is seriously menaced by a small but determined body of men lacking in moral or religious scruple, who are gradually filling many of the key position in the ALP. It is no answer to contend, as has been plausibly done, that the actual number of open and avowed Communists is small. That is perfectly true, but beside the point. At the last state elections the Communist party had to fight in the open against Australian Labor candidates, and its nominees were overwhelmingly defeated, as witness my own electorate of Balmain, where I myself polled 60 votes to every one recorded for the Communist candidate. Defeated in open contest these men resolved to seize control of the ALP by the less honorable but more effective method of organisation from within. Already their success has surprised themselves, and demonstrated the truth of Lenin's saying, 'that a small minority, if sufficiently unscrupulous and persistent, can capture most political parties' ... The situation may not be so clear in the other electorates, but the issue is perfectly clear in Balmain. It is this – whether the labour movement is to remain Australian in spirit and ideals, or whether it is to be secretly controlled by a Communist minority who are out to degrade, disintegrate, and destroy the labour movement of Australia.

On all sides, belief in the stability of society had been eroded by the Bolshevik success in Russia in 1917. The fact that a tiny group operating in the capital had seized a whole nation made communists everywhere sanguine and their opponents wary. The Old Guard never feared that large numbers of Australians would be won over to communism; its plans were devoted to ensuring that if there was a breakdown in civil order, however caused, communists should not have the chance to take advantage of it as they had done in Russia. Its task would be as much to maintain essential services as to attack communists directly. The fact that the communists were few, which the historians retrospectively inform anti-communists was reassuring, was not the point. It might have been more reassuring if the communists had organised openly on their own behalf and left other organisations alone. It was their failure to do this which led them to be judged cunning and unscrupulous. For the communists themselves, small numbers were not deterring. Lenin, after all, had counselled a small, tightly knit party and Marxist theory predicted crises and collapse in capitalism, which would give communists their chance. The hopes of communists and the fears of anti-communists were perfectly matched.

*

To plan a private military operation to protect liberal democracy may threaten the object that is to be saved. The leaders of the Old Guard were very well aware of this. They insisted that their movement was purely defensive – they would not stir unless there was a breakdown in civil order and/or an attempt at revolution; they hoped the civil power would not need their aid; they would act only in support of the constituted authorities. As Dr Moore justly notes, though they felt the impatience with liberal democracy which could lead on to fascism, they were moved more by what he calls an Anglo-Australian conservatism: an attachment to the British empire as a world-civilising force, to the monarch and parliamentary institutions with (though Dr Moore does not say this) the rights and liberties they guaranteed. The Old Guard had no novel agenda of its own to impose and in this was unlike that other anti-communist organisation, B. A. Santamaria's Movement.

The Old Guard considered all loyal citizens could support its aims and planned to enrol them 'irrespective of creed, party, social or financial position'. In Sydney the membership was small and from the elite; in the country, however, it was widespread ranging from pastoralists through small-town businessmen and tradesmen, to rural workers. The RSL club rooms were important recruiting grounds and a nucleus of organisation. These people were organised in a military hierarchy by district. Altogether there were 25,000 members in the country with substantial representation from every region and town, as compared with 5000 in Sydney. In the country the organisation was sometimes known simply as 'The Country' and it embodied in a new form the old determination that Sydney should not rule New South Wales.

The Old Guard must be distinguished from the much better known New Guard which secured its place in history when one of its members spectacularly up-staged Premier Lang at the opening of the Sydney Harbour Bridge. The New Guard was a movement of young turks, second echelon businessmen who rejected the Old Guard's purely defensive stance. They took the offensive, organised openly, paraded in public, broke up communist meetings and claimed the right to eject Lang from office. Its leader, Eric Campbell, was a fascist. The New Guard had a large membership in Sydney, but very few in the country. Dr Moore rates its military capacity as very low compared to the Old Guard which was a formidable force. The Old Guard was dismayed at the growth of this offspring, fearing that it would create the disorder which the communists could exploit.

*

The existence of two rival private armies leads Dr Moore to ponder whether our democratic history has been as quiet and untroubled as sometimes it is depicted. To strengthen this theme he makes a half-hearted attempt to show that the possessing classes in Australia have always over-reacted to working-class movements and denied their legitimacy. Of course the reverse is true. There was no social environment more conducive to the growth of working-class institutions than Australia in the late nineteenth and early twentieth centuries. The trade unions had legal protection and widespread community support, including frequently that of employers. Once the arbitration system was established (1904) they were fostered and protected by an organ of the state. The Labor Party won control of the national parliament as early as 1910.

If workers are liable to be sacked, bashed or shot if they form a union and yet unions are still formed, we have truly repressive owners and determined workers – and the very weak union movement of the United States. Given that employment relations under capitalism are so unequal, if unions become stable and widespread, this is *prima facie* evidence that employers are being restrained by society at large or are restraining themselves.

Certainly when working-class organisations began to be formidable, employers began to oppose them – in response to co-ordinated bodies of trade unions they formed employers' associations; in response to the Labor Party they attempted, for a long time unsuccessfully, to form a mass-based party to oppose it. It was only from 1917–18, as Dr Moore's researches make clear, that they began to dabble in paramilitary organisations, that is from the time syndicalists were threatening to dispossess capitalists through a general strike, and communists by revolution.

*

Why the resistance to communism should take the form of an unofficial militia is not a question which interests Dr Moore. For him the operation of liberal capitalist states are all alike and possess no mysteries. The owners of the means of production are quite simply the ruling class. One might have thought that if this is so, a word or two might have been given to explain why periodically the government of New South Wales was in the hands of the party organised by the working class, which in 1930–32 was led by a premier who was proposing to replace the currency with a device of his own and was refusing to pay interest on the overseas debt. Is Dr Moore suggesting that who controls the state is of no consequence or perhaps that Jack Lang was, according to the Marxist formula, actually the chairman of a committee running the affairs of the bourgeoisie?

The fact that the anti-communist militia was unofficial indicates how far the possessing class was from being a ruling class. From the time of the introduction of democracy to New South Wales in the mid-nineteenth century, men of wealth had found it difficult to get seats in the Legislative Assembly and increasingly had less desire to be associated with the rowdy low-bred fellows who composed it. With the formation of parties around the turn of the century, they were more closely associated with the organisation of the parties opposed to Labor, but still not very likely actually to hold a seat in the House. The colonial parliament, unlike the British, was not a gathering of the elite.

In the United Kingdom the body developed after World War I to cope with civil disorder and any attempt at revolution was the Supply and Transport Organisation, which drew on volunteer labour, but was organised officially and secretly by the British Cabinet and placed under the Ministry of Transport. It was used in the railway strike of 1919, the miners' strike of 1921 and the general strike of 1926. Dr Moore argues with some reason that this body was the model for the paramilitary organisations formed or proposed in Australia in the 1920s and of the Old Guard. However, he does not consider why in New South Wales the organisation was *unofficial*. What reasons can be suggested for this difference? That in New South Wales there was not a single governing class, surviving the changes of the party in office, ready to act against a militant working class; and the owners of wealth, rarely participating directly in government, felt they could only exercise control if they now took matters into their own hands. In short, there was no reliable political and military establishment. Having no institutional buttresses, the wealthy had to look for support to the volunteer efforts of those citizens they could persuade to join them. To be effective, especially in the country, they had to practise no social exclusion and press no agenda of their own.

Dr Moore considers the Old Guard an indication of the ongoing power of what he calls the ruling class; it more clearly demonstrates their comparative weakness. They had the power to defend the existing liberal democracy – but that's what nearly everyone else wanted. The width and depth of Old Guard membership in the country is one of the conclusions of his study which Dr Moore highlights. He does not see this popularity in any way threatening his claim that the Old Guard was a 'ruling class' organisation. According to him, those members outside the ranks of the ruling class did not realise where their true class interests lay!

The Old Guard in its composition and purpose was similar to the National Guard of the states in the United States. Had the Australian democracy had this form of protection, there would almost certainly not have been private armies. The polity of the Australian states was a hybrid: British in form but without an establishment; democratic in essence but without a regularised popular force at its command. One can understand why the state appeared vulnerable.

*

Like all good scholarly history, Dr Moore's work can be drawn upon by those who do not share its author's world view – as I have done here. Indeed, Dr Moore's scholarship is in danger of getting the better of his ideology. The more he uncovers of the Old Guard's operations, the less dangerous and disturbing it seems. Every working paper he cites reveals a cautious, level-headed, unalarmist organisation. The secrets of the Old Guard turn out not to be shameful secrets. Consider the instruction that went out to members in its last days. As the Lang government struggled to stave off bankruptcy, the Old Guard detected the shape of the crisis it had long expected – the massive numbers of the unemployed, deprived of their government dole, would riot or become an effective force under communist leadership. The orders for mobilisations were therefore revised – everyone should not only have a rifle at the ready but set aside money to feed the unemployed.

In his final chapter Dr Moore goes to great length in an attempt to demonstrate that Governor Game in dismissing Premier Lang was acting under orders from the Dominions Office in London. There is absolutely no evidence to support this; all the evidence he cites points in the opposite direction. Dr Moore has the odd idea that a British-appointed governor of a state with responsible government was the representative of 'British interests'. Governor Game in fact followed the British constitutional tradition of the Head of State supporting his government while it had a majority in the House. To the outrage of the Sydney bourgeoisie, he agreed to the creation of extra members for the nominated upper house to improve the government's chance of controlling it – and this while Lang was repudiating the British debt.

Governor Game dismissed Lang when he was refusing to comply with federal law that he pay the federal government the amounts it was paying to British bond holders on his behalf. Lang had challenged the law in the High Court, which had upheld it. He had withdrawn the state funds from the banks and to keep them out of the clutch of the Commonwealth stored them in the Treasury, guarded by members of the Timber Workers' Union. How was the Commonwealth government to get him to pay if he and state taxation and treasury officials refused to comply? Dr Moore has one doubtful piece of evidence, which he uses with due caution, indicating that the Commonwealth was contemplating enrolling members of the Old Guard as special peace officers to storm the state taxation offices. No doubt Dr Moore is correct – force of some sort would have been needed if Lang and his officers had stood firm. The Governor's dismissal of Lang made it unnecessary. The oddest thing in the book is Dr Moore's judgment on this possible use of force by the Commonwealth government to uphold the law – 'the real threat to "law and order" emanated from Australia's most respectable address: "The Lodge", Canberra'.

Dr Moore always puts law and order in quotation marks to indicate that the term does not have his endorsement. He has no respect for liberal democracy. He announces he will not berate the Old Guard for endangering it by organising a private army, for liberal democracy is simply a system of class rule. His own position appears to be that the working class would have benefited from a communist take-over in the 1930s.

This is an unusual position. On the left now the more common view is that the Communist Party's ideology and methods were totally inappropriate for the Australian democracy – and yet they still berate the past opponents of Australian communism. Donald Horne was one of the victims of this. Firmly progressive, he once reported that he was still regarded with suspicion because he was anti-communist in the 1950s. And yet, he lamented, he was only saying then about the communists what his left friends were saying now. It's wisdom after the event that is honoured.

The position of those who still complain about the strength of the anti-communist campaign seems to be this: communism had no prospect of success in Australia, the response was out of all proportion to the threat. A steamroller was being used to crack a nut. Such a view misunderstands the dynamics of the body we're discussing – an open, democratic society. If an organised group of people assume positions of prominence and influence, which the trade unions and the Labor Party allowed the communists to do, and proclaim that they aim to overthrow the existing form of society; if they tell a Christian people that in the new order there will be no religion; if they tell the large number of property-holders there will be no private property; if they offer the dictatorship of the proletariat in place of cherished human rights; if they tell the party of reform they will control or supplant it in the cause of the revolution – then there will be outrage, denunciation, clamour, virulence and counter organisation. This strong feeling, like all others, will be enhanced and exploited for a variety of purposes, like selling newspapers or winning elections. This is how society demonstrates that what is being offered is totally inappropriate to its needs – which is what the left now acknowledges communism was. There is no other way. Free societies are expressive bodies. Because they are open-ended, no-one can speak with full authority on their behalf; they have to make their own declarations. Because a threatening opinion cannot be silenced, it must be shouted down. There may even be some hysteria and paranoia. If you want quiet, measured, economical treatment of unwelcome opinion, choose a society with a well-developed apparatus of repression. If you want a society where there is not only freedom of expression, but a calm and rational assessment of all views, try a debating club.

The left historians cannot put out of their minds the vision of social justice which communism offered and the decency and dedication of individual communists. They also have to face the fact that the vision and decency were vitiated by the madcap scheme, sold in Moscow as scientific, of reaching justice and equality through violence and terror. So far, from that tension we are getting only tortured apologetics. The tragedy still awaits its historian.

1990

Who Tugged the Forelock?

isten to an Australian prime minister speaking in London at the heart of the British empire. His audience has been brought together by the Empire Parliamentary Association; the location is the Houses of Parliament, Westminster.

The prime minister says:

> We are a British community in the South Seas, and we regard ourselves as the trustees for the British way of life in a part of the world where it is of the utmost significance to the British Commonwealth and to the British nation and to the British Empire – call it by any name that you will – that there should be in the Antipodes a people and a territory corresponding in purpose and in outlook and in race to the Motherland itself.

Who is the speaker? You might think it was Robert Menzies. The sentiment could well be his, but it was not Menzies. Nine years before, Menzies spoke to the same association in the same place when he introduced himself as a proud son of the British race and took as his theme the origins of British freedom and parliamentary government and their spread around the globe. That was in 1935. Menzies was then Australia's attorney-general and his speech to the Empire Parliamentary Association was the high point of his first ecstatic visit to the mother country.

The sentiment could well be Menzies', but in fact, the speaker was John Curtin. The year was 1944. Yes, this was the same John Curtin who in 1941 turned to the United States, free, as he said, of any pangs as to our traditional links or kinship with the United Kingdom. Two years later Curtin was worried about the claims America was staking in the South Pacific. To counter these, Curtin wanted Britain to increase its participation in the war against Japan. That was one of his preoccupations when he was in London in 1944 and spoke those words. His chief business in London was the Commonwealth Prime Minister's Conference.

At the conference Curtin proposed that in order for the empire to act more effectively between conferences a secretariat should be established. The Australian view was that the empire needed greater coherence and organisation. This was also the policy of the Australian Labor Party, for Curtin, careful as always to carry his party with him, had organised for the Labor Conference to endorse his proposal before he left for London. When Menzies became prime minister again in 1949 he too suggested the formation of a Commonwealth secretariat. Neither Curtin nor Menzies had any success with his plan. Britain had some misgivings, and Canada had more. It did not want the Commonwealth to draw more closely together and its opposition killed the scheme.

Watching Curtin and Menzies mirroring each other on the British race in Australia, and on Australia in the British empire, reminds us how difficult it is to identify one party in Australia as an opponent of empire and one as its supporter. To imply, as the present prime minister, Paul Keating, has done, that it is only his opponents and their predecessors who supported the British connection is a gross distortion.

Consider the following:

1. At the outbreak of World War I it was a Labor prime minister, Andrew Fisher, who said that Australia would stand by Britain to its last man and its last shilling.
2. At the end of World War II, as we have seen, Curtin was desperate to bring the British empire back into the Pacific. To symbolise this bond with Britain he appointed the King's brother, the Duke of Gloucester, as governor-general. It is not generally acknowledged that it was a Labor prime minister who put a royal in Yarralumla.
3. Chifley, Curtin's successor, found it hard to adjust to the new name which the empire acquired when its dominions became sovereign

states – the British Empire and Commonwealth. For him it remained simply the British empire and he co-operated closely with Britain in economic and defence matters in the difficult postwar years.

4. For Evatt it had to be the British Commonwealth, for independence and equality of the dominions were vital. As foreign minister, he worked for the Commonwealth to become a third force in world affairs and he offered the maximum co-operation of Australia in the development of the British atomic bomb.

5. Arthur Calwell, the next Labor leader, had no great love for the empire-Commonwealth, but as minister for immigration he had reassured Australians that for every foreigner brought here he'd bring ten Britishers.

Now it is true that none of these Labor leaders was subservient to Britain; they did not tug the forelock. Though they accepted Australia as part of the British empire-Commonwealth, they had a lively sense of Australia's separate interests. But so did leaders on the non-Labor side of politics. To claim that the supporters of the British empire in Australia were tugging the forelock to Britain is the second of the Prime Minister's distortions.

*

Over the last forty years the changes in Britain and Australia and in the relationship between them have been so great that anyone under fifty needs a historian to explain why the British empire exercised such a hold over Australians. You are doubly fortunate – you have before you not only a historian but someone over fifty. When I was at primary school we proclaimed every Monday morning: I am an Australian; I love my country the British empire. How could we say both those things and mean both? That's the world we have lost and which I will now try to conjure back. I'm a historian and over fifty; I'm also a republican. You might think this a disqualification.

Multiculturalism is one barrier to our understanding of our British past. Let me say at once that I welcome multicultural Australia, wonderfully diverse, vital and tolerant. My quarrel is with the ideologues of multiculturalism, the multiculturalists, who are, by the way, not usually migrants. Multiculturalists are developing a history of Australia which characterises British Australia, Australia before the great postwar migration, as a long dark age. The people of these times are sneered at for being British; they are mocked when they worry that their way of life will be disturbed by mass migration of foreigners. Their desire to honour and preserve their tradition is wicked; on the other hand, the migrants' desire to preserve *their* culture is elevated into a right. This approach is carried to an absurdity in Al Grassby's recent book, *The Australian Republic*. He sets out to explain why the republic has been so long delayed, that is, why migrants from Britain did not declare themselves to be Australians and republicans immediately on disembarking from the boats. Having set himself a stupid question, he comes up with an absurd answer. They were tricked and bluffed and bribed into staying British by the imperialists in Britain and their stooges in Australia. It never occurs to this high priest of multiculturalism that migrants from Britain remained British for the same reason as Italian migrants remain Italian – for some time at least they couldn't be anything else and in strange circumstances they naturally held fast to known ways.

If an Englishman plants an oak tree in Australia he is a pathetic colonial unresponsive to his new environment; if an Italian migrant plants an olive tree he is making a valuable contribution to multicultural Australia. This is the position to which we are being led by the more extreme multiculturalists. It represents a lack of imagination and a gross prejudice totally at odds with the ideals of multiculturalism.

Another barrier to the understanding of our British past is the common view that our military history consists largely in fighting other people's wars. World War I, in which 60,000 Australians died, is considered not to have been our business. Of course Australia did have an interest in the outcome of that war. Britain was Australia's protector; Australia wanted to ensure a British victory and a continuing British commitment to defending Australia. There is a naive view abroad that the effects of war diminish with distance from the battlefields. In fact, when the great powers fight, the whole world, near and far, is affected by the outcome. How often were remote colonies bargaining chips at European peace conferences! So let us not hear from Prime Minister

Keating and others that the Australians on the Kokoda Track in 1942 were defending Australia and that the Australians fighting in France in 1916–18 were doing something else.

And yet when we look at the wild enthusiasm for Britain on the outbreak of war, we don't seem to be seeing a nation carefully calculating where its interests lay. This is because the calculation had been done some time before. In the middle years of the nineteenth century there was a general expectation that Australia would quickly be so strong that it would have no need of Britain; some reputable opinion-makers argued that Australia was already handicapped by the British connection because it could be dragged into British wars whose outcome could not affect Australia. All this changed from the late nineteenth century. Firstly, two of the European great powers, France and Germany, appeared in the Pacific and laid claims to islands in our region. Then Japan emerged as a great power, beating China in 1895 and Russia in 1905. Australia's prospects no longer looked so rosy. This was not to be a region isolated from great power conflict where we could look after ourselves. We faced potential enemies whose power was much superior to our own. Australia now had greater need of British protection.

*

We will understand loyalty to the empire better if we don't draw a fine line between sentiment and self-interest. The sentiment was stronger because self-interest was being served. Part of the sentimental attachment to Britain was that it was top dog in the world, the ruler of the waves, a matter very important to Australia, whose enemies would have to come by sea. Another ground for sentimental attachment to Britain was that it was an enlightened imperial power, allowing the colonies where British people had settled self-government. A second-rate imperial power which denied self-government would never have elicited the same enthusiasm.

Nor should we draw a firm line between Australia and Britain. Australians were not giving loyalty to another country, still less a foreign country, as Britain is sometimes now described; their loyalty was to Britain and its empire of which they were a part. They were Australian Britons whose country was Australia and the British empire.

This double loyalty is indeed an unusual phenomenon; and it is so because empires are not usually as enlightened as the British empire. When this loyalty is fully understood its oddity diminishes; in being loyal to the empire Australians were being loyal to themselves.

Not that there were not difficulties and ambiguities in the relationship. Australians spent a lot of effort to ensure that the empire to which they were loyal did not harm their interests and positively advanced them. There is little popular understanding of this aspect of the relationship. The cheering crowds and the troopships sailing away: these public events captured on film and constantly reshown suggest a mindless loyalty. The quieter battles within the empire now go unnoticed. Consider the activities of that very loyal subject of the empire, Sir Robert Menzies.

When Menzies became prime minister in 1939 Australia had the right to conduct its own defence and foreign policies. This had been conceded by Britain in the Statute of Westminster in 1931. However, Australian governments did not want to exercise this freedom. The dominions which had pressed for it, Canada and South Africa, were not as strategically vulnerable as Australia. Australian governments, needing Britain much more, wanted to co-operate with it in defence and take a part in the development of an imperial foreign policy. At the wish of Australia, the Statute of Westminster was not to apply here until the Australian parliament had adopted it.

Menzies signified this desire for unity in his declaration of war in 1939: 'It is my melancholy duty to inform you officially that, in consequence of a persistence by Germany in her invasion of Poland, Great Britain has declared war upon her, and that, as a result, Australia is also at war.' This is another public event; we can still hear the voice, and it speaks to the modern generation of Australia's abject status and of Menzies' grovelling to Britain. Great Britain is at war. Result: Australia is at war. This is tugging the forelock with a vengeance. But what follows?

Despite being under pressure from Britain and from within Australia to commit troops for service overseas, Menzies refuses. He explains that the situation is not the same as in 1914. Australia may be in direct danger from Japan. He will not release troops until he has an appraisal of Japan's likely intentions and a reassurance from Britain on its readiness to send a fleet to Singapore if Japan were to move south. Then there is the matter of finding the ships to send men overseas. Shipping is in short supply and Australia must use some of it to get its wheat and wool to England. Britain suddenly finds extra shipping and offers a deal on wheat and wool. Menzies still hesitates; he has Britain's assurance about a fleet for Singapore, but is it right about Japan's lack of interest in a southward move? Then his hand is forced. New Zealand decides to send troops to the Middle East. Australia can not do less.

Menzies' policy after all was co-operation with the empire, but he was annoyed at the excessive loyalty of the New Zealanders and the ready assumption in Britain that Australia would fall into line. This is the man who is sometimes depicted as being unable to distinguish between Australia's interests and Britain's.

While Australia was pursuing its interests within the empire, Britain of course was doing the same. From the late nineteenth century Britain lost its easy pre-eminence among the great powers; it needed the armed support which its dominions could offer. At various stages Britain wanted the dominions to build naval vessels for British fleets and to guarantee to send soldiers in the event of war. The dominions refused. They would give support but not on those terms.

Britain always had to weigh the interests of its empire against its desire to preserve peace with its European neighbours. Sometimes Australia seemed to want Britain to go to war with France or Germany to stop their territorial ambitions in the Pacific. Australians were angry and disappointed that the Germans gained a part of New Guinea and that France established itself in the New Hebrides.

In economic affairs there was a broad harmony of interests between Britain and Australia. Britain took Australia's agricultural products and Australia took Britain's manufactured goods. In the 1930s Australia wanted to exclude British manufacturers so that it could build up its own. It argued that it would be in the interests of the empire as a whole if Australia became a more diverse and stronger economy. Britain refused to budge from the arrangement settled at Ottawa in 1932: it gave special access to Australian farm products and expected to sell its goods in return. Menzies was one of the Australian ministers who visited London in 1938 to put the case for Australian manufacturing.

To be kept waiting for weeks and to be given nothing was very sobering. Menzies was very critical privately of the narrowness of the English, at their pursuit of material gain, at their lack of commitment to the empire. This was the line Australians always took when they didn't get their way with Britain: Britain was not being loyal to the empire. Since Australia would only count if the empire was taken seriously there was a touch of desperation to Australia's empire loyalty.

*

The critical test of Britain's loyalty to Australia came in 1942 when Australia was under threat from Japan. Despite all its earlier assurances, Britain did not send a fleet to Singapore. That impregnable base was easily overrun and Australia was exposed to the enemy. Prime Minister Curtin looked to the United States to save Australia. The present Prime Minister has pronounced on the significance of these events: the British deserted us; they didn't bother to defend the Malayan peninsula or Singapore. This view has some academic support in the book *The Great Betrayal* by Professor David Day. This is an angry book. Professor Day is not angry at the British; he is angry at the leading figures in the Australian governments of the 1930s and 1940s because not one of them shared his view of how Australia should have acted. He thinks our leaders should have realised that the British assurances about Singapore were obviously worthless because Britain rated its own interests in Europe and the Middle East much more highly than the defence of Australia, and if put under pressure would not send a fleet to Singapore; that our leaders should not have been conned into sending troops to the Middle East and should have concentrated all Australian forces for the defence of the continent.

Not only were the governments of Lyons and Menzies subservient to the British; Day is dismayed to find John Curtin was as well. On taking office he left troops in the Middle East; he made no proposal to move them even after Pearl Harbor; there is a story that Curtin fought Churchill to get the troops back, but that is a myth. Churchill proposed that the troops return to meet the Japanese threat; the argument between Curtin and Churchill was whether they should go to Burma or Australia. Curtin won that argument but he was still willing to allow some troops to be diverted to Ceylon and he still left the 9th Division in the Middle East and Australian airmen in Britain. Despite his look-to-America statement, despite the Singapore betrayal, Curtin still wanted Australia to participate in imperial defence.

It would be easy to be a historian if all we had to discover was that people in the past did not share our outlook. Why did our leaders act as they did? Clearly they doubted the British assurances about Singapore, for they returned to the issue again and again. What else could they do? They could spend more on their own defence – they did that, but even if Australia spent its whole budget on defence it could not defend itself against a first-class power. They could look for another protector – they did that, but in the 1930s the United States was not interested. They could seek to buy off Japan – they did that, but neither the UK nor the US would go as far in appeasement as Australia suggested. They were left then with the doubtful British assurances; better, they must have thought, to have a doubtful assurance from a great power than no assurance of outside aid.

Well before Japan entered the war the British told Australia that they were so hard-pressed in the Atlantic and the Mediterranean that a fleet would not be sent to Singapore. This did not mean that the British left Malaya undefended. There were British troops on the peninsula and at Singapore and the *Prince of Wales* and the *Repulse* on the ocean. All woefully inadequate: but there were more British troops lost and more British troops taken into captivity than Australian.

Curtin's task after Japan entered the war was to ensure the defence of Australia by acquiring troops and weapons from Britain and the United States who were jointly planning what had become a global war. Day wants Curtin to have withdrawn Australian troops immediately from every theatre around the globe, concentrated them in Australia, and then put the request that allied forces come to our aid. That is, he should have ignored the wider war, scorned planning and then approached the planners. That way he would have pleased simple-minded nationalists, but at the cost of endangering Australia. Curtin had to push for the protection of Australia within the overall plan, not to ignore it. Churchill and Roosevelt very sensibly considered that troops engaged in battle should finish their job before being moved.

So fresh American troops arrived in Australia while the Australian 9th Division continued to fight in North Africa. They remained there throughout 1942, the year of Australia's greatest danger, with Curtin becoming increasingly anxious. But he did not insist on their return until after their great victory at El Alamein. Churchill would have preferred to keep them in this theatre, but he sent them home with a generous message: 'The 9th Australian Division will carry with them from the African desert a splendid reputation and the honour of having played a leading part in a memorable victory for the Empire and the common cause.' If Curtin had forgotten the empire and the common cause, he would not have been a great wartime leader.

To persuade Curtin to leave the 9th Division in North Africa in 1942 Churchill repeated an earlier promise to Australia. He was confident that the Japanese would not attempt a full-scale invasion of Australia, but if they did, he undertook to cut his losses everywhere else and come to the aid of Britain's kith and kin. That promise did not have to be redeemed. Had Australia been invaded and Britain not sent aid, then respect for Britain might have evaporated overnight. But perhaps not. It was difficult to cast as betrayer a country which was itself as beleaguered and battered as Britain was in 1941–42. Australians did not feel betrayed by Britain because the desire for the continuance of the empire connection remained strong.

*

Australia never took a decision to leave the empire-Commonwealth; Britain's own strength declined and then it committed itself to Europe. But the Commonwealth as the loose association of the countries of the former empire continues, a reminder of the special qualities of that empire.

We are now constantly made aware of the cost of the empire connection in the lives lost in the empire's wars. But if we are to understand our forebears we must see the allure of empire. A small, vulnerable nation was to be protected by a great power and allowed a voice in the determination of its policies. Australia was frequently critical of Britain for not consulting it enough, but the ideal did take concrete form. In both world wars Australian ministers and prime ministers sat in British cabinets. Billy Hughes, the first to do so, did not confine his contributions to the conduct of the war. As the founder of the Water-side Workers Union he set the British cabinet right on how to deal with blockages on the wharves. When Prime Minister Bruce wanted to improve the process of consultation he sent the young Richard Casey to London as a liaison officer. Casey was located in the cabinet office and saw all the cabinet-papers. I know of no parallel to the closeness of these arrangements between separate states.

The evolution of the empire into an association of nations, equal in status, in no way subordinate one to another, though united in a common allegiance to the crown, was the last miraculous turn in the long evolution of the British constitution. The crown had been held to be single and sovereign; now there were several crowns on one head. The crown of Great Britain would take advice from British ministers; the crown of Australia would take advice only from Australian minis-ters. This development fascinated and excited the leading Labor lawyers in Australia, Dr Evatt and Maurice Blackburn. English law, for which they had tremendous respect, could bend so far as to allow full Austral-ian independence. And this unique association of equal nations, sharing common ideals of liberty and democracy, was an indication of what the world could be like if its separate nations ceased their mutual hostilities and suspicion. This was the empire, progressive and noble, which claimed the allegiance of the best minds on the left. Justice Michael Kirby comes from this tradition. He opposes an Australian republic because he is suspicious of nationalism and as an internationalist welcomes the sharing of the one monarch by a number of nations.

There was not of course universal support for empire. There were voices calling for an independent Australia, but mostly they did not represent a stronger attachment to Australia or a more careful appreciation of how best it could survive.

The small socialist movement in Sydney in the 1880s was republi-can. Its members were typically recent migrants from Britain and their republicanism was part of a radical agenda formed in Britain. They were using Australia as a platform to carry on their battle with the British monarchy and aristocracy. This was an opportunistic independence.

The Irish, especially after Easter 1916, could be found calling for the severance of the tie with Britain, but this was to indicate their abhorrence of the British treatment of Irish rebels. It was not a response to Australia's position within the empire. It was an act of solidarity with Irish independence.

Between the wars there were socialists and internationalists who were opposed to all wars and to capitalism and its empires which allegedly caused them. They did not want to spend any money on defence. They sought a defenceless independence.

There were communists who opposed all empires except the Soviet Union's, whose interests they were assiduous in serving. This was the independence of treason.

The Labor Party's attitude to empire was complex. In office Labor governments, as we have seen, gave it strong support, but many of its members were wary or suspicious of empire and some outrightly opposed it. There was a strong Irish and socialist component within the party. Labor's misgivings about empire showed itself in gesture, rather than any argued alternative, to use John Rickard's phrase. Between the wars Labor's suspicion of empire was at its height. Labor policy was to avoid entanglement in the empire's wars in Europe and to concentrate on the defence of Australia. But its capacity to do that was fundamentally flawed by its fanatical opposition to conscription. It had formed this policy in response to the plan to send conscripts to France in 1916, and after the party split on the issue anti-conscription became sacred. Conscription in all its forms was now illegitimate, not simply for overseas service; conscription to train in the militia was wrong; conscription to meet an enemy actually invading Australia was wrong. These positions, formed out of opposition to involvement in the empire's wars, were a severe handicap in developing policies for a nation which was meant to fight without the empire's aid. Labor offered not an independent Australia, but a hobbled Australia.

It cast off some of these hobbles when the war came, but its opposition to conscription for overseas service remained. This meant that Australia in World War II had two armies: one of volunteers who could fight anywhere, the other of conscripts who could fight only in Australia and its territories. This was terribly damaging to efficiency and morale.

Labor maintained its opposition to conscription for overseas service even when the service overseas was to push the Japanese back from the islands immediately to Australia's north. A tiny nation with two armies when a great power was on its doorstep – this was the independence of the sick joke.

Meanwhile the United States was sending conscripts thousands of miles to fight in Australia's defence. To stop American criticism of Australian policy, Curtin persuaded the Labor Party to make a small extension to the area in which conscripts could serve. It did not extend as far as to Japan whence the enemy had come. Menzies made a great contribution to the substance of Australian independence when he abolished the distinction between service within and outside Australia, for regular soldiers in 1950 and conscripts in 1964. Australia at last had one army which could be sent anywhere in defence of Australian interests.

Because the Labor Party had its doubts about empire, it took the initiative in developing the symbols of national independence. It appointed the first Australian-born governor-general in 1931; it opposed the awards of imperial knighthoods and created the Order of Australia; it gave us our national anthem. The current Labor government has espoused an Australian republic as the confirming symbol of our independence.

*

It is time we considered more closely this concept of independence. Already I have referred to the substance of independence, to fake independence in a variety of forms, and to the symbols of independence. How have these been related to each other?

Let's consider first another sort of independence, formal independence, the acquisition of sovereign status. It is very difficult to say when Australia became formally independent. Was it in 1901 when the Commonwealth was formed? No, because foreign relations were still in British hands and Britain kept the power, though never used, to veto Australian legislation. Was it then with the Statute of Westminster in 1931? More likely, though Australia requested that it not apply to Australia. Was it then in 1942 when the Commonwealth parliament adopted the Statute? Perhaps, but before this in 1940 Menzies had appointed Australia's first ambassadors, which is one of the tests of sovereign status. But if that is a test, was Australia independent when it sent delegates to the League of Nations in 1919? The experts can't agree. Ordinary people have no idea when their country became independent. Rather than try to settle the matter, we should examine what this uncertainty signifies. We get into trouble with this issue because of the special nature of the British empire which confounded the notions of dependence and independence by offering independence within the empire.

If we ask the question, 'When did Australians cease to feel that they were subordinate to the empire and were, rather, independent members of it?' then we go back a long way in our history. I would say to the 1850s and 1860s when the colonies achieved internal self-government and knew that if they wanted full independence Britain would not resist it. From the 1880s they conducted a foreign policy within the empire to ensure that it protected Australia's interests. In the 1890s they considered the option of forming a united Australia as a republic and rejected it in favour of federation under the crown. That put some restrictions on Australia. It deprived it of the formal trappings of sovereignty, but enhanced its substantial independence, in the sense of power to control its own fate. Australia wanted to prohibit Asian immigration; to maintain this policy it had to defy and insult a major power, Japan. It could not have done this without the backing of the empire. As Billy Hughes said, Australia was a nation by the grace of God and the British empire. Even those who disliked the empire knew this, which is why their distaste did not lead to realistic plans for Australia to manage on its own, but to pique, withdrawal and irresponsibility, to fake independence.

Since Australia had the substance of independence, to many it seemed there was no need for the symbols of independent nationhood. They were not only inappropriate but dangerous, since they seemed to deny the special dual loyalty. They were the more suspect because they were proposed by the Labor Party which did indeed contain people opposed to empire. So the symbols of nationhood were highly contentious. Labor proposed them and non-Labor attacked, ignored or resented them. One of the legacies of our life within the empire is this mismatch between the substance and symbols of independence. The symbols did not relate to political independence at all, which came without a struggle. The psychic need of colonials to show that they are as good or better than the parent stock was met when Australians beat England at cricket and when our soldiers fought so magnificently at Gallipoli.

*

We are in the same situation with the republic. To its opponents it seems quite unnecessary; they have no doubt of Australia's independence. Its supporters can offer no increase in the substance of our independence; it is a symbol merely. And though I am a supporter of the republic, a worker for the republic, I will make this concession, so long as Tony Abbott doesn't take it down and use it against me: The issue does not arouse widespread enthusiasm even though it has majority support.

However, the republican symbol is different from the other symbols of nationhood. The hurdle of the referendum means that if we become a republic it will only be after the issue has been long debated and the commitment has grown. It can't be implemented by one party; it will have to have bipartisan support. My hope is that in the process of Australia becoming a republic Australians will learn more about their Constitution and come to think of themselves more as citizens. Our national identity will acquire the civic dimensions which it now so conspicuously lacks. Thus this symbol will bring some substance.

If nothing else, I hope I have shown you that you can be a republican without denigrating Britain, the empire and Australia's former ties with it. The more you understand what that relationship meant, the more you realise how thin it has now become. Australians no longer think of themselves as British; Britain offers nothing in defence and is part of a hostile trading bloc. A British head wearing an Australian crown is a symbol that has lost its potency.

Now that you have heard my views, you will understand why I have mixed feelings about Prime Minister Keating. I admire the vision and the vigour with which he has advanced the republican cause; I appreciate his good sense in appointing me to his Republic Advisory

Committee; I regret that he has sometimes linked republicanism to an attack on Britain and those Australians who supported the empire. If the Prime Minister wants to attack the supporters of empire, he will have to attack not only Menzies, but Curtin, not only Casey, but Chifley, not only political leaders, but the great mass of the Australian people. They all sought within the empire to protect the substance of our independence. The difficulty they faced of being a European society in an alien and potentially hostile environment is the same situation we face. What substance we can now give to our independence will depend on our own strength, economic and military, and our skill in deploying it. I believe we will face that task better as a republic, but not one which mocks our forebears, who cared as much for the advancement and security of Australia as we do.

1995

Towards the Republic

One hundred years after federation, the Australian nation is debating whether it should be a republic. The decision of the founding fathers that the Commonwealth should be a union 'under the Crown' was not entirely uncontested. In the 1880s when the movement for federation began, republicanism was stronger than at any time until the 1990s. Sir Henry Parkes, who was responsible for the convening of the 1891 constitutional convention, had experienced the republican upsurge at close quarters.

In 1887 he had watched helplessly from the stage of the Sydney Town Hall as republicans created mayhem at a public meeting called to discuss the celebrations of Queen Victoria's jubilee. Neither he – the premier of the colony – nor the other worthies on the stage could gain a hearing. This was the second meeting on the jubilee. Republicans had taken over the first and voted down a plan to give schoolchildren a picnic in honour of the queen as a threat to democratic values. The mayor hurriedly closed that meeting and called another. To keep the republicans out special invitation cards were printed, but republicans forged them and so were able to occupy all the strategic spots in the hall and orchestrate such a torrent of boos, hisses and groans that the meeting never began.

A spectacular demonstration would be needed to offset these terrible blows to the colony's reputation for loyalty. A third meeting was held in Sydney's Exhibition Building. Volunteer soldiers, sportsmen, and university students were recruited to police the crowd and these admission tickets were harder to forge. The republicans had not given up, but finally they were outnumbered and, with only minor scuffles and dissent, a crowd of thousands proclaimed their love for their queen.

These nineteenth-century republicans were working people and small traders, autodidacts and dreamers, for whom republicanism was part of the coming social revolution. They were socialists and free-thinkers who saw the queen as a symbol of aristocratic privilege, inequality and superstition. It was not Australian nationalism that had carried them to republicanism. This movement was composed chiefly of recent migrants from Britain who had learned their republicanism before they boarded the boat. Compared to the regeneration of human-kind, the union of six Australian colonies was a small project in which they took little interest, though they would oppose those who wanted to unite them under the crown. The disruption of the Sydney meetings was the high point in their campaign. Over the next few years numerous republican organisations sprang up in New South Wales and Queens-land and soon faded away. They were part of a wider mobilisation of working people, but working people were not to be rallied by calls for separation from Britain.

There were other republican stirrings, more rooted in local concerns and attachment. The Sydney *Bulletin* blossomed in the 1880s; it was the first newspaper national in scope and readership. A republican form of government was the first point in its political program and mocking the royal family part of its staple fare. Like the working-class radicals, it took much from British radicalism but gave it an Australian bite and style. Throwing off the earnestness of radicalism it was breezy, slangy and funny and did not hope for too much.

Within mainstream politics effusive loyalty was the norm, but Australia's growing national aspirations inevitably called the imperial connection into question. Could the six colonies make themselves into a fully self-governing nation and not have its independence qualified by membership of the empire? Would membership of the empire minister to the new nation's interests, or would Australia be made to minister to Britain's interests? In the 1880s colonial leaders complained that Britain would not act decisively to forestall French and German incursions into the South Pacific because it put its other interests ahead of protecting Australia's. They wanted a more attentive Britain – but not too attentive. In Britain at this time schemes for a grand imperial federation were being floated. They received some support in Australia, but they spread much more alarm for they threatened to subordinate Australia's interests to the wider entity and to forestall the formation of an Australian federation.

It was not yet fully clear that Australians could be simultaneously 'independent Australian Britons', and that uncertainty encouraged the exploration of the independence option. In the New South Wales and Queensland parliaments there were parliamentary groupings styling themselves the National Party which did not advocate separation but were assertive about Australian interests and suspicious of British intentions. In Victoria the Australian Natives Association, strong advocates of federation, faced a crisis in 1888 when a few of its leading members refused to honour a toast to the queen.

In the parliaments of the eastern colonies, there were a few politicians who were known and declared republicans, most notably George Dibbs, leader of the Opposition to Parkes' government in New South Wales. In the late nineteenth century it was not improper, as it later became, for a politician to contemplate a fully independent Australia. To advocate immediate separation was unacceptable, but how could Australian patriots complain when told that their country would become a second United States, outstripping the mother country and parting from it on good terms when its protection was no longer needed?

These uncertainties about Australia's future relations with Britain were augmented by that arch-loyalist Sir Henry Parkes, recently promoted from Knight Commander to Grand Cross in the Order of St Michael and St George. In 1887 he fiercely denounced the republicans who would not honour the queen's jubilee. Yet in the following year, when Britain expressed misgivings about the Australian colonies forbidding Chinese immigration, he proclaimed, 'Neither for her Majesty's ships of war, nor for her Majesty's representative on the spot, nor for the Secretary of State for the Colonies do we intend to turn aside from our purpose, which is to terminate the landing of Chinese on these shores forever.' This was the language of the *Bulletin* and the National Party.

When Parkes launched his federation campaign in 1889, he suggested that Australia be guided by the federation of Canada, which was a union 'under the crown'. Strangely though, the resolution for union which he drafted for the first federation conference in 1890 did not include these words. The Victorians were quick to notice the omission and with Parkes' agreement had them inserted before the resolution reached the conference floor. In the conference Thomas Playford from South Australia went as far as to cast doubt on Parkes' loyalty, for which he received a withering reply, but the omission may not have been accidental. Parkes was well aware of the body of opinion, strong in his own colony and Queensland, which associated union under the crown with military ties and obligations and the hobbling of Australia for sinister imperial purposes. He may have wished to fudge the issue of the imperial connection for a little while longer. The Victorians wanted a definite declaration from the outset, which is what they achieved. During all the subsequent official deliberations on federation, union under the crown was accepted without question.

*

It took ten years for agreement on federation to be reached. During that decade republican sentiment declined. The fact that Australians were self-evidently in charge of their own constitution-making allayed fears of imperial manipulation. The working-class republicans were absorbed into the new Labor parties, which were wary of the imperial connection but not advocates of separation. The *Bulletin*, recognising that its brilliant advocacy was having no effect, dropped 'a republican form of government' in 1891 and accepted federation under the crown in 1894.

Yet the republican alternative still shadowed the federal movement. At the people's constitutional conventions at Corowa in 1893 and Bathurst in 1896 republican dissenters had to be dealt with expeditiously from the chair. There is a sense in which the federal movement was an explicit answer to the republican challenge: to forestall republicans harnessing nationalism to separation, loyalists created a nation within the empire.

In allowing the six colonies to claim a higher degree of self-government as a nation, Britain attracted an even firmer loyalty.

Australia expected and was granted full control of its internal affairs. Under the Constitution it also had power over defence and external affairs. However, it was not a sovereign nation. Britain remained in charge of foreign policy and Australia's business with other nations could be dealt with officially only by Britain. Australia's power over external affairs was the opportunity to influence British foreign policy. In defence Australia was expected to repel small-scale attacks, but its chief protector was the British Navy.

Australia's relationship with Britain was to take an entirely unexpected turn in the twentieth century. In the nineteenth century Australia was a young stripling, growing rapidly and likely soon to be able to look after itself. Then with drought and depression at the end of the century its growth slowed. It became more vulnerable with the rise of Japan to great-power strength. This increased its reliance on the mother country, which simultaneously was coming under greater threat in Europe. If Britain were distracted in Europe when Australia was attacked there might be a delay before Britain could come to Australia's rescue. So the new nation spent heavily to give its young men military training and to acquire its own navy. But that was not the form the crisis took.

During World War I, Australia was relatively safe while Britain faced not a distraction in Europe, but total defeat and ruin. Australia had to make an all-out attempt to save the mother country, its ultimate protector. Instead of growing apart the two countries fused together, a relationship which continued after the war. In the 1920s and 1930s the bedrock of Australia's foreign policy was that its destiny depended totally on the fortunes of the empire.

*

It was in these circumstances that loyalty to Britain passed from sentiment to stern duty, inculcated in the young and policed in adults. The open speculation about Australia's future outside the empire ceased. If there were republican members of parliament they had to be silent. And yet there was widespread resistance to these demands for loyalty, wider than in the nineteenth century when less had been demanded. Socialists, pacifists and Irish Catholics for different reasons did not want to give fulsome loyalty to the British empire. However, their dissatisfaction was not much more than passive resistance; they did not demand that links with Britain be terminated or offer a different version of Australia's place in the world. In these mean years, loyalty had a shrill edge and dissent became sterile.

Between the wars other dominions of the empire, Canada, South Africa and the Irish Free State, demanded full control over their defence and foreign policy – that they should be sovereign nations. Britain conceded this under a formula that declared the dominions were in no way inferior to the United Kingdom and that they were bound to it solely by a shared allegiance to the crown. The formula was drawn up at the 1926 imperial conference and enshrined in the Statute of Westminster of 1931. Australia looked askance at this development. It did not want formal independence for herself and saw danger in any weakening of the ties of empire. Much more vulnerable than the other dominions, Australia wanted to keep Britain obligated to defend her. At Australia's request, the Statute of Westminster was not to apply to Australia until the Commonwealth parliament adopted it. This did not occur until 1942.

During World War II, Britain's great naval base at Singapore fell to the enemy and Australia had to rely on the United States to repel the Japanese. This was the first in a series of blows to Australia following the contraction of Britain's power and then its abandonment of empire. It is notable, however, that attachment to Britain was so ingrained that it continued long after material advantages of the imperial connection were removed. Historians may mark an era when Prime Minister Curtin spoke in 1941 of looking 'to America, free of any pangs as to our traditional links or kinship with the United Kingdom', but never was loyalty to Britain so uncomplicated and widespread as in the royal tour of the queen in 1954. Prime Minister Menzies reaffirmed the solidity of the British world by having the queen unveil the monument which honours the United States for its defence of Australia. The withdrawal of British forces east of Suez, and Britain's entrance into the European Union, which put an end to its preference for Australian produce, were developments regretted in Australia, but they failed to lead to a critical assessment of what remained of the British relationship.

Very little remained. What had once been all-encompassing was now simply a cog in the constitutional machine. The queen, on the advice of the prime minister, appointed (and dismissed) the Australian governor-general. The slightness of the Crown's real influence was the best guarantee of its preservation. In truth Australia was a sovereign state able to make new arrangements in defence with the United States and in trade with Japan to replace the previous arrangements with Britain. No interest was threatened by this last connection to the British monarchy. What force could be summoned to break the nation of this harmless habit?

In the 1960s two leading intellectuals, Geoffrey Dutton and Donald Horne, found a reason for the creation of an Australian republic. They saw Australians' acceptance of the monarchy as symbolising their stuffiness, timidity and lack of realism about where their country stood in the world. A nation that threw off the monarchy would revitalise itself and overcome the cultural cringe, the deferring to metropolitan centres overseas and lack of faith in the local product. Horne made his republican declaration in his best-selling critique of Australian society, *The Lucky Country*, in 1964. Geoffrey Dutton edited a book of essays on *Australia and the Monarchy* in 1966. No organised movement for a republic followed and both authors were subjected to vicious personal attacks. Dutton, a descendant of an old South Australian pastoralist family, was thrown out of the Adelaide Club. One of his nineteenth-century ancestors had been a republican – and premier of the colony.

In the 1970s and 1980s Australian society ceased to be provincial British. The population became much more diverse as a result of European immigration. Most old Australians ceased to think of themselves as British as well as Australian. Britain no longer set the standard in the professions and the arts. The cultural cringe disappeared as Australian literature, art, film and dance flourished and gained international recognition. With that endorsement Australians moved to the easy assumption that in enjoying the local high culture they had not settled for the second-rate. These transformations had been achieved with the British monarchy still in place.

The Whitlam Labor government of 1972–75, coming to power after twenty-three years of conservative rule, was committed to erasing traces of Australia's past as a white dominion of empire, and to foster-ing a cultural renaissance. It made no move towards a republic; by amending the queen's title to simply 'Queen of Australia' and replacing 'God Save the Queen' with an Australian national anthem, it gave the monarchy another lease of life.

The dismissal of the Whitlam government by the governor-general on 11 November 1975 prompted the first significant republican movement since the nineteenth century. The queen played no part in the dismissal and refused an invitation to become involved, but the government had still been dismissed under the reserve powers of the Crown. To those enraged by the dismissal, some monarchist mumbo-jumbo had been conjured up to strike down a democratically elected government halfway through its term.

Their protests were not at first directed at the queen or even the British connection; Sir John Kerr, it was frequently said, had done what the queen would never do. The protestors wanted to strip this unelected viceroy of his powers and ensure that only the people could dismiss a government. They were moving to republicanism through their belief in the sovereignty of the people. The focus of the protest is clear from the name of the new body which emerged from it: Citizens for Democracy. Pioneer republican Donald Horne slipped in a republican resolution at the great protest meeting 'Kerr and the Consequences', at the Sydney Town Hall in September 1976. He was surprised at the level of support he received. By the following year during a visit of the queen, Citizens for Democracy were openly republican.

It seemed then to many people that democracy could not proceed in Australia without radical constitutional change. A reforming Labor government had been frustrated by a hostile Senate that had finally destroyed it by forcing it to an election at the time of the Senate's choosing. Labor stalwarts could see no point in playing the game under Kerr's rules. Many non-Labor people were shocked by the events of 1975 and wanted to ensure that the bitterness and division they created were never repeated. A spate of books examined the 1975 crisis and made proposals for constitutional change which included changes to the office of governor-general as surrogate of the British monarch.

There was no prospect, however, of this leading to any alteration in existing arrangements. In the political polarisation which the crisis had produced, the Liberals were enthusiastic supporters of the actions of Kerr and the reserve powers. Constitutional change in Australia is extraordinarily difficult. At a referendum a majority of the people and the states have to vote Yes. If a major party opposes a constitutional change it has little chance of success.

*

The Australian Republican Movement (ARM), formed in 1991, carried an ancient name, but was unlike all previous republican movements in Australia. It was a movement from within the new establishment of Sydney, comprising people from business, the professions, media and the arts who were, variously, wealthy, successful and famous. Citizens for Democracy had called to its support public figures, but was old-fashioned enough to think that a democratic movement should be able to rally the people. It had held monster meetings in Sydney and Melbourne. The ARM initially saw no need to organise a following. It would make its impact by its founding notables publicly and jointly refusing allegiance to the queen and urging the creation of a republic. This news would be carried in the media, in which they were practised performers. An impressive – and undeniable – array of well-known people was necessary for success. They were recruited in secret, the organisers fearing that a premature announcement would bring ridicule or vilification and defeat the movement before it began.

Once the notables had broken the taboo popular support would be measured in opinion polls. These polls had contained a general question on support for the republic for many years, but the nature of the republic had not been specified. Most people thought a republic and a president must follow the American model. The ARM wanted to maintain existing constitutional arrangements, except that a president would be created to do the same job as the governor-general. This would be a minimalist republic. The ARM lobbied the pollsters to start asking questions on republican options of this sort.

The narrowness of its aim also distinguished this movement from its predecessors. It had no wider social or political agenda. At the fish and chardonnay lunch where the plot to form the ARM was hatched,

Neville Wran, the former Labor premier turned merchant banker declared, 'The other thing I want to see happen before I bloody well die is an Australian Republic. And there will have to be something done about the reserve powers of the Crown, and the Senate's power of veto.' When it finalised its policy, though, the ARM did not propose to remove the reserve powers or reduce the Senate's power. To have done so would have made it impossible to secure the support of the Liberal Party or the smaller states, both of which were necessary for success. The most it requested was that before the powers of the governor-general were given to a president they should be clearly set out.

The organisers were well aware that many supporters of a republic would expect the movement to embrace other causes. To guarantee that its agenda would not be expanded, the ARM was organised not as a democratic association but as a company. The foundation members were the shareholders who elected a board of directors. Other supporters would be welcomed but would be given no power over the organisation.

The ARM notables had some difficulty in explaining why such a small change meant so much to them. Their concern was chiefly about status. They felt themselves and their country demeaned by the willingness to give the British monarch a part in the Australian polity. This was puzzling to those whose sense of self and nation was totally unconnected to the state or who understood politics as the satisfaction of material interest. Among these people, it transpired, were many who were not unhappy to see a change to a republic, but could not raise any enthusiasm for it or see the necessity of achieving it sooner rather than later.

The argument the ARM advanced was that it was simply anomalous for an independent country, which had to make its own way in the world, to borrow the monarch of what had become a foreign country. The British monarch could no longer symbolise the Australian nation; the nation should have one of its own citizens as its head of state. The message was to be a positive one with no attack on Britain or the queen. The ARM also held out the prospect that the making of the change would have a transforming effect. Formally independent, Australia in its spirit had not yet thrown off its colonial origins. The novelist Tom

Keneally, the ARM's first chairperson, declared that Australia must cease to divide its soul. And the first convenor in Victoria, wrote in *A Republican Manifesto*, 'Australia was born in chains and is not yet fully free.' When Australia threw off the deceptive demeanour of a colony, its identity would at last be settled and an increase in self-confidence and purpose would follow.

The Sydney republicans of the 1880s had forged invitations and disrupted public meetings. In July 1991 the new Sydney republicans unveiled themselves at an invitation-only reception for the media in a five-star hotel. Being well-connected, they had secured two officers from the police special branch to guard the door. After Tom Keneally had spoken, the naturalist Vin Serventy, the one dissenting voice, asked if the ARM would support the abolition of 26 January as Australia Day since it was offensive to Aborigines. Keneally ruled the question out of order. The ARM was committed to doing one thing only.

The founding members thought there was still a chance that they would be made pariahs. The media gave the launch good coverage and the response it orchestrated was the 'republican debate', which was vigorously pursued over the next few weeks and has been a staple fare since. There was opposition, of course, as debate required, but the ARM had immediately attained a chief objective: to legitimise the possibility of change. The media was generally sympathetic to the cause and the *Australian*, under the editorship of Paul Kelly, was an enthusiast. The polls showed a rise in support for a republic; one poll recorded over 50 per cent in favour by early 1992, another by early 1993.

The Sydney republicans knew that they would have to create a national organisation. Before the 1991 launch they had sounded out Melbourne notables and received many refusals. There the movement had to make-do with a second-eleven team. The same occurred in every other capital city. Only in Sydney was there an elite detached from old wealth and allegiance, cosmopolitan, progressive, eager to use its money and talent to put itself at the forefront of a new Australia. Outside of Sydney the ARM operated very differently. The first request from its Victorian branch was for a lowering of the membership fee; it was reduced by a quarter. State branches set up democratic structures for their own governance which operated per favour of the Sydney board which was not itself democratised. Tom Keneally did not survive long as its chair. He was supplanted by the lawyer turned merchant banker Malcolm Turnbull, who had become famous representing the Australian Peter Wright, former MI5 officer, when Thatcher's government accused him of breaching confidence in his book *Spycatcher*. Keneally was genial and conciliatory; Turnbull volatile and pugnacious. He was not universally admired, but his energy, brilliance and wealth carried the movement forward.

One year after the formation of the ARM, the opponents of a republic organised themselves as Australians for Constitutional Monarchy. What was interesting about its defence of the monarchy were its omissions: the monarchy was no longer a link to Britain or the wider British world, nor was it a standard of honour and probity or even a revered person – all the things that had made the monarchy strong in Australia. The defence quickly came to rest on the monarchy's role in the Constitution: it provided a head of state above politics which no possible presidential system could match. Against the nationalist cry that Australia should have one of its own as head of state, the monarchists replied that it already did: the governor-general. The queen, they explained, did not interfere in Australian politics; all she did was appoint a head of state on the nomination of the prime minister. Unique among lobby groups, they boasted not how much but how little was performed by the institution they were defending.

The participants in the 'republican debate' were usually at cross-purposes. The republicans argued that the queen was an inappropriate symbol while the monarchists accused republicans of undermining a Constitution which worked satisfactorily or, more than that, was the best in the world. Of course it was not a 'debate', but a campaign for change. The monarchists had retreated to the only safe ground where their battle cry was not 'God Save the Queen' but 'No Republic'.

Just days before the ARM was launched in Sydney, the national conference of the Labor Party resolved to support the creation of a republic by 1 January 2001, the same target the ARM was to set. The Sydney republicans were furious; they did not want their thunder stolen nor their movement identified as a Labor cause. In fact, the Labor decision did not arouse much interest. Republicanism for Labor was a cause from the past, one of the things it had inclined towards but was never able to act on. It had long accepted the monarchy and it passed this motion for its removal without enthusiasm.

When Paul Keating became Labor prime minister in December 1991, he moved republicanism to the centre of the Labor program. It was part of his vision of an Australia re-oriented to Asia and free of its old connections and allegiances. Though the underdog at the 1993 election, he boldly committed himself to the cause and promised to set up a panel of experts to examine how a republic might be achieved.

After his election victory Keating swiftly established the Republican Advisory Committee with Malcolm Turnbull at its head. It canvassed a number of options for a minimalist republic and favoured the ARM scheme of a president elected by a two-thirds majority at a joint sitting of the federal parliament. Keating delayed acting on the report, yet kept talking about the republic and goading the opposition for its indecisiveness on the issue. In the short term the republican cause was damaged by becoming a weapon in party warfare, although ultimately Keating did the cause a great service by forcing the Liberal Party to confront the matter. The Liberals were divided – almost half the parliamentarians were in favour, the party members were firmly against. The party made a virtue out of this division by committing itself to hold a convention so that the people could decide. It was reviving the mode by which the Constitution had been drawn up in the 1890s, though that convention had been fully elected. The Liberals proposed a half-elected, half-nominated body, which was enough to present themselves as democrats in contrast to the Prime Minister, who was accused of thrusting 'Keating's republic' on the people. In June 1995 Keating committed his government to a republic along the lines of the Turnbull report but, during the election campaign of 1996, he undertook to have the republic shaped by a bipartisan parliamentary committee.

Both major parties had now committed themselves to providing a route to the republic. The ARM's realism about how change was to be effected had been rewarded: mobilise the media rather than the masses, reduce the amorphousness of 'the republic' to a limited proposal which both parties could support or accept, show them through the polls that most voters supported change. The ARM had predicted one stumbling block with such a plan: idealists on the left would be unhappy with a minimalist republic. What they did not foresee, though, was strong popular dissatisfaction with its preferred mode of electing the president. The polls, which were now more searching, uncovered overwhelming popular preference for a directly elected president. The ARM and the political elite saw such a president as a potentially destabilising figure. With a more direct mandate than the prime minister, a president might be tempted to interfere in government. The ARM had settled on election by two-thirds parliamentary majority to ensure that the president would be, as the people wanted, a bipartisan figure not associated with a political party. A direct election, where the parties would inevitably run candidates, would be much more likely to produce a politician as president. But such was their loathing of politicians that the people would not entrust the election of their president to them. The ARM, aiming to win the elite with a limited measure, had unleashed a populist movement it could not control. It was obliged to modify its platform to accept popular election, if the people could not be persuaded against it, so long as the powers of the president were fully spelled out.

After its election win in March 1996, the Liberal–National government proceeded to organise a convention. John Howard and the minister he made responsible for the convention, Nick Minchin, were both monarchists. Since they had the appointment of half the delegates and planned a voluntary postal ballot to elect the other half, republicans feared they were contriving a stacked convention which would produce chaos or deadlock. Their fears were not realised.

The nominated delegates were broadly representative and not very different in their allegiances from the elected. The elected delegates were chosen by only 47 per cent of the voters, but mirrored the balance of opinion as represented in the polls – a little over half were republican, a third were monarchists and the rest uncommitted. Once the convention assembled, no doubts were thrown on its representativeness or legitimacy. Indeed, one of the government's rationales for the nomination of half the delegates was that it would make the convention more representative. Such has been the advance of identity politics that a fully elected body which did not contain the right proportion of women, migrants, Aborigines and young people would be seen as unrepresentative. The government chose its nominees disproportionately from these groups to make up for their expected under-representation among the elected delegates.

Those nominated also included politicians from both sides of the nation's parliaments which was a more controversial use of nomination. Such is the distaste for politicians that they are seen, perversely, as unrepresentative figures. Whether any of them could have commanded sufficient support among the voters to be elected to the convention was not tested because they were prohibited from nominating. (At the fully elected convention of 1897–98 all the delegates, bar one, were politicians.)

The ARM had opposed a half-nominated convention, yet its purposes were better-served by the presence of the politicians, whose support it had always sought, and with whom it openly worked at the convention. In some eyes this made the ARM unworthy of its noble cause. Further, the presence of the nation's leading politicians added weight and point to the convention and tied them more firmly to its recommendations. It would be they, after all, who would have to institute the formal procedures for change.

The original rationale for the convention was that it would allow the people to decide whether there would be a republic. By the time it assembled there was no chance of its voting to retain the monarchy. Far from playing a spoiling game, the monarchist prime minister then said he wanted the convention to agree on a republican model which he could put to the people. This would rescue him from his promise to hold a plebiscite on the republican issue if the convention came to no clear conclusion. At the plebiscite the people had been promised they could vote on whether there should be a republic and on what form it should take. A directly elected president was bound to do well in such a poll. To that republican option the prime minister declared himself implacably opposed.

The ARM secured the largest contingent of elected delegates. It spent a great deal on advertising, had high-profile candidates and enjoyed the support of the Labor Party's electoral machine, to secure which prominent positions on the ARM ticket were given to Labor nominees. However, it did much worse than it expected. Forty per cent of the republican vote went to other delegates who, under different banners, advocated a directly elected president. Among these were groups calling themselves the 'real' or the 'just' republic who wanted the new constitution to assert popular rights and sovereignty and reduce executive power. They advocated a new preamble and a bill of rights.

To secure a majority for a republican model the ARM had to make concessions to these delegates to its left. It also had to placate a group to its right who rallied to the scheme of Richard McGarvie, a former governor of Victoria. This proposed that the queen be replaced by a council of elders chosen automatically from the most recently retired governors-general, governors and judges. The council would appoint and dismiss the president on the recommendation of the prime minister. No other changes to the Constitution would be made. The vexed issues of the powers of the head of state would be left untouched, the guarantee of proper performance in the president being the prime minister's power to recommend dismissal. McGarvie argued with some force that the ARM's plan for the dismissal of presidents which required, as for their election, a two-thirds vote at a joint sitting, made dismissal too difficult. A head of state neither directly nor indirectly elected by the citizens scarcely deserved the name republican, but McGarvie's scheme was attractive to recent and reluctant republican converts and had strong support from politicians and other nominated delegates.

After two weeks of debate and back-room dealing, the ARM unveiled the model it hoped would have majority support. To accommodate the demand for direct election, any citizen or community group could nominate a candidate for the presidency. The nominations would be reduced to a shortlist by a mixed committee of parliamentarians and community representatives. From this list the prime minister would put a single nomination to the joint sitting. The powers of the president would be the same as those of the governor-general. The convention declined to codify the reserve powers, but recommended that as far as possible the Constitution should make clear that the president would normally act on the advice of ministers. Over-reacting to the McGarvie critique and desperate to attract his supporters, the ARM now supported dismissal of the president by the prime minister, subject only to an endorsement by the House of Representatives.

Although this was the preferred model of the convention it failed by four votes to win majority support from the delegates. Nevertheless, an in-principle resolution that Australia should become a republic was comfortably carried. The prime minister announced that he regarded these votes as a clear outcome; he would put the preferred model to the people. He would not have a plebiscite.

If the monarchist delegates had thrown their weight behind the McGarvie proposal as the least objectionable republican model, it would have been adopted by the convention. They were urged to this pragmatic course but declared that, having been elected to oppose a republic, they would support no republican model. In so doing they gained a great deal of respect. The monarchists further boasted that they would have no trouble in defeating the model that the convention adopted when it was put to referendum.

This model faces many difficulties. Some republicans have criticised the power of a prime minister to dismiss a president as unrepublican. This might be amended as the model is put into legal form by the parliament, though its failure to provide for direct election means it is bound to encounter republican opposition as well as that of monarchists. There is still strong popular support for direct election. The ARM had operated on the assumption that endorsement by the political parties was the pre-condition for success at a referendum, but since the feelings against politicians have grown so strong their endorsement may now be the kiss of death.

The defeat of this republican model, however, would not save the monarchy. Only a third of the citizens support the retention of the nation's symbolic head. A constitutional convention, summoned by a monarchist prime minister, resolved in favour of a republic. At the convention the leading members of John Howard's Cabinet, who had hitherto remained silent on the republic, came out in its support. In any government, Labor or Liberal, that is now formed, a clear majority of ministers will be opposed to the monarchy.

The referendum planned for November 1999 is not on whether

Australia should be a monarchy or a republic. It is the first referendum on the form that the republic should take. There may need to be others. The nation would be in a parlous state if, having disowned the monarchy, it had to live for any length of time with its failure to agree on a replacement.

1999

The result of the referendum held in November 1999 was a clear defeat for the republican proposal. Nationally 55 per cent voted No. In no state was there a majority for Yes. The monarchists and direct-electionists combined to run the No campaign. The queen was defended by the cry that this was a politicians' republic and that the people should be allowed to elect their president. No-one, however, could believe that the republican question was at an end.

2001

Five Fallacies of Aboriginal Policy

Think of an Aborigine. Not a pop star or a sportsman, an ordinary Aborigine. Most Australians cannot, because they are not closely acquainted with any. This is one reason why Aboriginal policy remains so unrealistic: the electorate is poorly placed to judge what the politicians tell it. Australians who do live close to Aborigines know the great gap between reality and policy. Most choose to remain silent; those who speak out are denounced as racists and are discredited. Indeed, some of them are or have become racists. In Aboriginal affairs we have contrived to reduce the policy options to two: unreality or racism.

If our policy is to be more realistic and effective, we have to sweep away the woolly thinking that supports the present policies. I identify five fallacies in the current official thinking about Aborigines.

1. All Aborigines Possess a Rich Culture

The liberal mind is generous to a fault; it not only hates oppression, it ascribes special virtue to the oppressed. In some circumstances oppression may ennoble a people, but if the oppression is close and relentless, if it has disrupted and broken all pre-existing ties among the people, if the people have been socialised by oppression, then its effect will be crippling rather than ennobling. Such a people will survive, but they will live by suspicion, cunning and mockery. What unites them is primarily their resistance to the oppressor; if the oppression is removed they are likely to fall into chaos and self-destruction.

In the far outback, Aborigines were killed and exploited, but their traditional culture survived. The European presence was slight and the world in large measure remained Aboriginal. The cattlemen made the young Aborigines work, they fed the whole mob who camped on their station, and did not interfere in traditional business. The missionaries did attempt to destroy traditional culture, but with singular lack of success. Now with the restoration to the Aborigines of the ownership of their land, they have the opportunity to stabilise and strengthen their traditional culture. From these areas come the Aboriginal art, music and dance which delight us and serve as an emblem of Aboriginality to Aborigines everywhere.

In the more closely settled areas, traditional Aboriginal culture was almost completely destroyed. The survivors, a tiny proportion of the original population, could not maintain traditional groupings and they became in effect a new people, intermarrying across tribal lines and with the Europeans. They lived by taking rural work and the meagre support offered by governments and missionaries. Their interests and preoccupations were similar to those of the white rural workforce – gambling, sport and drink – with this difference: there was a strong attachment to Christianity, as a result of the missions, and strong bonds between kin, the only significant survival from the traditional culture.

In the twentieth century, as the country towns became more prim and the preoccupation with racial purity more intense, the Aborigines suffered more severe restraints. The government reserves and missions became authoritarian in their control; if the Aborigines did not live on them they camped on waste ground, often the rubbish tip, outside the towns; inside the towns an informal apartheid system kept Aborigines out of the swimming pools, down the front of the cinema and at the end of the queue in the shops; in society at large an official apartheid system controlled movement, marriage and took children away. The present-day Aborigines in the country towns are the survivors of this regime and their descendants. They are bonded together by their experience of marginalisation and oppression and a determination not to become like their oppressors.

Aborigines now enjoy full civil and political rights, but the gap between them and the white country-townspeople is still vast. How the two groups live together in the towns of the far west of New South

Wales is described in Gillian Cowlishaw's book *Black, White or Brindle*. The rural jobs which Aborigines used to take are nearly all gone so most are unemployed. They have been unemployed so long that they don't look to be employed. Drunkenness, theft and vandalism are common. The townspeople secure a large contingent of police to control and limit these. The Aborigines complain of police harassment and victimisation. Though the Aborigines revile the police, they call on them regularly to break up fights amongst themselves. Aboriginal women depend on them to protect them from drunken and violent men.

A lot of money and effort have been spent to transform this situation, but with little effect. All projects for change founder on the strength of Aboriginal culture, which has been labelled by Dr Cowlishaw as 'oppositional culture'. These are the values and attitudes formed by the Aborigines to protect themselves from white oppression and scorn. For many Aborigines in these places, to be Aboriginal means to be regularly drunk, to scorn those who work, to treat school as a joke, and to welcome a term in jail. We may want Aborigines to be sober, well-educated and employed, but they are not necessarily seeking this for themselves. In the far west country towns, dedicated teachers who want to help Aborigines can still be called 'white cunts' and have their cars scratched.

This oppositional culture is rightly termed 'Aboriginal' for only Aborigines live within it, but who will say that it is rich? This is the worst thing Europeans have done in Australia, not to kill Aborigines, not to take their land, but to create this social deformity, each ugly feature of which mirrors the face we showed the Aborigines.

The problem we face seems intractable. The oppositional culture was formed when oppression was naked and unashamed; it persists even though now we desperately want to make amends. The townspeople who live with the Aborigines are not going to think well of them while they have to step around Aboriginal drunks in the street and go home to find their houses burgled by Aboriginal kids who should be at school. Aborigines still feel plenty of scorn which they now meet, not with meekness, but with defiance. This cycle could perhaps be broken if there were jobs Aborigines could aspire to, but there are no jobs in these places. One thing is clear: the Aborigines in these country towns cannot return to a traditional culture. The oppositional culture they do have nurtures unemployment, drunkenness, crime and violence. This culture will have to disappear if the Aborigines are to live a richer and more fulfilling life, less damaging to themselves and others.

There are situations worse than the far west country towns. Authoritarian control of Aborigines was most complete in Queensland, and with its removal, the Aborigines on some of the old reserves and settlements are now living in unsocieties, places of almost unimaginable chaos and destructiveness. I quote one passage from an Aboriginal report on these places prepared for the Royal Commission on deaths in custody which is sufficient to show how far the degradation has gone.

> There is little physical abuse of parents towards their children although there are cases of fathers burning their sons with cigarettes or trying to drown one boy in a bath tub. Neglect is the real problem and this lack of supervision leaves opportunities for children to be sexually abused. When I visited Community C, I was told that cases of sexually transmitted diseases are dealt with every day, whether it is testing or treatment. Monthly test reports are received from the Aboriginal Health Program Team 4 in Cairns which deals with STDs on all the communities. Cases of child sexual abuse on communities have been discovered because of the occurrence of STD in children as young as five years old. It is usually teenage boys who are the perpetrators abusing young girls and boys. Some young boys are violated with sharp sticks being shoved repeatedly into their anus. The children won't talk about it and are receiving no help besides medical treatment. The children are flown to Cairns Base Hospital if they do not respond to treatment in the community. Communities A and B and other communities have similar problems. In the last year there were two (2) reported child molestations at Community A and that is the tip of the iceberg.

Social scientists are very unwilling to make judgments about cultures; they tend to claim they are all equally valid. Even when faced with the culture of these settlements, one writer claims that 'Aboriginal people are actively seeking to maintain preferred lifestyles within the constraining limits imposed by a dominant white society'. The Aboriginal report rejects this. Calling things by their proper names, it declares: 'Homicide, suicide, domestic violence, child abuse and neglect, juvenile offending, alcohol abuse and early death from preventable diseases are hardly a preferred lifestyle for Aboriginal people.'

2. Land Rights Are the Key to Aboriginal Regeneration

Traditional Aboriginal groups should have the right to own their traditional lands if they have not passed into the ownership of someone else. This is now the law of the land since the High Court *Mabo* judgment.

Before and since that judgment, there has been a tendency to regard land rights as a cure-all. This is the more surprising because land rights have existed in the Northern Territory for almost twenty years, which gives us ample evidence for assessing their effect. That experience demonstrates that the ownership of traditional land does not allow Aborigines to become a self-supporting people. The simple fact is that the land, even if worked to the peak of economic efficiency, will not return to the Aboriginal people on it an income which remotely approaches what they receive in welfare payments. This land is not highly productive – that is why it was available for Aboriginal ownership. Nor are the Aborigines willing to live without a reasonable money income – even those who are living on the traditional land at outstations consume European food as well as bush tucker and operate out of four-wheel-drive vehicles.

Since the land won't support Aborigines, governments have encouraged Aborigines to set up businesses. Millions of dollars have been poured into these enterprises, most of which have failed. The basic reason for this is that there is little or nothing business can produce with advantage in these remote locations. Most small business enterprises fail; to succeed in the outback would be an extraordinary accomplishment; to expect success from Aborigines who are inexperienced in business and not given to the go-getting mentality which it requires was completely fanciful.

These failures do not in my view call into question the policy of restoring land to traditional Aboriginal groups. They have a claim as of right and with the land they have a better chance of living in a traditional way. How they are to support themselves remains to be considered. But these failures demonstrate the foolishness of believing that the key to regeneration for non-traditional Aborigines is that the government should buy land for them, as is now proposed. Take Wilcannia in the far west of New South Wales. Most of the town's population is Aboriginal and most of them are unemployed. If the Aborigines owned all the land within a fifty-kilometre radius of the town, it would not support them. Nor would they reach self-sufficiency if in addition they acquired every paid job in the town. The Aboriginal population of Wilcannia, which is growing rapidly, bears no relation at all to the local resources which might be utilised for its support. It grows because the welfare system supplies it.

The Aborigines of the outback and the country towns want to continue living where they do. If our policy is to support them in that, we must expect that most of them will remain unemployed.

The unemployment benefit was not designed to become the permanent support of people living where there are no jobs. In the 1950s and 1960s Aborigines in remote areas were considered ineligible for the benefit. The Whitlam government in 1973 reversed this policy, declaring that Aborigines were to receive the dole without the requirement that they should be prepared to move to take work. It took some years for this policy to be fully implemented because the civil service opposed it. They feared that if the dole became general all the existing schemes for the employment of Aborigines, run by governments and missions, which paid less than the dole, would become unviable. And so it has turned out. At the settlements and old missions are the ruins of these enterprises – piggeries, chicken runs, orchards, vegetable gardens, saw mills, bakeries, butcheries and brick-making plants. The dole has conquered all.

The rules of the dole had to be bent and still have to be bent to make it into a permanent payment for Aborigines. This privilege, it might be said, is small and much more than this would be required to make full compensation to the Aborigines. But of course it is not a privilege; it is a poisoned chalice. Not least of all the evils done to the Aborigines is the decision of our generation to pay them to do nothing.

The Aborigines were surprised at the readiness of the government to provide the dole, or 'sit-down' money as they termed it, and very soon some were worried about its effects. It was at the suggestion of Aborigines that the government created a work-for-the-dole scheme in 1977. These schemes have been widely used and are clearly valuable, but they provide no long-term solution to Aboriginal unemployment. The schemes can usually offer only part-time employment, they depend on extra funding to provide supervision, materials and equipment, and there is a limit to the number of projects which can be usefully carried out in remote settlements. The scheme might be used to build houses or a school, but when they are completed, the only work might be the collection of rubbish.

Aborigines deserve privileged treatment, and their privilege should be to have guaranteed access to proper jobs. The jobs would almost certainly have to be away from the traditional lands and the country towns. This is the place to confront the assumption that the maintenance of traditional Aboriginal life requires that all the group must remain on the traditional land all the time. This certainly has not been the practice since white settlement. But despite all the disruption and movement which that has caused, traditional ties and ceremonies were not forgotten. Adjustments were made to the timing of ceremonies to take account of absences and work commitments. Having all the group together in one place with no work to do is not traditional. If the men are drunk and the boys are sniffing petrol, traditional life will not be sustained and renewed.

Say the young men of eighteen to twenty-five, who are the most disruptive force in these communities of the unemployed, moved to some large centre to take work. They would have the opportunity to return regularly to their traditional land; at age twenty-five they might return permanently and take one of the jobs which local resources could support. What if a young man, denied the dole because there was a job for him elsewhere, refused to leave? Of course he would remain – there can be no forced relocation. But without welfare support he might work with more commitment at some local job – in the store or with the cattle – or in the gathering of bush tucker. Once the dole ceased to flow automatically, all sorts of enterprises would become more attractive. The vegie gardens and the piggeries might reappear.

There are already a plethora of schemes to train Aborigines and to encourage private and public employers to hire them. They are not fully utilised. Aborigines are understandably reluctant to leave their home communities to take advantage of them. But that reluctance will not be overcome while the dole is available. When it ceases, there would have to be a recognition of the special problems Aborigines face in moving into the workforce. I would envisage young people from the one settlement or country town being offered work in the same provincial town or city; there would be a hostel for them to live in and special arrangements to allow them to return regularly to their homes.

The home land and the country town will be better places as some Aborigines move out into the wider world and return with new skills, experience and funds. They will be a base and a refuge, not islands of despair.

3. Aborigines Are Naturally Co-operative

In traditional Aboriginal society goods were shared, but in a highly structured and ritualistic way. A kangaroo would be divided by unvarying rule, a certain portion going to a certain relative. The sharing was among kin. There was no generalised ethic of sharing. You looked after your own.

This is the practice still in Aboriginal society, both traditional and non-traditional. This makes Aboriginal society particularly unsuited to operate community co-operatives whose assumption is that each member has the same entitlements and obligations. Community co-operatives are nevertheless one of the cornerstones of policy for Aboriginal settlements. Aboriginal culture makes them very hard to run. An Aboriginal girl at the checkout in a community store is expected to let her aunts and uncles pass through without paying. An Aboriginal man who becomes store manager will be expected to pass out goods through the loading bay to his relatives and to employ only them in the store no matter what their suitability or commitment. If the community runs a cattle station, the clan which owns the land on which the cattle run will expect to control the enterprise and enjoy the profits.

These difficulties in the way of community co-operatives exist when the people are of one tribe. They become even worse when, as is often the case, the communities consist of people from different tribes. They were gathered together in one spot by pastoralists or missionaries, and when their control ended, the government declared these groups to be communities which would henceforth manage themselves.

The reasons for this were partly administrative convenience and partly the belief that Aborigines, being different from ourselves, were more disposed to sharing and communal behaviour. They are different from us, but in ways which make them even less likely than we are to run co-operatives satisfactorily. Aboriginal organisations are plagued by factionalism, nepotism and clan warfare, but the policy of co-operatives is maintained. Socialism has collapsed in Russia and Europe, the drop-out communes have dissolved long since, every day shared households break up in disputes over depleted fridges and inflated phone bills, but the Aborigines, poor bastards, must be co-operative and share everything equally. Only on these terms will they receive funding. But these Aboriginal communities are not to grow and flourish in freedom; all their activities are governed by the filling in of forms, the adherence to guidelines and proper accountability. The aim of present policy is to produce an Aborigine who is a cross between a hippie and an accountant.

Of course our own organisations are not free from feuding, factionalism and nepotism. But fortunately for us not so much depends on the smooth function of any one of them. The Aboriginal 'community' is expected to run the store, the housing, the school, the cattle station, the tourist business. Politics – the intense, personal politics of small groups – thus impinges on everything and feuds and walk-outs threaten everything.

The Aborigines would be much better off it they were allowed to segment their lives as we do. One clan could run the cattle station, another could run the tourist business, Coles could run the store, the Housing Commission the houses, and the community might be left with only the school. Politics would then cease to be so central and so harmful.

If for anywhere else in Australia it was proposed that the operation of businesses and shops, the repair of houses, the provision of water and the collection of garbage should be the responsibility of a neighbourhood committee, the proposal would be rejected as lunacy. Yet in Aboriginal Australia millions of dollars and hundreds of bureaucrats are pursuing this phantom.

If we want a world where Aborigines can look after themselves, we must give up our dream that they are a co-operative people.

4. Aborigines Should Determine Their Own Future

Aborigines, of course, should make choices about their future, but if they are to *determine* their future, they will possess more power than we have.

Much of the unreality in Aboriginal affairs arises because the policy of self-determination suggests that Aborigines can have whatever future they like. With the policy goes the commitment to consultation which encourages people to construct wish-lists. Aborigines, like the rest of us, if asked what they want, will list different things, contradictory things and things that cannot be had.

What is the situation Aborigines face? They all use goods and services from the capitalist economy; if they are to enjoy these without becoming dependent on welfare, they must work and invest in that economy.

A lot of commentary on Aboriginal affairs is devoted to evading this truth. The dependency on welfare is deplored, but the jobs for Aborigines must be where they want them and of the sort which they find congenial and which don't interfere with ceremonies and the attendance at funerals. That would of course be the ideal, but capitalism, as we know too well, does not offer its opportunities exactly according to our wishes. At this moment there are hundreds of engineers and architects who find they cannot work at their profession and live at home. If they are practising their profession it is in Singapore or Hong Kong; if they live at home they are driving cabs. Tens of thousands of people are unemployed because we have accepted that factories must close and work practices change if we are to have a secure economic future. Aborigines must make choices and adjustments too. No policy can rescue them from that fate.

The policy of self-determination has placed Aborigines in positions of authority. When they begin to exercise authority, they meet opposition and resistance from Aborigines. They are denounced as 'coconuts', dark on the outside, but white inside. Strangely, when some policy-makers and commentators see this, they side with the critics of Aboriginal authority. Like them, they have developed the notion that self-determination means that Aborigines should have whatever they want, without terms and conditions or considerations of the needs of other Aborigines.

The Aboriginal Development Commission was set up by the Fraser Liberal government. All its board members were Aborigines, who were appointed by the minister, and it was given a large budget to support projects for Aboriginal advancement. When Gerry Hand, the Labor minister for Aboriginal affairs, travelled around the country he heard complaints about the remoteness of this body and its bureaucratic ways, and of course gripes about particular decisions. The Minister decided to abolish this body and create an elected one in its place. We now have the Aboriginal and Torres Strait Islander Commission and exactly the same criticisms are made of it. Already these are being interpreted as signs of the failure of that body. Good grief! By these standards the federal Parliament and its bureaucracy would have been scrapped long since. Authority creates dissatisfaction: this is the noise of its operation.

One compensation outcasts have is the warmth of fellow-feeling among themselves. The oppressors order them around, but they never order each other around. As they cease to be outcasts, this fellow-feeling goes. This is why Aborigines are so ambivalent about joining our society and so suspicious of their leaders. Our position must be to support the leaders who are taking responsibility as distinct from those who are creating wish-lists.

ATSIC can no doubt perform better; it should be criticised, it may need to be reformed, but it should not be abandoned simply because some Aborigines do not like it. If the chief aim of policy is not to displease Aborigines, little will change.

My own inclination is to give ATSIC more autonomy. Free it from public service rules and strict accountability and let it respond in a more free-wheeling way to Aborigines and their needs. We broke all our own rules when we denied Aborigines civic and political rights; a strict adherence to our rules will not make a broken people whole. Canberra can regulate life, but it cannot create it.

5. *White Prejudice Is the Chief Barrier to Aboriginal Advancement*
There is still some prejudice against Aborigines, much less than a generation ago, and it is partially offset by a huge fund of goodwill. Prejudice is a very minor obstacle to Aboriginal advancement compared to the matters already discussed.

Why is the Aboriginal unemployment rate so high? – because so many Aborigines live where there are no jobs.

Why are Aborigines still so far from our standard of living? – because, understandably, they are in two minds about joining the society which oppressed them.

Why are Aboriginal communities poorly run? – because they are artificial communities and too much is expected of them.

Why are Aborigines unhealthy? – because many of them live in unsocieties.

Nevertheless, in the thinking of ministers of Aboriginal affairs white prejudice bulks large. It's easiest to blame this when things go wrong. Next time the Minister reaches an impasse, instead of lecturing us, he might try re-examining the assumptions on which present policy rests.

1994

The Distinctiveness of Australian Democracy

Democratic countries have their democracy in common, but how democracy works and what it means to the people differ from country to country. The society in which democracy operates is different in each country and each country has its own history of democracy: how it came about and what came before it.

France became a democracy suddenly when a movement to reform the royal government turned into a revolution in 1789. The first democratic parliament was elected in 1792. It supported a dictatorial government that kept itself in power by executing thousands of its opponents.

Britain became a democracy very slowly and peacefully. The violence in England took place in the seventeenth century when the parliament made itself supreme over the king. That parliament was elected and controlled by landowners. The franchise was first widened 150 years later in 1832 but it took a hundred years to establish full democracy. Since there was no payment of members until 1911, the rich landowners, their friends and relations continued for a long time to be the largest group elected to parliament.

The United States became a separate country by rebelling against Britain. It proclaimed that all men were created equal and set up a new republican form of government. To belong to this new nation was to believe in certain political principles. At first the United States was not democratic. It became so quite soon and without violence. Democracy became identified with America, the natural result of the principles of equality with which the nation had begun.

The Australian colonies became democracies suddenly (like France), peacefully (like Britain) and while remaining colonies (unlike the United States). These three circumstances, as we shall see, had a great effect on what sort of democracy it was and how the people related to it.

The democracies established in the Australian states are now almost 150 years old. The central democracy, the Commonwealth of Australia, is over a hundred years old. They are among the oldest and most stable democracies in the world.

This should be one of the things Australians are proud about, but Australians do not think of their political record when they think of what sort of people they are. Society itself in Australia is very democratic, but Australians have little regard for their democratic government. How this strange gap came about and how government works well despite it, are the questions we will now try to answer.

*

The answer begins with origins. Democracy – manhood suffrage for the Legislative Assemblies – was established rapidly in the 1850s immediately after the grant of self-government. There was no large-scale movement in support of it. British thinking on constitutional matters was orthodoxy with that extra tightness produced in a dependent society. Democracy was a dirty word.

Two factors nevertheless made for democracy. In 1850 the House of Lords was tricked into halving the qualifications for the franchise in Australia. It was told that under the existing rules rich ex-convicts got the vote and free working men recently arrived did not. A respectable electorate required a low qualification. The low qualification then set was made worthless by the inflation caused by the gold rush which began in 1851. The tenant of any hovel in Sydney and Melbourne got the vote. The franchise had become so wide without any change in the law that conservatives, who were in charge of drawing up the constitutions for self-government, added new qualifications based on salary rather than property and rent in order to give the vote to their household servants, clerks and managers. It was a desperate ploy: to stave off full democracy they were giving more people the vote. When manhood suffrage was introduced (with a residential qualification) it gave the vote to very few new people compared with the huge increases that had occurred under the processes I have just outlined.

South Australia was rather different. Manhood suffrage was established early – in the constitution for self-government. The great book on South Australia's early history, *Paradise of Dissent* (1957) by Douglas Pike, spoke of a democratic triumph and of democrats. If Pike was justified in using these terms my argument is wrong for South Australia. Pike's footnotes direct the reader to a press report of a meeting of democrats who formed an association to watch over the debates on the constitution. This was fifty working men in an Adelaide pub. They certainly had a very democratic program. Mr Morris outlined it in his speech: manhood suffrage (for both houses), vote by ballot, House of Assembly elected for three years with equal electorates, upper house to be elected by the whole colony, members to serve for six years. Mr Morris concluded his speech with these words:

> This association is not a Chartist, Radical, or Democratic one, or one
> to be called by any of those ugly names, but an association which must
> watch over the formation of a constitution which will secure prosper-
> ity and civil and religious liberty to us and our children.

Here too *democracy* was a dirty word.

To understand this founding movement properly we need to discredit an alternative explanation for the easy triumph of democracy. It runs like this:

The first settlers came from very unequal societies where inferior people had to show respect to superior people. Most of the migrants to Australia did not come from the superior upper classes; they were middle class or working people. They wanted to get rid of old-world distinctions and create in the colonies a world in which people did not have to know their place. Anyone in Australia who tried to pretend they were upper class was just laughed at. The old distinctions simply could not be re-established in the new land. People began to treat each other as equals and so democracy was the only form of government that would suit them.

This is very misleading. Society was not democratised first and then politics. It was the other way about. Politics was democratised long before society was.

It is true that the migrants rejected some aspects of the old society: they did not want position to depend on birth or education or knowing the right people. But those who came to the colonies to better themselves wanted to show off their success in the old ways. What other signs did they know; what other signs would be recognised?

The migrants did not want dukes or lords in Australia, but successful migrants claimed the title of gentleman. Gentleman was an English rank which proved to be an excellent import for the colonies. It was not quite definite; the qualifications were elastic and could be stretched. They were stretched a long way. The test for not being involved in business was easily dropped. Even true gentlemen in Australia – and there were some – were very closely involved in money-making. So that made it acceptable for others to be making money. But the test was not dropped altogether. It was shifted. If you made money as a merchant, that was all right; if you ran a shop and served the public, you could not be a gentleman. As to good breeding, the new gentlemen in Australia pushed their ancestors as far up the social scale as they dared.

The final result was that in Australia most men who had made money could be gentlemen. This was a huge change in the rules and it was not reached without great social turmoil, but the category of gentleman did not implode. The one definite test for a new gentleman in Australia was that he had to be wealthy and a wealthy man could look like a gentleman once he had a large house and a carriage and dressed like a gentleman with top hat and tails.

The first partly-elected legislatures in Australia were made up of landowners and squatters along with a few merchants and lawyers. They thought of themselves as gentlemen and were treated as such. They could appear as the local equivalent of the gathering of gentlemen at Westminster.

All this changed with the rapid move to democracy in the 1850s. The rich found it hard to get elected and were forced to retreat to the upper houses. Poor men of little education replaced them. Members heaped vulgar abuse on each other and some were only in parliament to benefit themselves.

Parliamentarians still dressed as gentlemen and hoped to be treated as gentlemen, but now there was an implosion: no-one believed that parliamentarians were gentlemen. The new democratic institution did not dress itself in its own clothes; it set itself up for a fall by putting on a distinctly undemocratic uniform.

Rich and educated people now regarded politicians as a low-class bunch of incompetents. They made fun of those who could not speak or write properly, who had done lowly work before they became MPs, and who had wives who could never be accepted into good society. If a rich and well-educated man did get into parliament, he was always apologising for keeping such low company. It did give him a lot of good stories to shock and amuse his friends.

These very ordinary parliamentarians had been elected by the votes of ordinary people. Their votes gave them the opportunity to show that they did not want parliamentarians to be just the rich and the well-educated. They elected parliamentarians who could not look down on them and whom they did not have to look up to. But they had not got rid of the idea that parliament was a place they should be able to respect. By their votes they had produced parliaments that they too despised.

Respect for parliament evaporated very quickly. In the Supreme Court in Sydney in 1861 the chief justice at the top of society and a criminal at the bottom shared a joke at the politicians' expense. The criminal was being tried for escaping from jail. Before the case began he asked that he be given another judge because it was the chief justice who had given him the harsh sentence that had put him in jail. The criminal said the chief justice might have 'prejudicial feelings' against him. The judge, thinking he had said 'political feelings', replied, 'Why should I have political feelings against you. Are you a member of parliament?' To which the criminal replied, 'Not yet.'

When the parliaments acted to protect their reputation, they discovered how little respect they enjoyed. The big man behind the bribing of the Victorian parliament in the 1860s was the squatter Hugh Glass. When the parliament committed him to prison, he became a popular hero. The Supreme Court set him free and the parliament took no further action. The most corrupt member of parliament was C. E. Jones, the member for Ballarat. While he was a minister, he took money to organise opposition to his own government. When this was discovered, the parliament expelled him, but Ballarat re-elected him.

The Ballarat voters thought he was no worse than the men who had expelled him, so they were not going to see him punished. A vicious cycle had set in. Parliament was despised, but voters continued to elect men who kept its reputation low.

In recent years, it is said, the reputation of politicians has fallen. If this is true, the change has been very small compared to the catastrophic collapse that can be dated precisely to the introduction of democracy in the 1850s.

*

So these are the inauspicious beginnings: a democracy ashamed to speak its name run by politicians who are held in contempt. But it need not have remained so. I consider a number of forces which elsewhere helped to attach citizens to the democratic state but which did not have that effect in Australia.

First is nationalism; it brought little credit to the state for reasons that are obvious. The independence of the state was readily granted by the metropolitan power and did not have to be struggled for. The Australian admiration for Britain increased after it had allowed self-government to the colonies in the 1850s and had encouraged the formation of the colonies into a nation in the 1890s. Australian nationality was formed in opposition to Britain but in other spheres – by the boasting about a more open society, by beating England at cricket, by producing superior soldiers. Australians are completely indifferent to the state as the symbol of their independence, as those who have tried to pluck this string for the republican cause have discovered.

One of the attractions of democracy for the common people of Britain and Europe was that it would give them the status of citizens rather than that of being the poor or the lower orders. In Australia, however, the common man was living well without needing to show deference to his betters before democratic politics began. Democracy was not needed to establish his dignity.

In the 1850s skilled building workers in Melbourne established the eight-hour day, the symbol of the higher status and rewards open to working men in this country. Soon afterwards all men acquired the vote, but it was the eight-hour victory that was celebrated annually by a public holiday, procession, picnic and sports, not the achievement of manhood suffrage, which had no heroes or heroics to commemorate. Working men used their vote to protect and extend their gains – to demand for instance that the state legislate for the eight-hour day or impose it on state contractors. With the collapse in living standards in the 1890s depression, working men used the Labor Party in an effort to get the state to guarantee what they had enjoyed previously. The institutional guarantor of a living wage became the arbitration system. Here was an attachment to the state, but not of a civic sort: the state was the guarantor of the living wage.

By the end of the nineteenth century there was a democratic movement openly proclaiming a democratic ideology. Its leaders were the progressive liberals who were committed to getting rid of the non-democratic elements in the colonial constitutions – like restricted upper houses and plural voting – who supported female suffrage, and who planned to establish the new Commonwealth of Australia on a democratic basis.

The progressive liberals gave serious attention for the first time to the concept of citizenship, the term that gives the people a civic identity; in the 1850s the term could not be used because the colonists were then unquestionably subjects of the Queen. The progressive liberals tried and failed to write a citizenship clause into the new federal constitution. The difficulty was that the starting point for the definition of citizenship was the status British subject – but you could not say that all British subjects in the Commonwealth were to be citizens because that would confer citizenship on Chinese born in Hong Kong and Indians. Against these people the colonies had enacted discriminatory laws and the new Commonwealth might well want to do the same. Safer then to do nothing. So for all its democratic elements the Commonwealth constitution was silent on citizenship – as it still is.

Early in the twentieth century support for Labor rose at an astonishing rate and by 1910 the Labor Party had squeezed out the progressive liberals and had taken the progressive mantle to itself. It was not overly interested in citizenship, for how could men and women under capitalism be considered equals until the Labor platform had been implemented? Those who were interested in citizenship regarded Labor's demand that members vote at the direction of a caucus as the antithesis of the independent judgment that a responsible citizen should exercise.

The new group that took citizenship seriously was the women's movement. Unlike men, women had had to struggle to get the vote and they based their case in part on the claim that they were already citizens, involved as they were in the care of children and the running of charities. After they got the vote the obligation of citizenship was their warrant for maintaining their own organisations and attacking the party politics of men. The women presented themselves as the more responsible sex, the true citizens, concerned for the common good rather than partisan advantage. The effort was heroic, but the women did not break the mould of party politics. Most women voted along the same lines as their men.

In the early Commonwealth progressive liberal governments introduced compulsory military training for boys and young men. Citizenship and soldiering were firmly linked. The name of the army for which they were being trained was the Citizens Military Forces. Billy Hughes in the Labor Party was a firm supporter of a citizens' army and with some difficulty he persuaded his party to accept it. Labor in office after 1910 implemented the policy of compulsory training.

In World War I, Hughes as prime minister tried to get his party to support conscription for service overseas. He argued that Labor had accepted in principle that all should contribute to the nation's defence; when the nation's fate was being decided in France conscription was the fair and efficient way to reinforce the Australian forces. The party organisation would not accept this and the party split. The Labor anti-conscriptionists were not, at least in public, opposed to the war; that would have been fatal. They had to develop a principled argument against conscription that would apply in any circumstances. The argument became that no more profound threat to individual liberty could be devised than making a man fight against his will. Conscription was undemocratic because it took away human freedom – an argument which has had no purchase in any other democracy since 1916–17. It remained a great force in this democracy. Labor took its argument seriously and after the war its platform declared against conscription in all circumstances not only for service overseas but even for the defence of the continent against invasion. In this matter the socialist Labor Party was the defender of voluntarism. It was their opponents who stressed communal obligation and preached against selfishness.

Labor people still honour their party's defeat of conscription in World War I. I regard it as a disaster on several grounds: it was damaging to the cause of progressive social reform, to civic life, to a coherent defence policy – in World War II, Australia had to have two armies, a volunteer army that could serve anywhere, and a conscripted one to defend Australian territory. And the effect most pertinent to our theme: it separated soldiering and citizenship. In the years since some men have volunteered to fight; others have been conscripted, but only for limited purposes. Australia has a strong military tradition but it is not a tradition associated with the state; it brings no lustre to democratic government.

*

The attitude of the Labor Party was also responsible for another of the dissociations that distinguish our polity: the welfare system is not a universal one based on the contributions of the people. The non-Labor parties planned such schemes between the wars and came close to implementing them. Labor was opposed to contributions for welfare: it wanted the rich to pay for the welfare of the poor. In office during World War II, Labor introduced welfare benefits paid for from general revenue – and so kept true to the party platform; but it began to subject the workers to income tax – which was against the platform. This has remained the Australian way of welfare. Here the welfare system does not bind citizens together as equals. It is a system where some people pay, somewhat reluctantly, for the welfare of others. The exception is Medicare to which all contribute according to their means and from which all benefit. The strong support for Medicare gives us an inkling of what we have lost by running the rest of welfare on other principles.

A similar situation has developed with schools. In some democracies – France, Germany, Sweden, the United States – government schools take children of all backgrounds and teach them that they are future citizens of the one country. The government schools symbolise a common citizenship. That hasn't happened in Australia because private schools have been strong and are getting stronger. The reasons for this can be given very briefly: the Catholic Church stymied the plan to have a common primary school system and until it was too late the Labor Party was not interested enough in secondary education to challenge the dominance of the private and church schools in that sector.

Australians of course don't see private schools as an anomaly. A visiting American educational expert in the 1950s saw it as highly anomalous: he wrote that he was always being told what a democratic egalitarian society Australia was. If that was so, he wondered, why did the private schools hold such a strong place in the education system?

Well might he ask. His mistake, though, was to think that egalitarianism is genuine only if it shows itself in formal institutions like schools. That is not the Australian way. Australians treat each other as equals. This is the egalitarianism they have perfected. Australian democracy is first of all a democracy of manners.

Some people claim that Australian society is not egalitarian because there are wide differences of income, which may now be getting wider. This misses the point of Australian egalitarianism. It is the way Australians blot out differences when people meet face to face. They talk to each other as if they are equals and they will put down anyone claiming social superiority. It is the feel of Australian society that is so markedly egalitarian, not its social structure. The democracy of manners was established when differences in income were much greater than they are now.

The democracy of manners developed slowly – and for most of its history it was a relationship among men; only recently have women been part of this equality. The democracy of manners owes nothing to democratic politics, but it has implications for politics. Politics is necessarily about power, about inequality. In democracies those who exercise power gain their authority by the votes of the people. That inequality Australians are reluctant to recognise. Their egalitarianism is a bond of equals, in part directed against the disruption of authority. Australians will recognise that a boss or a military officer must have power, though they will respect him only if he exercises power properly. But politicians have no excuse for wanting power; they have wilfully put themselves above the rest. They will have trouble therefore in gaining respect, no matter who they are or what they do. Many Australians seem to think politics exists only because there are a few egomaniacs wanting to be politicians.

The democracy of manners is a precious achievement. One of the reasons people fought for democracy was that they wanted respect for ordinary people, that they should not be humiliated and scorned. Australians achieved that outside politics and their egalitarianism is more deep-seated and genuine because it is not a political doctrine. But so that all men can be equal, politicians have to be dishonoured.

*

It is time to look to the other side of my original question: why does the democracy work well despite the people having no strong attachment to it?

The European settlers of Australia were very diverse. There were people from three nations – the English, Scots and Irish – and they followed two faiths – Catholic and Protestant. The Australian colonies inherited their history of mutual suspicion, prejudice and bitterness.

From the first the different people lived amongst each other. Unlike North America, there were no localities which were solely Scotch or solely Catholic. In the United States the Irish came late to a settled society and crowded into ghettos in the cities. In Australia the Irish were part of the founding population and settled throughout the country with everyone else.

When different people live in their own areas and maintain their own culture and faith, it is hard for them to agree to belong to the one country. They need some idea or principle or feeling to bind them together. If this does not happen the country might split up.

In Australia the people of the three nations and two faiths were thrown together from the beginning. The oddity of Australia for the new settlers was not simply the physical environment; it was having so many half-foreigners as neighbours. They all had to make their lives in this new, strange mixture. They created a harmonious society by setting their differences aside and being good neighbours, or work-mates or committee men. Australian society was integrated from the bottom up rather than from the top down. It did not need politics to unite it; sometimes politics was a destructive force.

From the earliest times there was a widespread determination to stop old-world hatreds from taking root here. Of course there were some who wanted to keep them alive. The ministers of the churches and their closest followers believed their faith was the true one and were ready to denounce the others as false. But even people who took their own religion seriously might not want to join in open warfare with others – unless something happened to reignite the old fears they usually kept under control. Fortunately, for the cause of social harmony, there were large numbers of people who did not take their religion too seriously.

Liberalism was a strong force in nineteenth-century Australia and it underpinned the task of keeping religion from disturbing the peace. But something much more positive was at work in Australian society: people actively worked to keep the peace by making sure that in community organisations there were representatives from all back-grounds and faiths. So there were Protestants and Catholics, English, Irish and Scots, on the boards and managing committees of hospi-tals and charities, friendly societies, sporting clubs and mechanics institutes.

This desire for social peace was not a political doctrine; it was not, as the political scientists would say, an acceptance of pluralism. The colonists accepted that there were differences between people that were not going to disappear, but they did not want simply to tolerate differ-ences and live apart from each other. They wanted to find ways to come together; they thought the peace would not be secure unless this happened.

Behind this desire was a shared memory of how much bitterness had been caused by religious and ethnic differences in the countries from which they had come:

Our children shall, upon this new-won shore –
Warned by all sorrows that have gone before –
Build up the glory of a grand new World.
—John Farrell, 1883

In politics it was harder to maintain harmony. Election campaigns often turned into battles between Catholics and Protestants. On a committee or in a parade, all groups could be represented, but elections were inevitably a contest. If a Catholic ran for parliament all Catholics were encouraged to vote for him. Protestants then became alarmed that Catholics – urged on, they were sure, by their priests – were attempting to take over the country. They tried to rally all Protestants to oppose the Catholic candidate. This could happen without there being a policy division between Catholic and Protestant. From the 1870s of course there was – a bitter division over policy on education.

I think historians have been too ready to read back from sectarian disputes in politics to deep division within society. Australian cities did not turn into a Beirut or Belfast where the two warring sides have their own areas. The conflict in politics and public life remained at a distance from the community. It did not so much reflect community division as save the community from division.

Protestants and Catholics still lived amongst each other. They interacted in the neighbourhood, at work and in playing and following sport. They interacted in the unions and the Labor Party. Intermarriage continued despite the opposition of the priests. There were still many people on both sides wanting to set aside their differences. The Australian style of dealing with difference did not disappear. It is the social foundation of the peacefulness and decency of Australian democracy.

The divide between Catholic and Protestant ceased to be important in the 1960s. It had no deep roots in the structure of society, so when both sides decided to treat each other as fellow Christians, the dispute disappeared.

*

After World War II, Australian society had to deal with new differences on a vast scale. A mass migration program began which brought to this British society non-English-speaking people, at first from Europe, later from Asia and Africa, the Middle East and Latin America. Australians applied to this new challenge the formula which had brought peace to their mixed society. The government, supported by the people, wanted the new migrants to mix in with the old population and not form separate enclaves. The government knew that this would happen only if migrants were welcomed. It told the Australian people to call the migrants New Australians and it set up the Good Neighbour Council which arranged for old Australians to help the New Australians settle in.

Old Australians were suspicious of the newcomers and a few were openly hostile, but on the whole Australians accepted them. If the newcomers wanted to make a go of it here and did not make a nuisance of themselves, they could be Australians. Migrants found that Australians were generally friendly, but they were puzzled that Australians were not interested in their culture and experience. They were encountering the Australian style of mixing where people remain friendly by not exploring differences.

The migrants did not mix in as rapidly as the government had hoped. In the inner cities they did form something like enclaves. But within ten years they were buying houses in the suburbs and scattering themselves widely in the process. After twenty years their children were marrying old Australians. Australian society was again being rapidly integrated from the bottom up.

*

Almond and Verba in their famous study, *The Civic Culture: Political Attitudes and Democracy in Five Nations* (1963) identify three orientations towards the state – the participant, the subject, and the parochial. Participants believe they can influence government; subjects accept government authority; parochials don't understand government but act to get what they want from it. A good civic culture requires a balance of participant and subject orientations. Almond and Verba judge the UK as strong, perhaps too strong, on the orientation as subject. They explain this British attitude by the survival of deference to a ruling class. My take on Australia is that, as in Britain, the subject orientation is strong, but the British reason for this can't obtain here. So how can egalitarians be compliant subjects?

Australians think of themselves as anti-authority. It is not true. Australians are suspicious of persons in authority, but towards impersonal authority they are very obedient.

This is the country which for a long time closed its pubs at 6 p.m. and which pioneered the compulsory wearing of seatbelts in cars. Its people since 1924 have accepted the compulsion to vote. Its anti-smoking legislation is so tough that smoking is prohibited in its largest sporting stadium, the Melbourne Cricket Ground, though it is open to the skies. At an Australian Rules football match, the fans yell obscenities at the umpire and then at half-time walk quietly outside to have a smoke.

Australian government was not created in Australia. The government came off the boat, in the person of the governor and his officials, carrying all the authority of the government in Britain. With only one exception settlers never had to come together and form a government. The authority which secured to them the benefits of their pioneering was not of their making.

Melbourne was the exception; it alone of the colonial capitals was an unauthorised settlement. For a few months the settlers did govern themselves. Then the governor in Sydney visited and installed a magistrate responsible to him.

The founding governments of the Australian colonies had the virtues of the British government that created them; they provided a secure world in which all people enjoyed protection of their property and liberty. The convicts of course did not have their liberty, but they were deprived of it by the law, which also set the term for their release and protected the property and persons of ex-convicts as if they had always been free.

The early Australian governments were actually better than the British. The British government was run by the aristocracy and gentry who rewarded their followers with government jobs. The job might pay well but have no duties. If the job did have duties, the holder was not obliged to perform them himself. He hired a deputy to do the work, but kept most of the proceeds for himself. Jobs frequently did not have salaries; the holder made his money by the collection of fees which he could manipulate to his own advantage.

This system was being reformed just as Australia was settled and so the new rules applied here from the beginning. All jobs had to be real jobs; the work could not be done by a deputy; the reward would be a fixed salary rather than fees. So the British officials who ruled under the governor's control were efficient and honest.

Government did not begin with taxation. The funds of the first governments came from the British taxpayer. The job of the Colonial Office was to get the governor to limit his spending and to raise money by local taxation. It was some time before the colonists in Australia were paying the full cost of their government. For the first hundred years they never really did that because their defence was provided free by the British navy. For most of human history defence spending has been the biggest item in government budgets. In the Australian colonies it was one of the smallest, which allowed government funds to be spent on the internal development of the colony.

Usually in empires, governors of colonies taxed the people and sent the proceeds back to the mother country. In the Australian colonies taxes were not sent to Britain. After the revolt of the American colonies Britain resolved not to tax its overseas settlers. Britain got its benefit from the colonies through the increase of its trade and the returns on the private funds invested in Australia. The governor's job was to promote the development of the economy, which would enable the colony to pay its way and bring more benefit to Britain. There was a basic harmony between what the British government wanted of the governors and what the settlers wanted.

Governors and their officials built roads and bridges, improved ports, encouraged exploration, surveyed land for settlement, and provided settlers with their labour force, at first convicts and later free immigrants. The British government which sent the governors did none of these things in its own country. So the function of government changed in Australia; it was not primarily to keep order within and defeat enemies without; it was a resource on which settlers could draw to make money.

The social character of the government changed too, or rather it did not have a social character. In Britain government was closely linked to the social order; the richest people were the great landowners and they and their friends ran the government. In Australia the government was one person, the governor, who was detached from, and superior to, all groups in the local society. Yet government was much more than the person of the governor; he embodied the full authority of the British government and was the representative of the monarch. So government was both more singular and more abstract.

Settlers of course attempted to influence the governor. The richer settlers had more influence than others and they occupied the positions in the early legislatures, which were at first appointed and then partly elected. But these bodies never controlled the governor, and the governors did not rule simply in the interests of the wealthy settlers. Several governors clashed with the wealthy settlers. The demand for self-government in New South Wales in the 1840s came from the rich squatters who objected to Governor Gipps attempting to make them pay more for their land.

In the mid-1850s governors and officials were replaced by premiers and ministers responsible to parliament. The transition was smooth. The public servants remained in place. The regular business of government remained the same: to provide the infrastructure for the development of the economy. Democratic government made it easier for more people to make demands for roads, bridges and local services. If people wanted something done, they went in a deputation to the minister, escorted by their local member. If the local member could not get results out of ministers, he lost his seat at the next election.

The democratic governments, like those run by the governors, were omni-competent; they took on everything. They ran the school system and the police, which in Britain and in many other countries were the business of local government. Local government in Australia was weak; it was established late and did not cover the whole country. Its chief job was the making of local roads and in the towns the collection of rubbish. Where there was no local government, the colonial government did all that was necessary. In most of the countryside of New South Wales there was no local government until 1906.

The colonial governments did all their work without imposing direct taxation. Until late in the nineteenth century there was no income tax and no company tax. All the money you earned you kept. Government was not a burden that you had to pay for; it was a magic pudding; you could cut slice after slice and there was always more.

The magic was performed by the government collecting its revenue from taxes that you were unaware of – duties collected on imported goods – and from the sale of crown lands – which was not a tax at all. Local government did not tax directly; its revenue came from rates collected on land. This was the chief reason why it did so little and why in many places it did not exist at all. No-one wanted to give local government more responsibilities because that would increase direct taxes.

The first government schools were built only if local people raised some of the cost of the building. That gave them some say in the running of the school. But from the 1870s the colonial governments, without raising any new taxation, were able to cover the full cost of school building. Local control of education disappeared. Who could quarrel with this when schools came for nothing?

The democratic governments were responsible for huge undertakings. The government railways were the largest businesses and biggest employers in colonial times. The provision of teachers and policemen throughout the colony and the sale and management of crown lands required large government departments.

Colonial politics did not look as if it would manage these large undertakings well. Members were concerned with getting benefits for their electorate and willing to trade their support to do so. Governments were short-lived and always had only a precarious hold on power.

But though politics was confused and unstable, administration was honest and efficient. Frequent changes of government did not matter much because there were no fundamental disagreements over what governments should be doing. The senior public servants had tenure and many of them were of outstanding quality. Ministers appointed public servants to reward supporters but incoming ministers did not sack existing public servants.

To their credit, politicians did not use politics to enrich themselves. A railway might be built to please constituents though there was little real need for it; a railway might even be built to run close to the property owned by members of parliament; but the money for railways did not go directly into MPs' pockets. The governor, still appointed from Britain, was a guarantor that proper standards were maintained.

Though the colonists had little respect for their politicians, their faith in government grew in the nineteenth century. In the twentieth century they created a national government which was meant to have limited powers, but quickly came to be used as an all-purpose facility like the colonial governments. It was to protect and foster industry, ensure workers received a living wage, and that farmers got a good return for their crops.

*

Government in Australia has been continuous; it has never broken down and had to be reconstituted. Except in the treatment of Aborigines, government has never been an oppressive force, something that large numbers of people feared. Government has never been simply a means of fleecing people; it has always been a supplier of services that people wanted.

There has been strong government but no ruling class. When the governors ruled, the rich landowners and squatters thought they would take over when self-government was granted. But when self-government came they were quickly defeated and democratic politics began. The democratic politicians were a very mixed bag indeed, not identified with any one group in society, so distinct that they were a group in themselves – the despised politicians.

Government is without social character; it is an impersonal force. That makes it possible for Australian egalitarians to give it the great respect that its record deserves.

The most distinctive characteristic of the Australian political system is compulsory voting. Polls show that a clear majority of people is in favour of compulsory voting. If there were no compulsion, there would be a reasonable turnout. But Australians want to be compelled to vote.

Those who write and comment on politics are overwhelmingly in favour of compulsion. In defending compulsion, they make a distinctively Australian contribution of political philosophy. To the objection that compulsory voting is a denial of liberty, they argue that governments regularly make citizens do things – to serve on juries, to pay taxes, to fight in the defence of the country. Of course governments compel citizens, but compulsory voting relates to another issue altogether: how governments are themselves created. Are citizens to be forced to create governments?

This argument has been developed in a society where the value placed on personal liberty and the responsibilities of citizenship has shifted markedly from that in other English-speaking democracies. The existence of government is taken for granted and the people can be forced to be citizens.

*

Australian democracy is certainly distinctive. There has been strong opposition to military conscription, but not to compulsory voting. Egalitarianism has not led to a universal welfare system nor prohibited the growth of private schools. Politicians have been held in contempt, but governments have been omni-competent and efficient. The people have been scornful of British snobbishness, but loyal to a British monarch. Men have been keen about mateship, leaving women to take citizenship seriously. There are no grand Australian statements about democracy, but the values that underpin it flourish in society at large.

All these characteristics have their causes. Taken together they account for that strange gap, that lack of attachment, between a democratic society and its democratic institutions of government, with which our enquiry began.

Another way of approaching the matter is to say that the movements for political democracy were not strong enough to command the society and to set its ideals. Manhood suffrage was achieved in the mid-nineteenth century when the word *democracy* could not be safely uttered. Democratic practice thus began without a democratic ideology.

A democratic ideology was certainly present in the second democratic movement at the end of the nineteenth century. Its carriers were at first the progressive liberals. It looked for a time as if the Labor Party that supplanted them could carry forward their ideal of an enlightened, democratic people shaping a new social order. Labor projected itself as the true national party and boasted of its moves to give the nation a strong defence force and to support compulsory military training. But in the Great War those who wanted Labor to be a class party for the workers took control, threw out the parliamentary leaders and gave Labor the pyrrhic victory of anti-conscription. Labor now carried the tag of being the disloyal party.

Labor recovered and was able on several occasions to govern well, but only as one party in a two-party system. It was not the standard-bearer of a wider democratic movement as it had been before the war. Indeed, the party system came to discourage wider democratic involvement. The small women's movement tried valiantly to keep alive the ideal of good citizens acting outside the party system – and failed.

Australia still awaits the moment when its natural democrats will become self-conscious citizens.

2002

Envoi: *Diversity and Unity*

As I was walking up Martin Place, I saw a Vietnamese busker playing a didgeridoo.

My theme is Diversity and Unity in modern Australia. Should the busker be set down under Diversity? Previously buskers in Martin Place were Anglo-Celts; now buskers can come from any nation and race on earth. Or does the busker better belong under Unity? Previously Aborigines played the didgeridoo: now Australians of all sorts play the didgeridoo.

The standard story of what is happening to our society is that it is becoming more diverse. But the marrying and partnering of people of all sorts across all boundaries is the greatest unifying force in Australia. The United States never saw such a rapidly melting melting-pot. It will produce before too long a new people who will have darker skins, much better suited to this place and our sun.

In fifty years there may still be buskers in Martin Place and they may play didgeridoos, but the observer will no longer be able to label them Anglo-Celt or Vietnamese; they will have no other name than Australian. I am sorry I will not live to see that day, for the Australians are going to be a beautiful people.

2001

Publication Details

'Changing My Mind' appeared in Stuart Macintyre ed., *The Historian's Conscience: Australian historians and the ethics of history*, Melbourne University Press, Melbourne, 2004.

'Australia's Absurd History: A Critique of Multiculturalism', *Overland*, no. 117, February 1990, pp. 5–10.

'Distance in Australia – Was It a Tyrant?', *Historical Studies*, vol. 16, no. 64, 1975, pp. 435–447.

'Women and History', *Quadrant*, no. 314, March 1995, pp. 35–43.

'Australian History and European Civilisation', *Quadrant*, no. 296, May 1993, pp. 28–40.

'How Sorry Can We Be?', written for this collection.

'Convict Society' is chapter subsection 'Convicts and Society' in *Convict society and its enemies: a history of early New South Wales*, George Allen & Unwin, Sydney, 1983, pp.78–82.

'Transformation on the Land' is an excerpt from 'La sociedad rural y la politica en Australia, 1850–1930' in J. Fogarty, E. Gallo, H. Diegue eds, *Argentina y Australia*, Instituto Torcuato Di Tella, Buenos Aires, 1979.

'Colonial Society' appeared as 'Keeping Colonial History Colonial: the Hartz thesis revisited', *Historical Studies*, vol. 21, no. 82, 1984, pp. 85–104.

'Egalitarianism', *Australian Cultural History*, 1986, Myths and Clichés, no. 5, 1986, pp. 12–31. Reprinted in S. L. Goldberg and F. B. Smith eds, *Australian Cultural History*, Cambridge University Press, Melbourne, 1988.

'The Pioneer Legend', *Historical Studies*, vol. 18, no. 71, 1978, pp. 316–337. The shortened version in this collection appeared in J. Carroll ed., *Intruders in the Bush: The Australian Quest for Identity*, Oxford University Press, Melbourne, 1982.

'Federation: Destiny and Identity', in *For Peace, Order, and Good Government: Papers on Parliament*, no. 37, Department of the Senate, Canberra, 2001, which draws on chapters 1 and 2 of *The sentimental nation: the making of the Australian Commonwealth*, Oxford University Press, Melbourne, 2000.

'Labor and Conscription' is excerpted from 'Australian Defence and Conscription: a reassessment', Parts I and II, *Australian Historical Studies*, vol. 25, no. 101, October 1993, pp. 608–27; vol. 26, no. 102, April 1994, pp. 39–56.

'The Gallipoli Landing' is an excerpt from 'Other People's Wars: Anzac and Empire', *Quadrant*, no. 270, October 1990, pp. 15–20.

'The Communist Threat' appeared as 'Communism and Australia's Historians', *Quadrant*, no. 265. April 1990, pp. 26–31.

'Who Tugged the Forelock?', *Quadrant*, no. 321, November 1995, pp. 10–16.

'Republicanism' appeared as 'Towards the Republic' in Robert Manne ed., *The Australian Century: Political Struggle in the Building of a Nation*, Text, Melbourne, 1999.

'Five Fallacies of Aboriginal Policy', *Quadrant*, no. 308, July–August 1994, pp. 11–16.

'The Distinctiveness of Australian Democracy', *Quadrant*, no. 392, December 2002, pp. 19–27, which summarises the chief arguments of *Australia's Democracy: a short history*, Allen & Unwin, Sydney, 2002.

'Envoi' is the opening and closing paragraphs of 'More or Less Diverse', in Helen Irving ed., *Unity and Diversity: A National Conversation*, The Barton Lectures, ABC Books, Sydney, 2001, pp. 110–129.

Books by John Hirst

Adelaide and the country 1870–1917: their social and political relationships, Melbourne University Press, Melbourne, 1973.

Convict society and its enemies: a history of early New South Wales, George Allen & Unwin, Sydney, 1983.

The strange birth of colonial democracy: New South Wales 1848–1884, George Allen & Unwin, Sydney, 1988.

The world of Albert Facey, Allen & Unwin, Sydney, 1992.

A republican manifesto, Oxford University Press, Melbourne, 1994.

The Oxford Companion to Australian History, Graeme Davison, John Hirst and Stuart Macintyre eds, Oxford University Press, Melbourne, 1998; revised edition 2001.

Discovering Democracy: a guide to government and law in Australia, Curriculum Corporation, Melbourne, 1998.

The sentimental nation: the making of the Australian Commonwealth, Oxford University Press, Melbourne, 2000.

Australia's Democracy: a short history, Allen & Unwin, Sydney, 2002.

'*Kangaroo Court*': *Family Law in Australia*, Quarterly Essay no. 17, Black Inc., Melbourne, 2005.

Index